PENSIONS POLITICS
AND THE
ELDERLY

PENSIONS POLITICS
AND THE
ELDERLY

Historic Social Movements and Their Lessons for Our Aging Society

Daniel J. B. Mitchell

M.E. Sharpe

Armonk, New York
London, England

Library of Congress Cataloging-in-Publication Data

Mitchell, Daniel J.B.
Pensions, politics, and the elderly: historic social movements and their lessons for our
aging society / Daniel J.B. Mitchell.
p. cm.
Includes bibliographical references and index.
ISBN 0-7656-0518-X (hc : alk. paper)
1. Old age pensions—United States—History. 2. Labor movement—United
States—History. 3. Social security—United States—History. 4. Individual retirement
accounts—United States—History. I. Title.

HD7105.35.U6 M57 2000
331.25′2′0973—dc21   99-087497

CIP

Printed in the United States of America

The paper used in this publication meets the minimum requirements of
American National Standard for Information Sciences
Permanence of Paper for Printed Library Materials,
ANSI Z 39.48-1984.

⊗∞

BM (c)   10   9   8   7   6   5   4   3   2   1

Contents

Figures and Tables

Tables

PENSIONS POLITICS AND THE ELDERLY

Chapter 1

Will the Boomers Have Their Ham and Eggs?

People are not going to be able to think about retirement the way
their grandparents did, which was that retirement is a right and
somebody will pay them to retire.

Dallas L. Salisbury, President,
Employee Benefits Research Institute (Barocas 1997, 26)

Demographic forecasting is founded on (some) known facts about the
future. That is, projected population trends are based largely on knowledge of those who are already born. These folks will simply age into
older brackets with the march of time and die off at reasonably predict-
able rates. But, of course, demographic forecasting has its risks, particularly as we go out into the distant future. Future birth rates and
immigration rates cannot be known with certainty.

For example, back in the mid-1930s, when Social Security was being
considered and its potential costs projected, estimates were made of
future population trends. According to the experts of that period, the
total U.S. population would level out at 151 million by the 1990s (U.S.
Congress, Senate 1935, 50). As it turned out, the actual population by
the mid-1990s was over 260 million and rising. Sadly, the forecasters
back in the 1930s knew nothing of the post-World War II baby boom to
come (nor even that there would be a World War II!).[1] And they could
not foresee the jump in immigration that would subsequently develop.
What they did know about was the low birth rate during the Great Depression and the restrictive immigration policies then being followed.

Still, forecasts about demographics are less tricky than forecasts about
the *implications* of demographics for the larger political economy. Spe-

cifically, what will be the reaction to future population developments? Even if we had perfect knowledge of future population levels and distribution, we could not know with any precision what impacts on the political process those trends would produce. An older population would surely require more medical care and other support than a youthful one. But how the economy and public policy would react to those costly health requirements is uncertain.

The Past Is Prologue

Despite these unknowns, this book suggests a scenario for the aging baby boom in the United States. It relies on past experience, namely developments centered in California in the 1920s, 1930s, and 1940s. In that time and place the politics of the elderly had a major impact on the local and national scene. In particular, California was the home of the "Ham and Eggs" movement, a plan to pay citizens fifty years old and over "$30 Every Thursday" in a new California currency. And it was home of other elderly-based pension movements as well.

In the next two chapters, I describe the Ham and Eggs movement and how it developed. I will show that the Ham and Eggs plan was a natural outgrowth of the elderly demographics of California. The creation of Ham and Eggs—and the related movements described in chapters 4 and 5—reflected the economic frustration of the elderly along with various currents of popular economic thought prevalent at the time. And I will argue that the retirement of the baby boomers will produce a twenty-first century counterpart to Ham and Eggs—that is, a political movement (or movements) coined from the thinking of that future era and earlier developments.

To be absolutely clear, I will *not* argue that someone in, say, 2030 will come up with a novel pension plan for folks over fifty to be financed by a newly created currency. We cannot know exactly what economic conditions will prevail at the time the boomers retire, nor can we know the path that popular and professional economic thinking will take between now and then. Inevitably, much speculation will be involved in the scenario I will be presenting.

But the story of Ham and Eggs and the other movements in California should serve as cautionary tales from the past. Those now discussing and making policy about Social Security and Medicare need to go beyond actuarial estimates. They need to consider political history and what it implies. There is an implicit assumption in policy circles that the baby-boom problem will be solved in the next few years through an interaction of reasoned reform options and the political process. Experts will research and discuss the issue, produce a consensus, and condition the political outcome by presenting feasible options. Politicians will then choose among the options. Once in place, the "solution" thus achieved will satisfy the aging boomers and the younger generations that must support their elders. History suggests it will not be so simple.

The Aging of the Baby Boomers

Everyone knows that the baby boom, which developed immediately after World War II, is pushing its way toward retirement in the twenty-first century, starting about the year 2010. As we go further and further out in the future, there are uncertainties concerning the exact proportion of the population that will fall into various age groups, as noted above. Trends in immigration, natural increase, rates of death, and factors yet unknown will determine the exact percentages. And the previously cited Social Security population projections of the 1930s should make us humble about very long-term forecasts.

Still, that there will be a growing elderly population after 2010 is not a controversial proposition. As Figure 1.1 illustrates, the best guess is that the United States will become what one observer termed "a nation of Floridas." That is, the proportion of the elderly in the future is expected to rise to levels similar to that of today's state of preference for retirees (Peterson 1996).

Already the foreshocks of this bulge in the elderly population can be seen. Discussion in Congress on success in balancing the federal budget focuses on target years *before* baby boomers will retire. The reason is obvious: the Social Security and Medicare portions of the budget, no matter how well pre-funded they might be, *must* go into deficit as the boomers reach eligibility age.[2] Even a fully funded system, however that phrase is defined, must *save* (run a surplus) before the boomers retire and then *dissave* (run a deficit) once they do.

In any event, Social Security and Medicare both are targeted for various degrees of fiscal overhaul; this is because the boomers' retirement is not fully funded. Remedies proposed for this underfunding range from increases in payroll taxes and reductions in benefits to more exotic forms of "privatization" (Aaron 1997; Kotlikoff and Sachs 1997). Schemes

Figure 1.1 **Percentage of the U.S. Population Aged Sixty-Five and Over: Middle Projection**

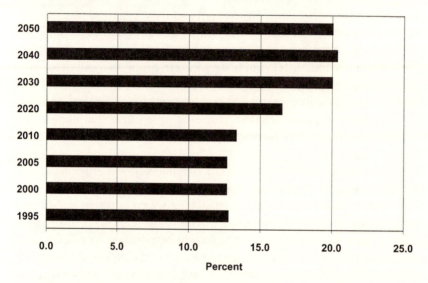

Source: Estimates from the U.S. Bureau of the Census.

are proposed to invest the trust funds or some new individual accounts in the stock market where they will (it is hoped) earn a higher return or to "reform" the Consumer Price Index (CPI) so as to reduce cost-of-living adjustments. But the end result of all these plans is that there is likely to be a reduction in benefits below what is currently promised to the boomers. In addition, younger generations will have to pay more into the systems or support their elders in some other fashion. These implications—which are likely to hold whatever Congress and the president decide—will be discussed more fully in the final chapter.

What will be the social and political reaction to these changes in the existing social contract? It is to that question that California history provides tantalizing insights.

Who Will Provide the Resources?

Politicians often focus on the Social Security and Medicare systems as if they were private benefit plans. They worry about inflows to, and outflows from, the federal trust funds just as the trustees for some private plan would do. In contrast, economists tend to concentrate on the issues the systems pose for national saving (Aaron 1982, 40–52). It has never been clear whether Social Security in fact substitutes for private retirement saving or whether the system is an add-on. That is, if Social Security or Medicare benefits were reduced, would individuals then save more for their retirements? And if they did save more, would they save enough completely to offset each dollar of reduction in Social Security and Medicare liabilities with an equivalent amount of private saving? The issue has long been debated. However, it is likely that improving the funding of the system—or adding some type of compulsory supplemental retirement saving plan to it—would add to net national saving.

Yet there has been political reluctance to improve system funding by an explicit payroll tax increase. When federal budget surpluses began to be projected, those who wanted to do least to Social Security and Medicare proposed "diverting" the surplus to these programs. In effect, such diversion adds to government saving. Overall, however, combined national saving from all sources (government, business, private households) has fallen short of investment in the United States for many years. This shortfall phenomenon, in turn, shows up as increased net U.S. international borrowing.

During the 1980s, the United States became the world's largest international debtor. The taxpayer revolt of that era led to considerable expansion of the federal deficit—that is, to increased negative government saving (dissaving). Retiring the boomers in the twenty-first century can only reduce net saving in the United States, producing a propensity to continue running up net debt to the rest of the world. Institutionalized saving through Social Security—as noted earlier—will have to turn negative. There will also be increased drains on private pension plans. And the boomers will want to draw down the personal savings assets they control directly. Someone will have to buy the previously accumulated assets released from the public, private, and personal systems of saving.

In the popular literature the problem posed by this asset sale has been termed "the Big Chill" for financial markets. Questions are raised about who will buy the real estate liquidated by the boomers, not to mention their stocks and bonds (Sterling and Waite 1998). One thing is clear: The ability to borrow in world markets to finance the asset sell-off will be limited. Other developed countries have demographic bulges similar to America's baby boom. Only Ireland—with a unique demographic profile—is an exception. Indeed, many nations, including (notably) Japan, face a much big-

Figure 1.2 **Change in Public Pensions as a Percentage of GDP in 1994 Prices**

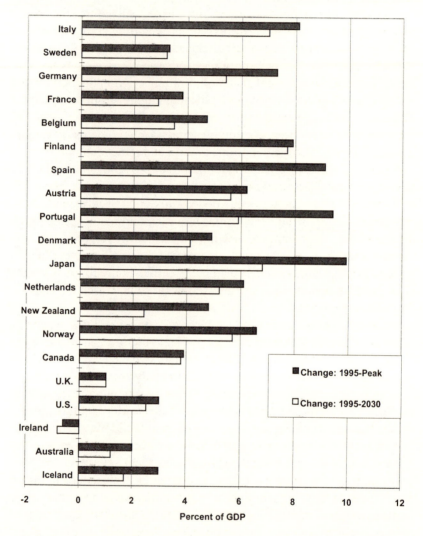

Source: Estimates from the Organisation for Economic Cooperation and Development.

ger jump in public pension spending on the elderly than does the United States, as can be seen in Figure 1.2 (OECD 1996). It is unlikely that the American boomers can collectively draw their retirement resources from foreigners.

What Can Be Afforded?

The kind of evidence just described has led some observers to predict economic calamity when the boomers retire. It is assumed that the United States cannot "afford" the final life-cycle stage of the baby boom and that somehow an economic collapse will ensue. But in fact, the United States can readily afford the retirement of the baby boom as a technical matter. If the Social Security and Medicare systems are viewed as stand-alone plans, changes in payroll tax rates, diversions of budget surpluses, changes in age requirements, or reductions in benefits can always be made to keep the programs solvent indefinitely. Indeed, as can be seen in Figure 1.3, many countries *today* spend a higher fraction of their GDP (Gross Domestic Product) on public pension systems than the United States is projected to spend at the peak of its boomer retirement (if no changes in pension promises are made). And, as noted, almost all developed countries will face increased expenditures from their current bases in the future.

Medicare's problem—if Medicare is also taken as a stand-alone system —is more immediate than the pension component of Social Security. But in principle, Medicare's problems can be solved with more money and/or more controls and rationing. However, saying that changes *could* be made as a technical matter is not the same thing as saying that such changes *will* be made. Nor is it equivalent to saying that large political fallout will be avoided if these changes are made or attempted.

The current elderly population has become a formidable lobby, with its major representative, the American Association of Retired Persons (AARP), seen in Congress as a group with which it is risky to tangle. In former House Speaker Tip O'Neill's famous phrase, Social Security and Medicare have become the "third rail of American politics" (Morris 1996, xi). Congress became more conservative after the 1994 elections than it was in Speaker O'Neill's days. Nonetheless, the politics of the late 1990s became a contest between the president and Congress over whose plan to "save" Social Security was best. Despite the rhetoric, the true implications of reforming, or saving, or doing little or nothing about Social Security and Medicare will not be known until the boomers experience the results. Even if the voltage in the third rail was reduced in the 1990s relative to earlier decades, the power in that rail will surely increase again by 2010.

If the boomer retirement issue is viewed as a national saving problem

Figure 1.3 **Public Pensions as a Percentage of GDP in 1994 Prices**

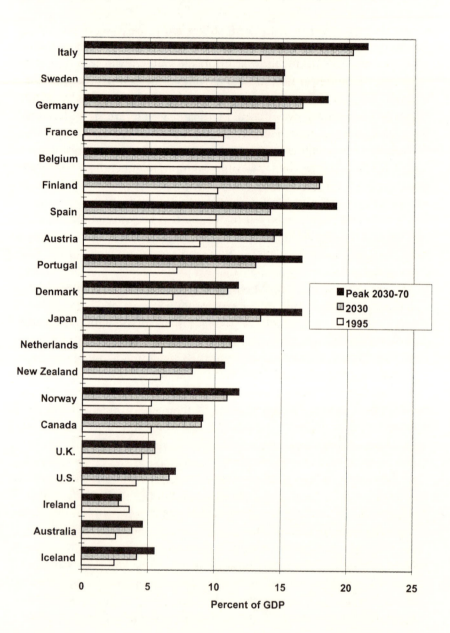

Source: Estimates from the Organisation for Economic Cooperation and Development.

rather than as one of the solvency of particular public institutions, it is again wrong as a technical matter to say that the United States cannot afford the retirement of the baby boom. The United States "afforded" World War II, during which the federal government consumed upwards of 40 percent of GDP for the war effort (at a time when real GDP per capita was much lower than today). Indeed, as those who downplay the boomer problem are fond of pointing out, America's dependency ratio (nonworkers/workers) was higher in 1960 than it is projected to be at the peak of boomer retirement. That earlier peak in the dependency ratio occurred because there were more children per worker than are projected for the future. Those children were, of course, the very same boomers (in their pre-Woodstock years!). And there were also more nonworking women back in 1960 (Aaron 1997, 19).

Virtually anything can be afforded if people are willing to make the sacrifice, as the World War II example demonstrates. However, *willingness* to afford is another matter. For example, opponents of welfare reform often (and correctly) pointed out that welfare for the poor amounted to only a small percentage of the federal budget and an even tinier fraction of GDP. Similar arguments have been made in defense of U.S. foreign aid, yet both programs have been squeezed as a matter of political decision. When it comes to what can be afforded, much depends on how issues are framed and who is doing the affording.

The predominantly male breadwinners of 1960 were willing to afford *their own* nonworking wives and children. Will the wage earners of the twenty-first century—male and female—be willing to afford the upkeep of *someone else's* parents? Or will they insist on cutbacks of such expenditures? And what will happen if such insistence is met by political resistance from the elderly? The answers to these questions cannot be known with any assurance, but a nasty political collision seems a strong possibility. And there will be temptations for politicians to pose remedies that seemingly are costless. California's pension movement history points in that direction.

In part, the outcome will depend on the economic circumstances prevailing during the boomer retirement period. However, it is clear that simply making actuarial estimates of future Social Security and Medicare outflows and inflows does not address these issues of political choice. Nor do debates about the adequacy or inadequacy of U.S. saving rates provide the answers.

One view about this potential collision—the most sanguine—is that the boomers will simply take care of themselves through private arrangements. They will "realize" before retirement that they need to save more, thanks perhaps to the plethora of articles on retirement planning now appearing in the popular press. Some polls indicate that current workers expect less from Social Security and more from personal and employer-based savings plans than earlier cohorts did (Barocas 1997, 27).

The difficulty is that such polls and articles in the press are not in agreement with actual economic behavior. As can be seen in Figure 1.4, U.S. personal saving rates as officially measured—which include saving through employer-based pension systems, 401(k) plans, and similar programs—have not shown any dramatic increase in the 1990s; quite the contrary. Where is all this reported boomer saving?

Saving rates as officially measured have been criticized as analytically inaccurate. Issues can legitimately be raised, for example, about the treatment of the inflation element over time in interest rates as a component of personal income. However, even with such adjustments, it is hard to turn the decline in officially measured saving into an avalanche of newly developed baby boomer prudence (Gale and Sabelhaus 1999). At most, one can say that there has been some decline and then hope that offsetting capital gains will turn out to mean real and permanent resources to support the elderly in the future.

At the same time that public social insurance systems are being questioned, changes in workplace institutions are making reliance on private employers as a source of retirement security more risky. A shift is occurring away from defined-benefit pension plans (which typically pay a guaranteed income based on age, seniority, and final earnings levels) and toward defined-contribution plans. Defined-contribution plans are essentially workplace-based savings plans (which receive favorable tax treatment). The monthly income that such plans will eventually provide is uncertain; that will depend on such unknowns as the total returns to plan assets before retirement, interest rates prevailing at the time of retirement, and actuarial factors. On the health care side, employers have been cutting back on retiree health insurance, in part because of changes in accounting standards.[3] Indeed, health coverage for current employees is also slipping, which may increase future dependence and drains on public health systems.

Turning Toward History for Clues

Forecasting, whether economic or political, often involves looking to the past for clues. Economic forecasting, for example, is often under-

Figure 1.4 **Personal Savings as a Percentage of Disposable Personal Income**

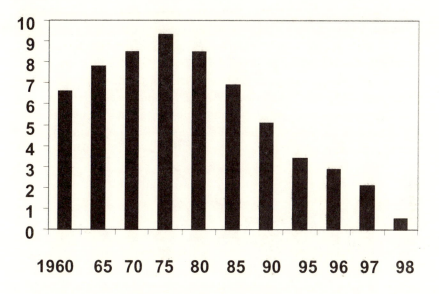

Source: Data from the U.S. Department of Commerce.

taken through complex multi-equation models. These models' structural relationships are econometric estimates based on earlier data—history, in short. As it happens, just as with economic performance, there is past evidence available on the politics of the elderly. It comes from the 1920s, 1930s, and 1940s, particularly from California.

California might seem a strange place to search for such evidence. The state today is associated with youth culture and, indeed, it now has a younger than average population when compared with the other forty-nine states. But as Figure 1.5 shows, this youthful age profile is one that developed in the mid-1950s. Before that time and beginning in the 1890s, California was what Florida is today. California was a place for older people to retire in the sunshine.

Indeed, it was California's elderly profile that helped to establish the state's reputation for unusual happenings and social movements. Having reached a stage in life when health was an important issue, California residents were susceptible to entrepreneurs selling various quack remedies. Thus, Gaylord Wilshire—the colorful "socialist" land specu-

Figure1.5 **Percentage of the Population Aged Sixty-Five and Over: United States Versus California**

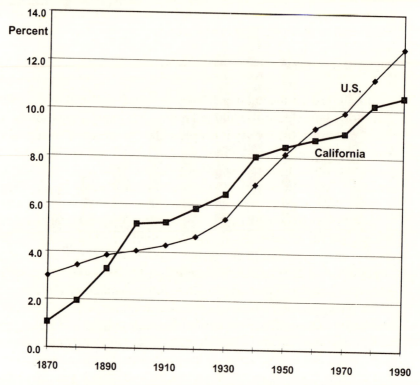

Source: Data from the U.S. Bureau of the Census.

lator after whom one of the main boulevards in Los Angeles is named—could tout his I-ON-A-CO electric belt in the 1920s as a "short cut to health" (Davis 1967). As one's health declines, hopeful—even if fanciful—remedies become attractive.

Even if Wilshire's electric belt delayed the inevitable, Californians who were still worried about their eventual place in the cosmos had a choice of novel religions. These ranged from Aimee Semple McPherson's Foursquare Gospel in the 1920s to the Great I Am in the 1930s to Scientology in the 1940s. The phrase "New Age" was first applied to California spiritualism in the early 1900s; the variants of the 1970s and 1980s were simply new variants of much earlier movements (Schwartz 1998, 176). At a more earthly level, Forest Lawn cemeteries—founded in 1917—were designed and marketed to be as "unlike other cemeteries as sunshine is unlike darkness, as Eternal Life is unlike Death" (McWilliams 1973, 230–31, 259–65; Davis 1992, 59–62). Until Forest Lawn came along with its local customer base, no one had thought of cemeteries as profit-making businesses.

Direct Democracy

California had an institutional feature in place well before the 1930s that allowed the elderly—while still mortal—to express themselves: so-called direct democracy. As it happens, the "progressive" electoral reforms of the initiative, referendum, and recall did not originate in California; South Dakota was actually the first state to install direct democracy. Nonetheless, direct democracy came early to California (Crouch 1943; Key and Crouch 1938; Allswang 1991).

In 1898, John Randolph Haynes founded the Direct Legislation League and pushed for direct democracy within the City of Los Angeles. The drive in the city was ultimately successful and became merged into a larger effort at the state level, carried on by the so-called Lincoln–Roosevelt League. Fierce opposition to direct democracy was mounted by the liquor industry (fearful of prohibition initiatives) and the Southern Pacific Railroad (then a major force in state politics and the target of reformer wrath). However, the election of Republican Hiram Johnson as governor in 1910—a one-time lawyer for the Teamsters Union—led to a triumph of the progressive agenda. Johnson had begun his reform career prosecuting a local scandal in San Francisco (Schwartz 1998, 157). In 1911, with Governor Johnson playing a leading role, the initiative, referendum, and recall were installed at the state level. Along with direct democracy came other progressive reforms of the day including women's suffrage and a state workmen's compensation system.

Once direct democracy was installed, an avenue opened for a variety of causes to be presented to the public. On the economic side, these included such issues as the eight-hour workday, proposals to limit chain stores (pushed by competing independent retailers), antimargarine regulations (pushed by competing dairy interests), single-tax proposals (pushed by the followers of nineteenth-century economist Henry George, who believed that the property tax should be the basis of all taxation), utility regulation, and a variety of conventional tax and bond measures. Social issues also appeared on the ballot. These included prohibition of alcoholic beverages, proposals to permit bibles in schools, and antivivisection laws.

Note that up to the mid-1930s, about two-thirds of the initiatives and referendums placed on the ballot by voter petitions were subsequently rejected by the larger electorate (Crouch 1943, 565). Nonetheless, California voters, including the elderly, had a system of self-expression that could be readily employed by organized groups and promoters. And politicians could win or lose office based on their position on the more controversial ballot propositions. Even if a particular proposal failed at the polls, endorsing it could gain a politician needed votes from the proposition's supporters. A politician might win (or lose) based on endorsement of, or opposition to, a ballot proposal, regardless of the fate of the proposal itself.

Pension Politics in California

One thing elderly Californians, or residents of any other state, did not have until the 1930s was a national social insurance system. The closest the United States had come to such a system prior to the Great Depression was a Civil War veterans pension plan, a plan with some precedents in pensions provided to Revolutionary War veterans (Skocpol 1992, 105). One view is that reformers had come to see the Civil War plan—which consumed over 40 percent of the federal budget in the mid-1890s—as the epitome of corrupt patronage. As such, according to this view, it inhibited proposals for other, more general national social insurance arrangements.

On the eve of World War I, Civil War pensions still accounted for over a fifth of the federal budget, and over 90 percent of living veterans were receiving them (Skocpol 1992, 109). Initial rules for eligibility were not precise, and the machinery for verifying eligibility was limited. Later, as lobbying for the pension program intensified, the program shifted toward being age based rather than injury based. As a result, many good-government types may have seen the activities of Congress in defining pension eligibility for constituents as vote buying.

Veterans could receive pensions based on age alone as young as sixty-two years by 1907. Typical Civil War pensions replaced about 30 percent of the income of unskilled laborers. About a fourth of the population aged sixty-five and above benefited from veterans'—or veterans' widows'—pensions by 1910. Indeed, elderly veterans had a valuable asset, dependent pension eligibility, to offer young brides. Some of these brides were still collecting benefits as late as 1999 (Tawa 1999)!

A considerable lobby developed through veterans' groups to enhance the pensions and keep tariffs high to provide federal revenues for them. Conversely, protectionist interests saw veterans' pensions as a vehicle for retaining high tariffs needed to pay for them. Although Confederate veterans were not eligible for the federal plan, some southern states provided pensions to them. But northern veterans were eligible for special state as well as federal pensions in many jurisdictions (Costa 1998, 11, 32–37, 49–50, 160–66, 184–85, 197–212; Skocpol 1992, 139–43).

According to some researchers, the upper- and middle-class reformers who might have been expected to push for federal social insurance in fact rejected it (Orloff 1993, 233–36). The Civil War system was viewed as a semi-corrupt form of vote buying. Reformer rejection was so strong—according to this view—that World War I veterans were denied pensions to avoid a repetition of the Civil War experience. This atmosphere at the national level left the question of any public support for the elderly to the states and localities. The only federal pensions that reformers could stomach were those for civil servants; these were seen as a way of cleaning out deadwood and thereby part of more general civil service reform (ibid. 275–76).

But there are other interpretations of the comparatively late development of a Social Security system in the United States. The issue was sometimes seen as one of competition by government with the private employer pension plans—limited though they were—of this period. Congress did face a controversy in the 1920s over a proposal by Metropolitan Life Insurance Company to have the federal government mandate employer-provided pensions. This proposal would have created major business for Metropolitan Life and other insurance companies as administrators of such plans. The plan was strongly resisted by the business community and was killed. Nonetheless, the existence of some nascent employer plans and the issue of how these would fit into any proposal for government pensions created sufficient controversy to prevent adoption of any federal plan (Sass 1997, 70–72).

Evidence for overt corruption in determining veteran pension amounts and eligibility under the Civil War plan is limited—much of it may well have been eliminated as the system was professionalized. Nonetheless, anecdotes of corruption and abuse circulated (Skocpol 1992, 143–48). Corruption and lobbying are not the same thing, although some reformers may have perceived them as similar. Recipients of veterans' pensions were more likely to retire than were nonrecipients and may have set an example for those interested in creating (or receiving) more generalized old-age pensions. But for a complex of reasons activity in this area was confined mainly to the states and, especially in the 1920s, plans began to be passed by state legislatures.

California—17 percent of whose population aged sixty-five received Civil War veterans' pensions in 1910—was part of this process (ibid. 541). And even if social reformers were discouraged by the Civil War pension experience, other groups took that experience as a model. Thus, the American Federation of Labor (AFL)—although at the time traditionally opposed to government programs—endorsed a de facto federal old-age pension plan in 1909. The plan would have nominally conscripted the elderly into an "Old Age Home Guard" for unspecified "duties," really a subterfuge for receiving pay from the government (ibid. 212–17). Giving the plan a military aspect provided a possible avenue to avoid constitutional objections that a more general social insurance system might have faced at the time.

Interest in political matters relating to the elderly had a long history in California, predating the era of direct democracy.[4] As early as 1850, the state legislature made grants for relief of various needy categories of persons (Bond et al. 1954, 39–53; Fitzgerald 1951, 1–4). An 1883 law—reinforced by various court decisions—provided state support for institutional care of the elderly (i.e., poorhouses). However, politicians in this early era—which anticipated California's shift toward an older-than-average population—proved fickle on matters dealing with the elderly. In 1895, the law was repealed—owing to the deep economic depression of that period—and relief for the elderly was again in the hands of county governments. Eventually, county aid was shifted away from poorhouses and toward direct monetary payments to the indigent elderly at home, so-called outdoor relief. Prior to the Great Depression, this payment system, varying county by county, coexisted with poorhouses in California.

State relief for the elderly ran into the same kind of resistance from many reformers as did proposals for national social insurance. State and local political regimes were seen as corruptible and patronage-prone as was Congress. California, which had seen a victory by Republican progressives at the state level in the early twentieth century, was not immune from such thinking. To progressives, social insurance for the aged—if it were ever to come—would have to await a reform of government itself. Once out of the hands of corrupt politicians, perhaps government could undertake new responsibilities (Orloff 1993, 236–37; Skocpol 1992, 267–78).

However, various California groups sought to enhance the local relief approach by the 1920s. These groups were generally affiliates of national organizations with the same goals. Particularly active in California was the Fraternal Order of Eagles (FOE), which pushed various proposals in the state legislature. The Eagles and other fraternal groups had been ridiculed in Sinclair Lewis's 1922 novel *Babbitt.* According to one account, they thus decided to take up the cause of the elderly as a demonstration of their public service (Douglas 1968, vii). But other accounts do not mention this motivation and suggest that doing "good works" was rather a device to attract new members (Quadagno 1988, 66–72).

In any event, the Eagles did embark on their mission for the aged in 1922 (Epstein 1928, 195–96). Such efforts had support of the California State Federation of Labor (Skocpol 1992, 234–35). And California might have seemed a likely target for old age pensions, even apart from its demographics. It had been one of the early states to adopt "mothers' pensions" (essentially the forerunner of modern "welfare") in 1913 (ibid. 446–47, 453–54).

The proposal by the Eagles to raise the elderly pension payment level or ease eligibility, however, met stiff resistance. Conservative governors and legislators viewed such notions as socialistic attacks on private thrift and personal responsibility. The elderly, or their families, should provide for their own retirement. There was an odd three-way alliance against state pensions. It was composed of social Darwinists, those who believed that private, employer-based welfare capitalism would solve social problems, and—some argue—many good-government progressives affronted by the Civil War pensions.

In 1929, despite the strong resistance, an FOE-sponsored plan for means-tested pensions for those aged seventy and over was adopted in California. The new law *required* the counties to participate in the program and to bear 50 percent of the costs, with the rest coming from the state. As such, California had enacted the first mandatory state outdoor relief system in the country. However, the payments were not referred to as "pensions" as the term offended conservatives. "Pension"—to them—connoted an employment-related earned entitlement, whereas a term such as "relief" implied government-funded charity. As late as the early 1950s, local government administrators were complaining, nonetheless, that the elderly referred to the payments as pensions and resisted application of means testing (Bond et al. 1954, 313, 339). Seen by these recipients, the payment was—or should have been—an entitlement.

Note that even in the early 1950s, more than 60 percent of those over age sixty-five in California had no more than a grammar school education (ibid. 25). It can be surmised, therefore, that educational attainment would have been even lower two decades before. Thus, it was unlikely that administrators would have succeeded in explaining the distinction intended by the legislature to recipients back in the 1920s and 1930s. At that time, moreover, the terminology was not as clear-cut as it is today. In contemporary usage, distinctions are made between "welfare," "Social Security," and employer-provided "pensions." But in 1929, there was no Social Security, few employers provided pensions, and what we now call welfare was a hodgepodge of diverse state and local arrangements.

Despite the terminological concerns, California's 1929 law was liberalized in 1931 by the (William) Hornblower Act, named after an FOE activist and state assemblyman. Under Hornblower, the criteria for eligibility were eased, although the minimum age remained seventy. By then, California along with two other states (New York and Massachusetts) accounted for the bulk of state old-age pension expenditures (Quadagno 1988, 72). But with the tax base substantially eroded by the Great Depression, California's state government shifted all funding and administration of relief, including relief for the elderly, to the counties in 1933. The budget for the state's administrative agency, the Department of Social Welfare, was cut.

Under the new system, with the elderly lumped in with other indigents, the notion of relief as a "pension" was made harder to sustain. The 1935 federal Social Security Act, with its subsidy of state old-age relief, however, breathed new life into the program by providing a federal subsidy. By the end of 1938, about 29 percent of the state's population over age sixty-five was receiving aid under California's program of Old Age Assistance (Fitzgerald 1951, 8).

Age and Votes

Because of the age distribution of the population in California, the elderly accounted for a significant proportion of the potential electorate in the 1930s. The number actually receiving relief was small but rose from 5,600 in 1930 to 18,000 by 1934. However, the number of older persons

Figure 1.6 **Age Distribution of the California Population Aged Twenty-One and Over: 1940**

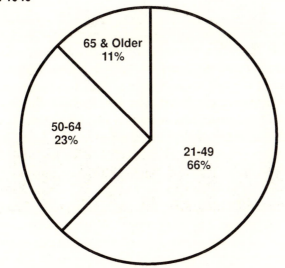

Source: Data from the U.S. Bureau of the Census.

who felt threatened by potential impoverishment had to be many times those actually receiving payments.

As can be seen in Figure 1.6, if the population aged twenty-one and over is taken as an indication of the voting age population, those aged sixty-five and over accounted for 11 percent of the total. More significantly, particularly in the light of the "Ham and Eggs" pension propositions that appeared on the ballot in the late 1930s, the population aged *fifty and over* accounted for a third of the potential electorate. Many people in the years approaching traditional definitions of old age could potentially be mobilized politically if the "elderly" age bracket were extended.

The elderly were dispersed throughout the state, but California's population as a whole was geographically concentrated. About 40 percent of residents lived in Los Angeles County, including a roughly equivalent fraction of the elderly (using sixty-five years as the cutoff). Good data on the exact toll the Great Depression was taking on the elderly are limited. Because of the concern about unemployment, a repeat of the April 1930 decennial Census was taken in Los Angeles and selected other cities in January 1931. Although the definition of "unemployment" utilized at that time does not precisely correspond to that currently in

Figure 1.7 **Unemployment Rates in Los Angeles: April 1930 and January 1931 (%)**

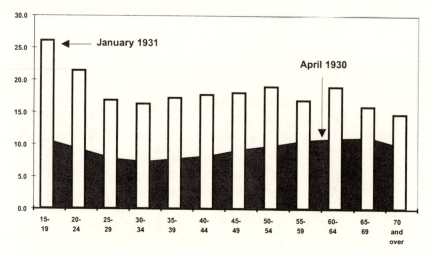

Note: Unemployment rates for both dates based on gainful workers as of April 1930. The graph omits data for 10- to 14-year-olds and those of unknown age.
Source: Data from the U.S. Bureau of the Census.

use, some sense of the impact of the early stage of the Depression is apparent from Figure 1.7.

Figure 1.7 shows that the elderly had comparatively high unemployment rates in April 1930—a few months into the Depression. At the time the overall unemployment rate stood at 8.8 percent, but the older age brackets had still higher rates. Thus, opportunities for employment as a source of income were already limited. By January 1931, the city unemployment rate, had risen to 18.1 percent. At that point, the younger brackets had caught up with the elderly. All age groups shared in the already very high unemployment rate, which would inevitably rise still further as the Depression worsened.

With conditions deteriorating, there were many older—and now frustrated voters—in close geographic proximity in southern California. Retirement in the sunshine was not working out as planned. For others in the ages approaching sixty-five, a forced retirement (without the necessary or expected income) was being imposed by the Great Depression. The elderly and near-elderly could be mobilized if the right leaders came along. And come along they did.

Chapter 2

Ham and Eggs

> Then one day—just three short weeks before the (1938) Califor-
> nia primaries—the Pension Plan presented Frank C. Jordan,
> Secretary of State, with the largest list of petitions in the history
> of California: 789,000 voters—25% of the registration—were
> demanding a chance to vote for Ham and Eggs for California.
> California politicians sat up with a jerk. It wasn't possible! Over
> three quarters of a million voters. Who were these people?
>
> *(Moore and Moore 1939, 77)*

At first glance, the story of Ham and Eggs is one of those truth-is-stranger-than-fiction tales that one might expect to originate in southern Califor-nia. The world has come to be unsurprised by such regional events as the 1997 mass suicide of castrated, computer-programming "monks" seeking to join a mythical space ship following behind the Hale-Bopp comet. Yet as already noted, California in the late 1930s—the era of Ham and Eggs—was a different state in one important respect. Unlike its current stereotype as a center of youth culture, in the 1930s and be-fore, California was a place to which one retired.

It is my suggestion that the rise of the Ham and Eggs movement is actually not so strange, given the then-prevailing age demographics in California and the economic and political winds in the atmosphere of the period. Moreover, the history of Ham and Eggs provides a preview of an oncoming event, the retirement of the baby boomers. I do not argue that history will repeat itself in some mechanical fashion, but I will nonetheless suggest that some futuristic version of Ham and Eggs will play itself out as the United States (and many other countries) at-tempts to cope with a bulge in the elderly population.

Whatever that version will be, it will not be the 1930s Ham and Eggs plan itself, as that scheme was a product of its age. It will instead be woven out of the institutions, economic conditions, and currents of thought of the coming era. And because California will likely retain its youthful bias in the future, whatever developments occur in, say, 2030 may well originate in some other part of the country.

Ham and Eggs: An Introduction

The chances are that you have never heard of the "Ham and Eggs" movement. Few contemporary Californians could identify it. Indeed, a scholarly study on problems of the aged in the state, written only sixteen years after Ham and Eggs first appeared on the California ballot in 1938, describes the episode as "all but forgotten" (Bond et al. 1954, 255, note 13). Many Californians—sharing that historical amnesia—would tell you that the notion that someone could make a lot of money by putting propositions on the state ballot is a discovery of the 1970s and 1980s. They would cite that discovery as a result of the so-called taxpayer revolt of the late 1970s, not something that goes back to the 1930s.[1] But they would be wrong.

The Ham and Eggs movement roiled California state politics decades before the state's taxpayer revolt. And it amply demonstrated the commercial possibilities of promoting ballot initiatives and political causes.[2] As later commentators on Ham and Eggs noted, its creators "were the first to introduce business principles into political campaigns by requiring that each promotional activity defray its costs" (Pinner, Jacobs, and Selznick 1959, 6).

In the rest of the United States today, the political goings-on in California of the late 1930s are certainly long forgotten. Yet arguably, a by-product of Ham and Eggs was the eventual elevation of California Governor Earl Warren to chief justice of the U.S. Supreme Court. There he presided over such monumental legal decisions as the desegregation of the American public school system and a host of other cases that gave the judiciary a liberal tilt. As in chaos theory, a little event somewhere can have major (unforeseen) effects elsewhere.

And, at the time it occurred, Ham and Eggs *did* draw national attention; it was not just a little event. President Franklin Delano Roosevelt was drawn to criticize Ham and Eggs in one of his radio fireside chats. Columnist Westbrook Pegler, covering the Ham and Eggs campaign in southern California for his national readership, wrote that "the USA would be better off if . . . Los Angeles could be declared incompetent and placed in charge of a guardian like an individual mental defective" (Starr 1996, 207; 1997, 197). The country, in short, took note of Ham and Eggs during the late 1930s.

Many readers *will* be familiar with the fictionalized version of Los Angeles water politics as dramatized in the 1974 film *Chinatown*. Perhaps it is best to put Ham and Eggs in cinematic perspective, so appropriate for Los Angeles. To start, it is worthwhile noting that the eminent California historian Kevin Starr (1996, 203) has argued that the Ham and Eggs "melodrama of skullduggery, greed, mass manipulation, and politics" would make at least as fine a film as *Chinatown*. And there would be no need for the fictional characters that *Chinatown* added for color and drama. The straight story is sufficiently colorful without embellishment.

Indeed, the definitive contemporaneous study of Ham and Eggs declared that the movement "out-Hollywoods Hollywood" (Moore and Moore 1939, 29). And one film of that era—Frank Capra's 1941 *Meet John Doe*, starring Gary Cooper and Barbara Stanwyck—already included some elements of the Ham and Eggs story. That film's dialogue even contains an off-hand remark about the Ham and Eggs movement.

Ham and Eggs: The Cast

Given the film reference, perhaps the best way to introduce the Ham and Eggs movement is to provide a listing of its cast of characters. In addition, the list of characters in Ham and Eggs is lengthy, so itemizing the principal players prior to the tale itself will be helpful. After the cast is presented, the drama will follow.

Robert Noble, originator of the Ham and Eggs California Pension Plan. Noble was a Los Angeles radio commentator with a listener-following. He also had a bit of a past, although accounts of that differ. Noble may have at one time been sequestered in a mental institution under the delusion he was Jesus Christ. Or it may have been his mother who was the inmate. He was also said to have been a Navy deserter. Given the spectrum of enemies Noble acquired, it is hard to know what is truth and what is fiction. In any event, touring New Orleans on behalf of the Los Angeles Chamber of Commerce, he discovered Louisiana Senator Huey Long's populist wealth-sharing movement. Noble named himself Huey Long's California representative and advocated the Long plan on his return. In 1935, Noble made a scene at Long's funeral by throwing himself over the grave. And he was identified with the third-party Lemke campaign for president in 1936, discussed in the next chapter (Putnam 1970, 90; Zimmerman 1980, 78).

In Los Angeles, Noble was given to denouncing on the radio the corrupt regime of Mayor Frank Shaw and Shaw's brother and "confidential secretary" Joe. This habit would eventually get Noble and the later offshoot of his pension plan scheme into trouble. Noble supported the candidacy of muckraker Upton Sinclair for California governor in 1934 in the so-called EPIC campaign, although he later turn against Sinclair. He read approvingly from speeches by demagogic radio priest Father Charles Coughlin on his own radio program. And he campaigned against chain stores in contrast to the rival Townsendites who took the pro side. (More on Long, EPIC, Coughlin, and Townsend in chapters 3 and 4.) Noble was imprisoned for pro-Nazi seditious activities during World War II.

The Allen brothers, Willis and Lawrence, promoters of "Grey Gone" hair tonic, an enterprise that led Willis into legal difficulties when the tonic turned out to destroy hair rather than recolor it. Willis got two years' probation for the hair tonic scam. In that episode he was following in the family tradition; the Allens' father spent five years in prison for embezzlement. Lawrence—in contrast—seemed to escape such problems and was the attorney for both his father and brother when they were convicted (President's Personal File 3385). The Allen brothers owned a building in Hollywood in which Robert Noble rented space. From this building, the brothers operated the Cinema Advertising Agency, which did not seem to have anything to do with cinema other than the Hollywood location.

Brother Lawrence reportedly had a certain affection for Adolf Hitler but, surprisingly, also had a Mexican wife who spoke little English. Both Allen brothers believed there would be money to be made in owning a high-powered Mexican radio station that could beam into southern California with programming for various political causes. Sadly, they lacked the money to obtain a Mexican license until Noble came along as a tenant in their building. By forging a document, however, the Allens hoped to surmount their money problems and put the station on the air.

Earle Kynette, a captain in the Los Angeles Police Department intelligence unit, sometimes known as the "Red Squad." Kynette became aware of the Allens' forgery and, exercising a bit of blackmail, offered to make their resulting legal problem go away if (1) the Allens would make him a silent partner in the Ham and Eggs movement, and (2) the

Allens would take Noble off the air, thus halting his criticism of Mayor Shaw. Kynette made the mistake, however, of bombing the car of an investigator from a civic group seeking to recall Mayor Shaw, and he was imprisoned for attempted murder. The Allens' failure to live up to the spirit of their agreement with their imprisoned partner may have led to the first electoral failure of Ham and Eggs.

Raymond Fritz, treasurer of the Ham and Eggs movement, who deftly moved incoming political contributions from the elderly faithful into the coffers of the Allens' Cinema Advertising Agency. As did Lawrence Allen and Robert Noble, Fritz maintained Nazi sympathies.

Sherman J. Bainbridge, the radio voice of the Ham and Eggs movement. He had previously worked with Roy G. Owens (see below) in various schemes. Bainbridge's radio broadcasts were interrupted by a severe automobile accident that occurred as he departed from the funeral of a martyr of the Ham and Eggs movement, Archie Price (see below). Nonetheless, Bainbridge was able to obtain labor union support for Ham and Eggs. But when the Kynette matter came to light, he made the mistake of trying to force the Allens out of Ham and Eggs. For his trouble, he ended not only up being expelled from the movement but also denounced as a traitor to it.

Archie Price, an inadvertent martyr to the Ham and Eggs cause. Price walked into a newspaper office in San Diego and told the staff that at age sixty-four he had no job and no pension and would therefore soon commit suicide.[3] When he later made good on his threat, Price was given an extravagant funeral by the Ham and Eggs movement to symbolize the plight of the aged in California. Price may never have heard of Ham and Eggs, but when Bainbridge learned of his suicide incident and publicized it on the radio, Price's postmortem conversion to the movement was assured.

Roy G. Owens, a high-school dropout who nonetheless styled himself the "engineer-economist" of the Ham and Eggs movement. Owens had previously been involved in the Utopian Society and drafted a "dated money plan" for it.[4] He was also involved with the cult of Father Divine and had a girlfriend (an "angel") in the group. (Father Divine proclaimed that he was God and developed a devoted black following.) Owens honed his legislative skills—later to be used for Ham and Eggs—drafting something called the "Righteous Government Act of 1936" for the cult. Among other features, the act would have put an "engineer-economist"—guess who?—in charge of the nation's monetary affairs. Owens managed to escape a sex scandal involving an underage angel known as "Virgin Mary" and a close friend of his whose Divine cult name was sometimes "John the Revelator" and sometimes "John the Baptist."

Bainbridge brought Owens into Ham and Eggs. The pair had been associated earlier in the "Plenocracy" movement. Plenocracy was a Ponzi-type scheme, possibly associated with the "Great I Am" religious cult of the period. It promoted investments in farms that were supposed to return a 30 percent "natural increase" based on the "Universal Creative Principle." Unfortunately for Plenocracy's promoters, the Securities and Exchange Commission shut down the operation.[5] Owens and Bainbridge were also previously involved in the Utopian Society (discussed in the next part) before coming to Ham and Eggs.

Gertrude M. Coogan, originally an economic adviser to radio priest Father Coughlin, joined Ham and Eggs and became a major spokesperson for the movement. Unlike Owens, she had some academic credentials, specifically a master's degree from Northwestern University. Coogan had written a book, *Money Creators*, with a foreword by a former Oklahoma banker and U.S. senator. Her theories involved "invisible forces" controlling the government and the Federal Reserve. These forces, according to Coogan, were part of a conspiracy to destroy Christianity dating back to the Bavarian "Illuminati" in the 1770s and involving the Rothschilds.

Both Adam Smith and Adam Weishaupt, leader of the Illuminati, were exposed in Coogan's book as having been financed by the same "international money." Using these ill-gotten resources, Adam Smith foisted on the world unethical capitalism and Adam Weishaupt, socialism. In their modern form, these same dark forces were seen by Coogan as preventing the United States from going on a silver currency standard and instead maintaining American attachment to the evil gold standard. The Federal Reserve should be abolished, she argued. Banks should be prohibited from creating money. Instead, money should be created by a new national institution and used for such worthy purposes as veterans' bonuses and pensions.[6]

George McLain, organizer and Los Angeles County manager for the Ham and Eggs movement in its later period. He used his Ham and Eggs connections to initiate his own political enterprise, which continued to create ballot propositions well into the 1950s. As will be seen in chapter 5, McLain was the first pensionite actually to pass a ballot initiative in California.

Apart from these individuals, there were numerous other colorful characters involved in Ham and Eggs, not to mention the many elderly contributors sending in their scarce pennies and dollars. And there were various state politicians.

These included:

Sheridan Downey, former candidate for lieutenant governor who ran with author Upton Sinclair on the EPIC slate in 1934 ("Uppy and Downey"). After the defeat of EPIC, Downey involved himself in the Townsend Plan (although Townsend had opposed EPIC). He decided to run for the Democratic nomination for U.S. senator from California in 1938, endorsing Ham and Eggs as part of his campaign. In contrast, Downey's opponent—William Gibbs McAdoo—made the mistake of denouncing Ham and Eggs. McAdoo, a former Secretary of the Treasury, had been instrumental in the nomination of Franklin Roosevelt as president in 1932 (Burke 1953, 2). But McAdoo's opposition to Ham and Eggs led to an upset loss to Downey in the Democratic primary despite an endorsement of the former by Roosevelt. As the Democratic candidate for senator, Downey won the 1938 election despite the defeat in that year of Ham and Eggs. He remained in the Senate for many years, pushing various versions of the Townsend plan.

Frank Merriam, Republican governor of California. Merriam had been elected lieutenant governor in 1930 with running mate James ("Sunny Jim") Rolph, a former San Francisco mayor. Rolph became (in)famous as governor for endorsing a lynching in San Jose. When Rolph died in office in 1934, Merriam became governor. He then had to face Upton Sinclair (running with Downey) and his EPIC campaign in the gubernatorial election that year. Merriam endorsed the Townsend plan, thereby obtaining a share of the pension vote, and he defeated Sinclair after a massive effort was waged on Merriam's behalf by the panicked business community. Although he opposed Ham and Eggs, Merriam seemed to have links to the Allens.

Culbert Olson, successful Democratic candidate for governor in 1938 against incumbent Frank Merriam. In his native Utah, Olson became an ardent supporter of the "free silver" presidential campaign of William Jennings Bryan. He became a Utah state senator before moving to California in 1920 and involving himself in local Democratic politics (Burke 1953, 9). Olson was elected to the California state senate in 1934 on an EPIC platform. He had earlier been elected chairman of the California Democratic Party during the convention that nominated Sinclair for governor. Olson seemed friendly to the Ham and Eggs movement in 1938. But later he appeared to Ham and Eggs supporters to have double-crossed them during the election campaign of 1939.

Earl Warren, Republican attorney general and later governor of California. Warren defeated Culbert Olson in the gubernatorial election of 1942 with assistance from angry Ham and Eggs supporters. Although he did not favor the Ham and Eggs plan, he won pensionite support by making promises to do something about the old-age pension issue. Warren is most famous for his subsequent service as Chief Justice of the U.S. Supreme Court, a post he would not have achieved without succeeding in the 1942 election.

Ham and Eggs: The Movement

Given the cast of characters above, what exactly was the Ham and Eggs movement? Surprisingly, the movement developed over an extended period with only a vague program. Its genesis began when Robert Noble stumbled across an article by Irving Fisher, the famous Yale monetary economist. Professor Fisher is still credited as a pioneer in monetary theory, inventing such concepts as "money illusion." He was also a pioneer in the development of index numbers for economic analysis.[7] But he was—in addition—the unwitting and unwilling father of Ham and Eggs.

Stamp, Stamp, Stamp

Fisher was interested in various social causes such as the prohibition of alcoholic beverages. His view of the Great Depression was that a monetary "reflation" was needed for economic revival—that is, a rise in prices that would undo the deflation that accompanied the economic slide of 1929 to 1933. Deflation transferred wealth to creditors from debtors and often caused bankruptcy of the latter. Reflation would reverse that process. In that context, Fisher wrote favorably of experiments in various small towns and cities to create "stamp money" (Fisher 1933). Although various versions of stamp money were tried, the version favored by Fisher had particular characteristics.

A municipality would persuade its merchants to agree to accept a locally issued scrip that would be used initially to finance some public works. The scrip notes would have a face value of $1 that the merchants would agree to accept *at par*. However, on a given day each week, the notes would officially become "worthless" unless a special two-cent stamp was attached with the two cents payable in U.S. currency. After a year's worth of stamps were affixed, the scrip note could be redeemed for a "real" dollar from the municipality. The municipality would have collected $1.04 in stamp taxes and would therefore have the dollar to redeem the scrip note plus a four-cent surplus to cover printing and distribution.

The weekly two-cent tax would also provide incentive to use the scrip rather than hoard it; the way to avoid the tax was to spend the scrip before the tax was due. This spending, it was argued, would stimulate demand and boost the Depression-ridden local economy. These beneficial effects depended, of course, on successfully encouraging people to accept at par a currency that effectively depreciated by more than 100 percent within a year. Users were being asked, after all, to accept an asset that cost $1.04 over the course of a year to maintain, after which it would be worth $1. Nonetheless, Fisher believed the U.S. Treasury should issue $1 billion of such a currency as an experiment to see if what a small municipality could do might be duplicated at the national level.

Noble Visions

In the hands of Robert Noble, Fisher's stamp scrip became the financing mechanism for a proposed state pension scheme. Under the Noble plan every jobless citizen in California aged fifty and over would receive "$25 Every Monday" (a significant sum in those days) in stamp scrip. The recipients would spend these scrip notes or "warrants" quickly owing to the stamp feature, thus stimulating the state's economy. Trumpeting this plan on his Los Angeles radio program, Noble developed an avid following of elderly listeners in the late 1930s. Clubs were formed to push for adoption of the Noble plan, and cash contributions began to flow in. An appealing element of the scheme is that it seemed to provide resources costlessly (i.e., without taxing anyone). Of course, it would in fact collect $1.04 in stamp revenue—a form of tax—for every $1 of pension warrants (which might turn out to be worth a lot less than a dollar).

It should be recalled that at the time, although the Social Security Act had been enacted in 1935, the Social Security system itself was not originally scheduled to pay out any pensions until 1942.[8] Employer-provided pensions in that era were comparatively rare, having gradually evolved from early experiments for civil servants, railroad workers, university professors, and other specialized groups. Moreover, some employer pension plans had been terminated during the Great Depression. Many private plans were limited to higher-paid white-collar workers and managers, particularly as pensions came to be seen by executives as potential tax shelters (Sass 1997, 18–112). But for those elderly without any pension on which to rely, income was scarce. Work opportunities for the elderly (or anyone else) were limited by the Depression.

A typical indigent elderly person on Old Age Assistance in California in that period would have received about $20 a *month* from county authorities as compared with Noble's $25 a *week* (Douglas 1936, 237). Average weekly wages of a full-time factory worker were also below the level promised by Noble.[9] And at the lower end of the wage scale, the newly enacted federal minimum wage in 1938 of 25 cents an hour was the equivalent of $10 per week on a forty-hour basis. Thus, there would have been strong incentive for many workers aged fifty and over to quit their jobs and rely instead on the proposed California pension. By retiring such workers, job opportunities—it was argued—would be created for the young. And, of course, those unemployed over fifty and individuals already retired would have been delighted to receive such an income.

At about $1,300 annually ($25 × 52 weeks) for eligibles over fifty, the cost of the plan would have been about $1.1 billion on the conservative assumption that only half of those Californians over fifty would choose not to work to be eligible. Such an amount would have been about one-fifth of the state's gross domestic product.[10] Of course, this estimate assumes that individuals from other states would not flock to California to achieve eligibility for the pension. In an echo of arguments made against the earlier EPIC movement (discussed in the next chapter), opponents argued that Ham and Eggs would attract indigents from outside California (Zimmerman 1980, 83). But even under conservative assumptions, a state stamp currency issued in the volume required (apart from constitutional issues that might be entailed) would raise considerable questions about its value in the marketplace. It would, after all, compete against regular money that bore no tax.

There was probably only about $350 million in regular U.S. currency in circulation in California and perhaps $2 billion in narrowly defined money (currency plus demand deposits).[11] It is one thing to get the major merchants in a small town to agree to accept a modest increment of local stamp scrip at par. It is quite another to obtain such an agreement—and for a flood of new quasi-money—in a large state of well over 6 million people. Irving Fisher himself denounced the child he had inadvertently sired, citing this problem (Putnam 1970, 95). He even wrote to President Roosevelt trying to disown Ham and Eggs.[12]

As for the name "Ham and Eggs," there are different stories concerning its origin. One is that Sherman Bainbridge shouted at a rally that "We want our ham and eggs!" (ibid. 93). A variation is that the phrase "ham and eggs" was the equivalent of "pie in the sky"; the phrase was thus used by critics with that negative meaning until Bainbridge gave it the positive connotation of the elderly having a good breakfast (Starr 1996, 206). A third version relates the phrase to a ritual at a local breakfast club in which members greeted strangers with "Hello Ham" to which the stranger was to reply "Hello Egg" (Lindsay 1960, 89). Finally, there is a version that a pro-pension speaker promised at a rally that during the election campaign, the plan would become as familiar to voters as ham and eggs (Weaver 1967, 131).

Whatever the name's origin, a pattern developed of chanting "ham and eggs" at rallies, a practice compared by critics to the ritual incantations at Nazi gatherings (McWilliams 1973, 305–6). As the scheme evolved, local Ham and Eggs clubs were kept under tight control. Buttons, pamphlets, and other paraphernalia sold through the clubs provided significant revenues. Thanks to Ham and Eggs treasurer Raymond Fritz, these revenues passed through the Cinema Advertising Agency, the sole authorized supplier. And, of course, the revenue was collected in U.S. currency, not some ephemeral state scrip.

The Noble Loss to the Allen Wrench

The Allen brothers—Willis and Lawrence—became partners with their tenant Robert Noble in his rapidly expanding pension enterprise. They persuaded Noble to invest in a scheme to set up a powerful Mexican radio station that would carry his and other programming into southern California. The Allens' interest in having a radio voice is not surprising, given their ambitions for the pension program.

Radio was the latest electronic medium in the 1930s; about 70 percent of households were estimated to own radios by 1936 and the proportion was continuing to increase rapidly (Kazin 1995, 115). The public reported in surveys its satisfaction with radio as an entertainment medium. Moreover, and much to the distress of newspaper interests, there was a growing reliance on radio as a source of information (Cole 1985, 22–66, 210–27). Just as some folks today believe in what appears on the

Internet because it comes from a computer, so too did people then tend to give credence to what they heard on the radio.

Several years prior to the Ham and Eggs movement, radio's use as a political tool had been demonstrated by President Roosevelt, who communicated directly to the public through his regular fireside chats. And by 1938, the ability of radio to convince its audience was amply illustrated by the impact of Orson Welles' famous *War of the Worlds* simulated news broadcast; Welles reported an invasion from Mars and produced a nationwide panic. Listeners, after all, could hear a live report from New York City describing the city's destruction, complete with the asphyxiation of the announcer by Martian gas.

At the time, broadcasters to the United States could evade Federal Communications Commission (FCC) regulations on station licensing and power by operating across the border. American broadcasters complained of interference from stations in Mexico (as well as Cuba and Canada). Public health officials complained of quack remedies being touted on stations along the Mexican frontier. A treaty known as the North American Broadcasting Agreement was signed in Havana in the mid-1930s. However, the Mexican senate refused to ratify the treaty until 1940, apparently under the influence of the American-aimed border broadcasters. In the interim, Mexico granted a license in 1937 for a 100,000-watt station in Rosarita Beach, backed by a former Mexican president. Rosarita Beach was a resort—not far from the California border—founded in 1928 by one Manuel Barbachano and his brother. It was frequented by Hollywood stars of that era (Fowler and Crawford 1987, 209–10).

The new license created an opportunity for the Allen brothers. The Hollywood radio station that Noble—and later the Allens—used for Ham and Eggs programming was a relatively low-powered 1,000-watt station (KMTR). A Mexican "border blaster" could send their pension message to a much wider audience and would in any case be a profitable venture.

To launch their proposed new station, the Allens obtained a Mexican partner as required under Mexican law; it was none other than developer Manuel Barbachano. Other partners were also involved, including the colorfully nicknamed J.A. ("Foghorn") Murphy and a former San Diego city attorney. The Allens, however, found themselves short of the funds needed to obtain the Mexican radio license. Their American broker in this deal, George Berger, was unaware of the Allens' limited financial resources when he located Barbachano for them. Berger was even more surprised to learn that the Allens had forged his signature on a document to convince their Mexican partner to put up his own money as a temporary loan.

Various skirmishes occurred involving the partners in the radio scheme. J.A. Murphy believed he was being cut out of the deal and tried to stop construction through a court order. But the other partners managed to spirit the transmitter across the border before the court could act. Murphy then sued his partners for $450,000.[13] Litigation involving Barbachano and Willis Allen was still in progress as late as 1951![14] The upshot of the initial skirmishing was that Berger went to the police to file a complaint about the forgery. And the forged document wound up in the hands of Los Angeles City police captain Earle Kynette.

Captain Kynette turned out to have a special interest in the Allens and the pension enterprise they were operating with Noble. He offered the Allen brothers a deal they could not refuse. If the Allens would get their pension partner Noble—with his broadcasts attacking Mayor Frank Shaw—off the air and if they would bring Kynette in as a silent partner in Ham and Eggs, the unfortunate forgery matter could be made to disappear. Kynette also reportedly gave Willis Allen money to buy more radio air time (Zimmerman 1980, 84). He apparently was willing to invest in his new business venture as well as draw from it.

Captain Kynette had learned how to get folks to do what he wanted through direct experience. He had started his career as a pharmacist but moved on to work for a fellow who controlled a "chain of whorehouses" in Los Angeles. His patron had gotten him a job in the police department. As a cop, Kynette had subsequently been arrested for shaking down a prostitute. But the matter was quickly dropped and Kynette was soon promoted to sergeant. He became known as the "dirty-job man" of Police Chief James Davis. Chief Davis, in turn, was widely seen as an ally of Mayor Shaw, although there have been reports that the mayor was effectively blackmailed by the *Los Angeles Times* into keeping Davis on the job (Richardson 1954, 221–22; Domanick 1994, 44, 55; Gottlieb and Wolt 1977, 219–20).

The Allens, in short, were lucky that Kynette offered a carrot along with a stick. And given Kynette's carrot-and-stick offer, the Allens called a rump meeting of the board of the California Pension Plan Association. The meeting took place in a cafeteria ironically owned by one of the leading figures in the effort to unseat Mayor Shaw.

At the rump meeting, the Allens managed to take control of the organization and kicked Noble out of the movement he had created. When Noble and his followers attempted a public demonstration to protest the coup, the unsympathetic police broke up the rally and arrested him. But Noble was not finished as a pensionite. Like an angry bee displaced from its hive, he continued buzzing around the outskirts of the Allens' pension enterprise, making trouble at key points. As a swan song to his career, he became pro-Nazi and pro-Japanese as World War II approached, sentiments that did not make him a popular character after the attack on Pearl Harbor. (He called for Roosevelt's impeachment four days after the attack.)

Curiously, among Noble's partners in this unpatriotic endeavor was a former director of the local American Civil Liberties Union in Los Angeles. Both were arrested by the FBI and then released in late 1941. But by mid-1942, both were convicted of sedition and imprisoned (Schwartz 1998, 348–49; Bennett 1969, 247). Other charges against Noble included income tax evasion and stealing coins from a pay phone (Fitzgerald 1951, 35). But more of that in chapter 5.

With Noble out, the Allen brothers needed a new broadcaster and they found Sherman Bainbridge, who also brought with him his friend Roy Owens. Bainbridge soon discovered that the Allens, despite having achieved a considerable elderly following, actually had no formal pension plan other than Noble's vague idea about using Fisherian stamp money. Bainbridge set Owens to draft a bill that could be put on the California state ballot. But in a rapid first strike, Noble got hold of the Owens draft and took that and the accompanying slogan "$25 Every Monday" to the California Secretary of State, acquiring exclusive rights to both. This preemptive action, however, proved to be only a temporary inconvenience for the Allens.

The Allens incorporated under the name "Retirement Life Payments Association." They changed their slogan to "$30 Every Thursday" and had Owens draft a revised bill with the higher amount. As $30 was greater than $25, Noble's version of the scheme was dead. Under the Allen-Owens plan, anyone qualified to vote in California and aged fifty years or older without a job would receive $30 of warrants each week. Each $1 warrant would require a two-cent tax paid weekly to keep the note valid until redeemed. (A cost-of-living escalator was included to adjust the $30 figure for any subsequent inflation.) The warrants would be made legal tender for payment of state taxes in an effort to keep the notes circulating at par. Transactions in warrants would also be exempt from sales tax. An administrator of this system would ultimately be elected. But the ballot proposition made it likely that Roy Owens (the "engineer-economist" of the movement) would be named interim administrator until such an election was held (California, Secretary of State 1938). Then, as the incumbent, he would likely be installed by the voters more permanently.

Things initially went well for Ham and Eggs. The necessary signatures were quickly gathered by the faithful and Ham and Eggs went on the ballot as Proposition 25 in November 1938. With the suicide of Archie Price—a pauper who had no pension—the Allens had a martyr to the cause. So well were things going for Ham and Eggs that the state's business establishment was in a panic by early September. Banking and business representatives announced that they would not accept the proposed stamp scrip (Hanne 1998, 197).

But the business community had to contend with new personalities joining in support of Ham and Eggs. Gertrude Coogan enlisted in the movement after leaving radio priest Father Coughlin. She provided Ham and Eggs with an air of monetary expertise and learning. The major official Ham and Eggs book has a long question-and-answer section dealing heavily with monetary matters, written in the style of Father Coughlin's pamphlets of the period (California Pension Plan 1938, 39–71). Undoubtedly, Coogan was the contributor. Apart from writing, Coogan turned out to be an inspiring speaker to boot.

Word of the Ham and Eggs movement spread beyond the state. As a result, Coogan was not the only non-Californian attracted to the cause. Francis H. Shoemaker, a former congressman from Minnesota, joined the cause. Shoemaker had a background as colorful as that of the other Ham and Eggs leaders. He had been expelled from the Progressive Farmers of America in the 1920s on grounds of misuse of funds. He had also been convicted of sending defamatory materials through the mails to a local banker, accusing the banker of being a "robber of widows and orphans." A suspended sentence for that charge was converted to an actual term in Leavenworth Prison for persisting in the vituperations.

After Shoemaker's spell in prison, he won a seat in Congress. However, he was nearly blocked by the House from taking office because of his prison record. Defended before the House by North Dakota Congressman William Lemke (a character in the next chapter), Shoemaker took his seat in 1933 and served one term. His career in Congress was also notable for various unusual incidents. One involved a trial for punching a cab driver after having rammed the cab from behind with his own car and pushing it through an intersection. Other incidents of violence and trouble with the law marked his later career (Johnson 1989).

Shoemaker reportedly was a powerful speaker for Ham and Eggs. He could reel off figures and could pack in listeners to movement meetings. The Allens especially liked Shoemaker because he donated his time for the cause and did not cost them a cent. If there was a fly in the ointment, it was that Shoemaker had an unfortunate habit of including in his speeches lines such as "When I was in the penitentiary . . ." (Moore and Moore 1939, 97–98). Nonetheless, Shoemaker could boast to an audience that he had gone to the White House and been given a pardon personally by FDR.

Strength in Union

Ham and Eggers were able to capitalize on support of the expanding labor union movement and the surrounding turmoil. In the mid-1930s, the national American Federation of Labor (AFL) and the Congress of Industrial Organizations (CIO) were split into contending factions, while union membership itself rapidly expanded. The AFL unions tended to be more conservative politically than the new CIO unions. The CIO unions—with their creed of mass industrial unionization—were generally on the left, often with Communists in key positions. Particularly in Los Angeles, with its long-time anti-union business establishment, labor–management tensions were at a peak. Federal legislation, specifically the Wagner Act of 1935, now favored unionization. And the U.S. Supreme Court, in an about-face on New Deal legislation, had upheld the constitutionality of the act in 1937.

For the business community, the federal tilt toward organized labor meant that combat against unions would have to take place at the state and local level. Business groups such as the Merchants and Manufacturers Association set about forming various anti-union front groups under such names as the "The Neutral Thousands" and "Truth Not Terror." Within the City of Los Angeles, business pushed for anti-picketing ordinances. At the state level, various options were possible, including, of course, ballot initiatives (Perry and Perry 1963, chapter 12; Gottlieb and Wolt 1977, 217–19).

Not all of these efforts were successful. A business-supported group called "Women of the Pacific" pushed for a state proposition that would have sharply limited union activities. But it failed to obtain the necessary petition signatures. In a local court case, various executives of the anti-union *Los Angeles Times* were cited for contempt for interfering with labor litigation through certain editorials. And Los Angeles Mayor Frank Shaw vetoed an anti-picketing ordinance, bringing him the support of the AFL faction. Not surprisingly, during the recall campaign against Shaw (see page 42) the rival CIO endorsed Shaw's (successful) opponent, Judge Fletcher Bowron.

However, the business community was successful in putting Proposition 1 on the ballot in the November 1938 election, where it appeared along with Ham and Eggs' Proposition 25. Proposition 1 regulated picketing, boycotts, and displays of banners. It aimed at preventing "abusive statements and threats of violence" and at the then-prevalent (though illegal) tactic of sit-down strikes. Culbert Olson, the Democratic candidate for California governor, opposed Proposition 1, winning CIO support. The split in organized labor, however, led to (some) AFL support for Olson's rival, incumbent governor, Republican Frank Merriam.

Despite their split on candidates, both the AFL and the CIO could see the virtue of opposing Proposition 1. Thus, an alliance was forged between the Ham and Eggers and organized labor, with the assistance of Sherman Bainbridge. Labor and the Ham and Eggs crowd would both endorse Proposition 25 and both would oppose Proposition 1. They were successful in the latter endeavor; "Prop 1" received 42 percent of the votes.

The Big Bang

Opponents of Ham and Eggs were unsuccessful in an attempt to have the California Supreme Court bar the Ham and Eggs proposition from the ballot. Money kept rolling into Ham and Eggs headquarters in response to schemes such as casting a new "Liberty Bell of 1938" (Hanne 1998, 202). But despite their good fortune both financially and in court and despite their ability to attract allies and outside speakers, the Allen brothers had problems. President Roosevelt let it be known that he viewed the Ham and Eggs proposition as a "short cut to Utopia" and opposed it.[15] In a press conference on "background," FDR hinted that there might be constitutional impediments to a state issuing a quasi-currency. Roosevelt also circulated a report on Ham and Eggs from the Controller of the Currency. The report attacked the plan (although it curiously did not mention the constitutionality issue).[16]

Brother Willis telegraphed the president offering to send a representative—either his "economist-engineer" Roy Owens or pensionite Congressman John Dockweiler—to explain the plan.[17] And a letter-writing campaign to Roosevelt was started urging him to reverse his position. (See Figure 2.1.) Meanwhile, Roosevelt's famous quote that "this generation has a rendezvous with destiny" appeared (though unattributed) on the inside cover page of the major Ham and Eggs propaganda book (California Pension Plan 1938). The quote gives a false impression of a Roosevelt endorsement of Ham and Eggs.

Presidential opposition was not the only problem. Another difficulty was that the Allen brothers were greedy. They neglected to pay Social Security taxes for their staff (leading to federal investigations), and sometimes neglected to pay the staff any wages at all. While ex-convict Shoemaker may have helped the Ham and Eggs campaign, another person currently in jail began creating difficulties for the cause.

Police Captain Kynette was jailed for planting a bomb in the car of an investigator of corruption in the Mayor Shaw regime. The victim, Harry Raymond, was a former police officer himself; indeed, he had been police chief of Venice, California, when it was an independent city, and of San Diego. On what Raymond thought was his hospital deathbed, he had called in a journalist/friend for some last words. The following dialogue—out of some *film noir*—reportedly ensued:

> "Who did it, Harry?"
> "That son of a bitch Earle Kynette. . . . I want you to promise you'll get him for me."
> "I'll get him for you, Harry."
> "They told me they would get me. They put Kynette on me. . . . Kynette takes his orders from the City Hall and they wanted me out of the way. He's the one who rigged the bomb." (Richardson 1954, 220–21)

The charges against Kynette came not only from Harry Raymond. As it turned out, Kynette had been spying on Raymond's house for some time. A neighbor, spotting Kynette and other men from Kynette's Red Squad, had asked them to leave. He was beaten up for his intervention and told to keep quiet. But at Kynette's trial, the aggrieved neighbor testified about the surveillance and beating. Sadly for Police Chief James Davis, he, too, was called to testify:

> My memory is not sufficiently clear to state that I directly ordered Captain Kynette to keep Raymond under surveillance . . . but I did not order Kynette not to do so (quoted in Domanick 1994, 77).

Figure 2.1 **Three Sample Letters to President Roosevelt from the 1938 Ham and Eggs Campaign**

Your Honor
I am asking in this letter. A very great favor. And that is this. That when you make your National Broadcast some time in the near future, that you will speak in good terms concerning the Calif. Pension plan, or Retirement payments Act, which is to be voted in to our constitution. For if there is any thing done to help the aged it is now. So will you consider?
I thank you.
Mrs Virginia Devers, Mrs Eany Mae Devers,
Mr. Mack Devers (Los Angeles)

Dear Mr. President:
I am writing this humble letter with reverence hoping that in your speech on Nov. 4th you will say something in favor of the California pension plan. . . . We are going to win on Nov. 8th by 85 percent by our own power, but with a helping hand from you Mr President we would like to win by 95 percent or better. I am to old to get a job, and to young for pension.
Very Sincerely Yours,
Joel E. Westlund (Los Angeles)

Dear Mr. Rosevelt,
I am writing you asking for a favor. Won't you please speak a good word for our California State Retirement Live pension plan named Ham & eggs for California. I am a U.S. Citizen past fifty was born in good old U.S.A. and have worked hard from child hood up, and I do feel that we are in a age when the machine is taking the place of labor, and it is so hard for people even above 40 to get work and so many of our younger generation goes through school then has nothing to look forward too and I know that our Plan is one that will help all. So please give it a Series though and speak a good word for it in your Address before election. Please give this a series though.
Respectfully
Mrs Nora Dack (Los Angeles)

Source: President's Personal File 3385, Franklin D. Roosevelt Library.

Such equivocal testimony appearing in the newspapers daily made it unlikely that Kynette would be around in person any time soon to claim his share of Ham and Eggs revenues. So with their silent partner in jail and likely to remain so, the Allens began neglecting to make payments to Kynette's wife. This failure to keep the money flowing to Mrs. Kynette proved to be a big mistake in retrospect. It turned their silent partner into a very noisy one.

Recall campaigns against mayors were not new to Los Angeles. A recall had been tried against Mayor Shaw's predecessor, John C. Porter. But Porter, a used auto parts dealer elected in 1929 on a platform of keeping Los Angeles as "the last stand of native-born Protestant Americans," survived the effort (Rasmussen 1997). Shaw was not so lucky; the jailing of Kynette for car bombing turned public opinion against the mayor.

Shaw's opponents began their recall campaign radio broadcasts with the sound of a simulated explosion followed by screams, to remind listeners of the Kynette bombing (Caplan 1947, 114). Shaw declared himself "too busy with real work and real problems to give any thought to this curious combination of commercial advertising, poor sportsmanship, subversive activities and backfence gossip" (Henstell 1984, 55). But despite his pretended aloofness, the recall was successful. A new mayor was installed who soon forced Police Chief Davis to resign and—for a time—abolished the Red Squad. Significantly, the city recall election was held in mid-September 1938, only a few weeks before Ham and Eggs was on the November state ballot.

Kynette was surely angered by what had come of his misadventure. He was also enraged about the failure of his wife to receive payments from the Allens. In revenge for this financial neglect, he began to cooperate with authorities. Kynette told about his links to the Allens, about the forged document, and about the Allens' failure to pay him his share of the "profits." With these disclosures, both the Ham and Eggs organization and the campaign were endangered.

To make matters worse, Lawrence Allen was sued by an elderly woman for slapping her. And the Allens seemed to be using Ham and Eggs in an effort to discredit Mayor Shaw's opponent in the recall election that had been set in motion. They also appeared to have links with the incumbent Republican candidate for governor, Frank Merriam, even though Merriam had openly come out *against* Ham and Eggs. And, conversely, they would not officially support Democratic candidate Culbert Olson, who at least was seemingly friendly to Ham and Eggs.

Armed with this information, Sherman Bainbridge attempted to get the Ham and Eggs board to oust the Allens just as the Allens had once ousted Robert Noble. But Bainbridge was not as successful an organizational manipulator as were the Allens; he ended up being ousted himself, although after the election. As might have been expected, the Allens branded their new opponent as being in the hands of dark money interests. Bainbridge remained loyal to the pensionite cause, however. After his ouster, Bainbridge had to seek new employment. He found it at the national office of the Townsend Plan as "General Manager" of that (federal) pension scheme.

It might be thought that the unfavorable publicity, along with the internal power struggle, would lead to an electoral disaster. Yet despite the internal turmoil, bad publicity, and massive opposition by the state's business establishment, Ham and Eggs Proposition 25 was defeated by a relative narrow margin of 1,143,670 to 1,398,999. Ham and Eggs had come remarkably close to popular enactment with 45 percent of the vote. Surely, had it not been for the outrageous conduct of its proponents, Ham and Eggs would have passed.

Ham and Eggs: Once Again

The 1938 defeat was not the end of the Ham and Eggs story. For the Allen brothers just to close up shop would have meant killing off their money machine. With the narrow electoral defeat and with an intact organization, the Allens got the necessary petitioners together to put another Ham and Eggs proposition on the ballot in 1939. Indeed, their 1939 election petition carried over 1.1 million names, more than in the petitions for the 1938 election and about equal to the votes cast in 1938 for Ham and Eggs (Zimmerman 1980, 89). The new version, drafted (again) by Owens, included an income tax of 3 percent except for income received in warrants, and it would have created a state bank with Owens in charge, along with the requisite warrants and $30 weekly pensions (California, Secretary of State 1939).

Proposed creation of a bank caused Gertrude Coogan to walk out in a huff, since banks were generally to be distrusted in her approach to monetary affairs and conspiracy theories. Owens, who had felt eclipsed by the more educated Coogan during the first Ham and Eggs campaign, was pleased by her departure. But the split endangered the prospects of the revised Ham and Eggs proposition. And the addition of an explicit tax to the plan was not likely to attract wavering voters.

Culbert Olson, as a mere *candidate* for governor, could afford to take an ambiguous position on Ham and Eggs in 1938. He had sent the Ham and Eggers a statement saying "Please express my gratitude for the support given me by the supporters of the California Pension Plan and my assurance of fidelity to the course that compels them on in the fight for retirement" (Hanne 1998, 200, note 73). But as a former EPIC campaigner, Olson had followed Upton Sinclair in opposition to the federal Townsend pension plan scheme while serving in the California State Senate. On the other hand, although opposed to the Townsend Plan, Olson advocated making pensions a federal matter (Burke 1953, 9, 12).

In the 1938 gubernatorial campaign, Olson said he was not sure Ham and Eggs would work. But then again, he noted, how can one be sure anything will work before giving it a try? He even had nice words for the Townsend people by 1938. As a candidate for governor, Olson wanted to play down the Ham and Eggs issue in his campaign but at the same time—as a campaign aide later put it—not "alienate" the pensionite vote (Earl Warren Oral History Project, 1976a, Clifton, 11).

During the 1938 California State Democratic convention, although Olson chaired the platform committee, Willis Allen let him off the hook on the Ham and Eggs issue. Perhaps this was because the Allens' links to Republican Governor Frank Merriam might have been compromised had the Democrats endorsed Ham and Eggs; it is hard to know. In any case, Willis Allen declared that the issue was nonpartisan and should not be in a party platform (Burke 1953, 16–17, 24, 26–27).

The straddling of the Ham and Eggs issue of *candidate* Olson in 1938 would not ultimately be possible for *Governor* Olson in 1939. In his inaugural address, Olson had said that the state relief pension for the elderly was inadequate but suggested that fiscal resources were insufficient to raise it (ibid. 42). Thus, he did not have a strong pro-elderly record from which to oppose the reincarnated Ham and Eggs proposition.

When first presented with the petitions putting the measure back on the ballot, Olson spoke to a Ham and Eggs rally and promised the enthusiastic crowd a special election on their new proposition. But he included some evasive language indicating—again—he was not sure the plan would work (ibid. 108). Nonetheless, holding a special election just on Ham and Eggs would have increased its chance of passage; an election with just one narrow issue would have attracted mainly the faithful to the polls.

Olson's ambiguity invited political criticism. Initially, Olson defended his promise of a special election on grounds that because so many people wanted the vote, it was best to have the matter settled quickly. But somehow, the new proposition, now designated as Proposition 1, ended up on the fall election ballot despite Olson's initial promise for an earlier vote.

In the end, Olson came out against Ham and Eggs, although the lieutenant governor, Democrat Ellis Patterson, supported it. The market for municipal bonds shuddered as it contemplated the possibility that Ham and Eggs might rise from its 1938 defeat like a phoenix (Leader 1972, 84–85).

Meanwhile, Ham and Eggs followers were treated to an all-out campaign with the usual rallies and radio broadcasts. One grand event was scheduled in a public park in Los Angeles. To promote attendance, a Ham and Eggs broadcast promised that "as you enter the main gate, you will go up Ham and Eggs Boulevard; wander down Retirement Warrants Lane; turn out Thirty Thursday Street, and find yourself entering Security Highway" (Cleland 1947, 236).

On the other side of the country, the Roosevelt administration again became concerned about the issue, as it had been in 1938. This concern developed partly because the Ham and Eggs campaign included literature purporting to show a Roosevelt endorsement. "'Try Plan,' says Roosevelt," read one leaflet.[18] The president had actually said only at the time of the previous campaign that ultimately Ham and Eggs was a state matter for Californians to decide.[19]

Despite the fears of financial markets, Ham and Eggs lost in 1939, receiving about a third of the votes. The drop in percentage was due partly to an absolute decline in yes votes from the 1938 level and to a decided increase in no votes. There was again a link between organized labor and the Ham and Eggers in the 1939 campaign, but this time it was decidedly looser. First, no anti-union initiative was on the ballot in 1939, unlike 1938. Thus, there was less reason for an alliance from the union side. Second, there was language in the Ham and Eggs initiative making it unlawful to curtail the flow of goods and services. Some labor officials believed this feature could be used to limit strikes. The weakened labor connection undoubtedly contributed to the decline in the "yes" percentage.

Still, CIO-affiliated unions generally supported the revised plan. And members of the Communist Party were active campaigners on its behalf (Perry and Perry 1963, 494). As a result, the House Committee on Un-American Activities came to Los Angeles, claiming there was a secret Communist plot to take over the movement, and through it the state (Zimmerman 1980, 87). And the Roosevelt administration, exasperated with Ham and Eggs, forwarded a letter it had received to FBI director J. Edgar Hoover. The letter, from a Los Angeles doctor, complained that the Allens were working with the Communists to take over California and then the United States.[20]

Would Ham and Eggs have done better in 1939 if Governor Olson had scheduled a special election as he initially indicated he would? Many at the time believed it could have passed in a special election (Cleland 1947, 240). Angered at Governor Olson's betrayal and seeking revenge, the Allens backed an immediate recall drive against the governor. However, the recall effort was abortive, and some petition circulators wound up convicted of fraud (Schwartz 1998, 294). Labor support was not available for the recall drive; Olson was by this time seen as pro-union. And parts of the Ham and Eggs movement split away from the Allens after the 1939 elections and opposed the recall. These groups—having seen the electoral handwriting on the wall—decided to go with Olson, who promised to work for higher Old Age Assistance (Zimmerman 1980, 91). But this erosion did not seem to discourage the Allens.

Partly to embarrass Governor Olson, the Ham and Eggers ran a slate of delegates in the Democratic presidential primary in 1940, pledged to Willis Allen for president (Burke 1953, 142). However, Olson showed himself willing to compete for rank-and-file pensionite votes, even if pensionite leaders opposed him. Immediately after the 1939 defeat of Ham and Eggs, he announced support for a "Sixty-Sixty" plan, really a recommendation to Congress (à la Frank Merriam's support for Townsend). Sixty-Sixty was a recommendation that Congress raise the Social Security pension to $60 a month and cut the age of eligibility to sixty. Olson said he supported a reduction in the California age to sixty for California Old Age Assistance. This proposal was meant as a goodwill demonstration to Congress, but it was never passed. Olson's lieutenant governor—a previous Ham and Eggs supporter—now went on to endorse Sixty-Sixty (Putnam 1970, 120–21). Eventually, a California version of Sixty-Sixty became part of the 1942 gubernatorial campaign, as we will discuss in chapter 5.

The slippage in support for Ham and Eggs, first for the actual Ham and Eggs proposition, and then for the gubernatorial recall, points to the oft-seen life cycle of quixotic movements. Enthusiasm is hard to sustain after defeat. Opponents are strengthened. And more conventional political action is hard to resist. Thus, in more recent times, for example, the Ross Perot popular vote dropped from 19 percent in 1992 to less than one-tenth in 1996. And, a century before, William Jennings Bryan's first run on a "free-silver" platform in 1896 earned him more votes than in his two later runs for the presidency. Faced with the same erosion of support, the Allen brothers would have to wait for revenge against Olson until the regularly scheduled gubernatorial election of 1942.

Buckeye Eggs and Ham

Not only was Ham and Eggs beaten in California in 1939, but a variant of it also lost in Ohio—another state with an above-average concentration of the elderly. The Ohio proposal was known as the Bigelow Plan. Herbert Seely Bigelow, a Congregationalist pastor, had long been involved in Ohio and Cincinnati politics. He pushed such causes as free silver, pacifism during World War I (subjecting himself to vigilante action and a U.S. Secret Service raid), and the Single Tax movement of popular economist Henry George. Bigelow linked himself with radio priest Father Coughlin in the 1930s, using the resulting Coughlinite support to get himself elected to the Cincinnati city council and even to Congress for one term. (See the next chapter for more on Father Coughlin.)

Bigelow apparently had a lifetime interest in old-age pensions; the World War I Secret Service raid uncovered a plan for such pensions in his safe. But it was not until 1939 that he actually placed a pension initiative on the Ohio ballot. Bigelow's plan would have provided single persons in Ohio aged sixty and over $50 a month and $80 a month for couples.

Rather than using a state currency to finance the plan, Bigelow relied on his favorite Single Tax of Henry George (a tax on property valued at above $20,000). But the tax was the undoing of the Bigelow proposal. Ohio farmers and other landowners mobilized to defeat the Bigelow plan, which garnered only a quarter of the vote (Beaver 1957; Brinkley 1982, 188–90).

Ham and Eggs: Fade Out

The Allen brothers probably were little concerned about their Ohio counterpart. There were new efforts to put Ham and Eggs initiatives on the ballot shortly after 1939, but these failed owing to legal technicalities. The California State Federation of Labor endorsed a variant on the Ham and Eggs plan by Willis Allen in 1941, in exchange for Ham and Eggs support for an employer-backed proposition that organized labor was opposing (Taft 1968, 138–39). Labor leaders apparently viewed Willis Allen with caution as someone seeking money for his own purposes

(Earl Warren Oral History, 1976c, Haggerty, 38–39). But brother Willis's Ham and Eggs variant never made it to the voters.

Ham and Eggers had a more significant impact on subsequent California gubernatorial politics. Their activities in the 1942 gubernatorial election will be described in more detail in chapter 5. But a brief preview is in order. In 1942, incumbent Governor Culbert Olson faced Republican Attorney General Earl Warren in the contest for the governorship. The two candidates feuded over various issues including those related to California's defense preparedness. Warren was an ambitious state politician who set his sights for electoral office high. He eventually became the Republican vice presidential candidate on a ticket with Thomas Dewey in 1948 and hoped to become president one day.

After the attack by Japan on Pearl Harbor, Warren played on anti-Japanese sentiment in California and attacked the local community of Japanese-origin residents as a likely fifth column. Olson equivocated on the issue, sometimes calling for tolerance, sometimes citing the need for Japanese farmers for wartime agriculture, and sometimes endorsing evacuation. The issue was clearly Warren's, and it put him in an excellent position to oppose Olson (Burke 1953, 194–206).

But defense was not enough to guarantee a Warren victory over incumbent Olson. Ultimately, Warren decided to push for the pensionite vote. While never endorsing Ham and Eggs, Warren declared that the elderly "are entitled to pensions . . . as a matter of right" (Bond et al. 1954, 77). Such statements were enough to obtain for Warren the Ham and Eggs support he needed against the traitor Olson (even though the Ham and Eggers had run Roy G. Owens in the Democratic primary against both Olson and Warren) (Burke 1953, 217–18). During the post-primary campaign, backers of the Ham and Eggs movement scheduled regular radio broadcasts favoring Warren.

Olson charged that Lawrence Allen had offered to support him in exchange for $50,000, which Olson refused to pay. However, in the end, Warren was elected with 57 percent of the vote. From the governorship, he eventually became Chief Justice of the U.S. Supreme Court, and the rest—as they say—is history. Throwing their support to Warren may have been the most influential decision the Ham and Eggers ever made!

Toward the end of the campaign, Warren had added a promise to the pensionites. He pledged to appoint a state pension commission with representatives from Ham and Eggs, the Townsend group, and others. And after the election, Warren had to implement his promise. The Ham and

Eggs and Townsend folks did get to sit on an official commission. For them it was the high point of their public visibility, official recognition courtesy of an ambitious Republican governor. But included as a member of the new pension committee was Hollywood-born George H. McLain, former Ham and Eggs organizer and stepson of a famous California rainmaker (Fitzgerald 1951, 61–62). McLain, by this time the head of his own pensionite group, used his temporary elevation into respectability to become Mr. Pension in California—to the eventual regret of Governor Warren.

As for the Ham and Eggers, and particularly the Allen brothers, they were never able to deal with wartime and postwar prosperity. After all, a key element of the Ham and Eggs plan was that it would end the Great Depression in California. Meanwhile, a more agile McLain adapted to the changing political landscape. The Ham and Eggers continued trying to put propositions on the ballot, always unsuccessfully. Their propositions were bizarre concoctions involving such disparate elements as gambling and margarine regulation, along with pensions, children's allowances, and payments to college students. At least, by including the young in some of their schemes, the Allens could see California's changing demographics!

The postwar Ham and Eggs movement descended into the kind of conspiracy theorizing once favored by the long-departed Gertrude M. Coogan. Now the monetary institutions created by the Bretton Woods conference, the gold standard, tariff cuts, and aid to war-torn Europe became the villains. The Allens linked up after the war with the notorious anti-Semite Gerald L.K. Smith, who in the prewar years had denounced FDR as "Franklin D. Jews-Evelt." Smith had been cited by the Justice Department for printing seditionist propaganda during World War II. And in his postwar incarnation, he was soon calling for deportation of Jews and blacks.[21] With their tactics and allies increasingly out of fashion, the Allen brothers and Ham and Eggs faded from public view, while George McLain assumed center stage. Proponents of the Ham and Egg movement had never passed a California ballot proposition on pensions. But McLain was destined to do so.

Chapter 3

The Nonpension Ingredients
of Ham and Eggs

[T]he solid opposition delaying our President from driving the
money-changers out of the Temple and from restoring
normalization to our currency money originates from these
Federal Reserve banksters in whose vaults there reposes the great
bulk of the interest-bearing war bonds. The ghosts of the four
horsemen of the apocalypse are to this day riding roughshod over
this nation—Mellon, Mills, Meyers and Morgan—the "M"
standing for money.

(Coughlin 1933, 24)

Although the Ham and Eggs movement was the brainchild of Los Angeles broadcaster Robert Noble, his invention was in fact the product of
related contemporaneous and earlier social and political movements.
Not all of these were related directly to pensions. Various notions were
in the air at the time, out of which Ham and Eggs was developed. These
included (1) *monetary and currency theories,* (2) notions about
underconsumption and income distribution as causes of the Great Depression, (3) depression-alleviation schemes such as *spreading around
limited opportunities for employment,* and (4) movements *promoting
payments to worthy groups* such as veterans, the aged, and widows.

I will take up these four themes below. But more generally, I will
argue that the Ham and Eggs movement—bizarre as its particulars may
seem in retrospect—was a caricature of the New Deal. Roosevelt's New
Deal, in fact, contained monetary elements, underconsumption remedies,
employment spreading, and social welfare payments as part of its agenda.
The United States moved to the political left with the coming of the

New Deal. But "left" in the American context meant simply that the economic remedies of the day were to be found in interventionist government policies.

When the mainstream shifts in such a fashion, a certain receptivity develops in the larger society to other proposals that have characteristics similar to those now seen as centrist. Whether these proposals are put forward by "serious" proponents or by promoter-charlatans is not the main issue. Off-center ideas, such as Ham and Eggs, may not "win" elections per se, but they can influence mainstream politicians trolling the electoral seas for votes. As such, mainstream political outcomes are influenced by off-center movements that might not have had any impact in other eras.

There have been other, more-recent episodes of shifts in the center of American politics. The Cold War brought with it a mainstream of anticommunism, producing at its fringes such politicians as Senator Joseph McCarthy and such groups as the John Birch Society. The shift to the right in economic policy in the 1980s and 1990s unearthed various militia and antigovernment groups. Basically, there are always doctrines and fringe groups on the edge of the political center. Shifts in the center allow some of these doctrines and groups to gain prominence, particularly in the hands of "political entrepreneurs" such as Robert Noble and the Allen brothers.[1]

Ham and Eggs had its monetary side, namely the stamp-money warrants the State of California was supposed to create. It had its underconsumption and redistribution of income elements in the form of the pension payments themselves. It had a worthy target group: the elderly. It would have discouraged work among this group, thus spreading employment opportunities to younger people. And it clearly relied on government intervention, albeit at the state rather than federal level. Moreover, as will be seen below, there was a veritable stew of political and social movements during the 1930s and before from which Ham and Eggs could draw sympathizers and ideas. Figure 3.1 summarizes a number of these movements to which more detailed reference will be made below.

Monetary Notions

Ham and Eggs's monetary side, the idea that currency manipulation could cure economic problems and that dark monetary interests were in oppo-

Figure 3.1 **Social Movements of the Ham and Eggs Era and Earlier**

• **Populists** and the **free silver** movement. A late nineteenth-century inflationist movement dedicated to elimination of the gold standard and substitution of free coinage of silver. Democratic presidential candidate **William Jennings Bryan** first ran on a free silver platform in 1896 and left a strong residue of silver and currency agitation in the Democratic Party, which remained in place during the 1930s.

• **Bonus Marchers**. A group of veterans who marched on Washington in 1932 to demand early payment of a bonus otherwise due in 1945. Military means were used eventually to oust the demonstrators.

• **Father Charles E. Coughlin** and the National Union for Social Justice. Coughlin was a Roman Catholic radio priest championing various monetary manipulations such as free silver, a mix of social doctrines concerning a just distribution of income, and other notions similar to Social Credit. Anti-Semitic and pro-fascist diatribes by Coughlin eventually led to his silencing by the Church.

• **Social Credit**. A British movement involving various monetary theories and notions of underconsumption. It became popular in western Canada, and a Social Credit government was elected in Alberta in 1935. Various Americans may have been influenced by Social Credit ideas coming across the border. Although stymied in its major proposals by the central Canadian authorities, the Alberta Social Credit government pushed for control of banks, a provincial quasi-currency, government payments to citizens, and debt-burden reduction.

• **Senator Huey Long** and his Share-Our-Wealth clubs. As governor of Louisiana Long built a mass movement attacking wealthy individuals and corporations and calling for income redistribution. He was assassinated in 1935, and elements of the movement were taken over by anti-Semitic preacher **Gerald L.K. Smith**. The movement included a call for generous pensions.

• **Dr. Francis E.Townsend** and his Old Age Revolving Pension Plan. Townsend, a Long Beach, California physician, and his followers supported a national plan to pay everyone aged sixty and over a pension of $200 per month, financed by a tax on "transactions."

• **The Union Party**. An alliance of Coughlin, Gerald L.K. Smith, and Townsend, which ran Congressman **William Lemke** for president in 1936. The Townsend pension plan became loosely linked to the campaign, along with limits on individual income and monetary manipulations.

• **The EPIC Campaign** (*E*nd *P*overty *I*n *C*alifornia). In 1934, author and muckraker **Upton Sinclair** ran for governor of California on a platform that mixed Technocracy ("production for use"), worker cooperatives, money creation, and pensions.

• **The Utopian Society**. A secret society based in Los Angeles with elements of EPIC, Social Credit, Technocracy (see below), and monetarism in its program as well as unusual ceremonies and rituals.

• **Technocracy**. A movement based on applying engineering principles, rather than market mechanisms, to production and distribution. It had many California adherents, notably at Cal Tech.

sition to the needed reform, has obvious earlier roots. The Populists of the latter part of the nineteenth century eventually fused with the Democratic Party in 1896, or some would say were captured and co-opted by it. In any event, William Jennings Bryan's Democratic presidential candidacy in 1896 (and twice thereafter) on a platform of free silver marked the height of the Populists' influence. But the Populist message endured for decades and was certainly alive and well during the 1930s.

The Legacy of Populists and Earlier Monetary Movements

Essentially, the original Populist movement was an alliance of farmers (who as debtors would benefit from quick inflation) and silver mining interests (who would benefit from a high official price of silver). The Populists saw the gold standard as an international banking conspiracy centered in England (the former colonial master) and sometimes described in anti-Semitic terms (Hofstadter 1955, 77–81; Harvey 1963, 57–67). In turn, Populist pro-inflation ideas were an outgrowth of the earlier "Greenback" movement.

Greenbackers, also largely rural, recalled with fondness the erosion of the real value of their debts and the high agricultural prices that had prevailed during the Civil War. As part of its wartime financial strategy, the United States (Northern states) had gone off the gold standard and used paper currency creation to finance military expenditures. (The rebel South did the same.) A constituency for inflation arose thereafter, especially during the deflation of the 1870s.

There is a still longer history of suspicion of banks (creditors) and bankers going back to the administration of President Andrew Jackson in the 1830s. Jackson fought a successful major battle to kill the Second Bank of the United States, the budding central bank of his era. He also fought to discourage issuance of nonspecie (i.e., bank-issued) money by requiring that payment for public lands had to be made in specie. Jacksonian suspicions of financial interests were subsequently reflected in state laws limiting banks to single branches or otherwise constraining their size. As illustrations of the persistence of economic thought, such state laws remained on the books until the deregulation era of the 1970s and 1980s.

Even the Jacksonian monetary/bank controversies had earlier roots. Shays' Rebellion during the 1780s in Massachusetts centered on demands that the state legislature issue paper currency and prevent mortgage foreclosures on farmers by banks. When the demands were not met, troops from the state militia were used to quell the sometimes violent reaction. Thus, a century before the Populists arose, their concerns over money, banking, and the clash of interests between debtors and creditors were clearly foreshadowed.

The capture of the Democratic Party by Populist thinking in the 1890s left a residue of monetary activism and political interest in currency matters. Creation of the Federal Reserve System in 1913 rekindled monetary passions. It revived the conspiracy theories that persist today, especially among the more anarchistic elements of the radical right. The Democratic Party's Populist monetary inclinations were still strong at the time of the New Deal, especially in Congress.

Father Coughlin and Social Justice

As noted in chapter 2, part of the monetary element of the Ham and Eggs movement can be linked to the stamp-money proposals of Irving Fisher, a Yale economist, thus making Fisher the unwitting father of the movement. But a more general willingness to fiddle with the currency entered the movement through other social currents of the period. Father Charles E. Coughlin, a Roman Catholic priest in the Detroit area, pioneered in the use of radio for religious purposes along with other figures of the era such as Los Angeles evangelist Aimee Semple McPherson. However, Coughlin's broadcasts soon took on a political complexion and developed a large following. The CBS radio network, which originally carried these broadcasts, became nervous about the politics and dropped his programming. This development forced Coughlin to develop his own chain of independent radio stations. In succeeding in developing his own ad hoc network to carry his programs, Coughlin was a communications pioneer.

Coughlin's "National Union for Social Justice" (established in 1934) called for abolition of the Federal Reserve, creation of a new government-owned central bank charged with maintaining the cost of living and (somewhat in opposition) issuance of sufficient currency to buy back the national debt. Also on the agenda was nationalization of "public necessities," a position he somehow differentiated from socialism. Coughlin was influential enough so that the Roosevelt administration catered to him and tracked his political strength carefully, drawing, for example, on reports of the Post Office Department to monitor the volume of mail Coughlin was receiving (Schlesinger

1960, 13, 37). During the period Roosevelt took the United States off the gold standard (early 1933 to early 1934), several members of Congress and the Senate—including Senator Huey Long—pushed the president to send Coughlin to an international monetary conference in London as a U.S. delegate (Nixon 1969, 221, 225–26).

Father Coughlin's notions about money blended traditional anti-usury teachings of the Catholic Church with more recent American Populist concepts. Coughlin commissioned papers from Brookings Institution staffers and relied on Gertrude Coogan, his economic adviser, to develop various seemingly authoritative monetary tracts. He applauded Roosevelt's temporary departure from the gold standard and called for a silver standard (Coughlin 1933). But Roosevelt's eventual return to the gold standard led Coughlin to turn vehemently against the New Deal (Coughlin 1936, Appendix VII). He labeled the president the "great betrayer and liar" and "Franklin Double-Crossing Roosevelt." The Roosevelt administration at one point took the offensive against Coughlin. It disclosed that the treasurer of the "Radio League of the Little Flower," Coughlin's broadcasting network, was speculating in silver futures and stood to gain from his proposed move to free silver.

Anti-Semitism had been on the edge of Coughlin's views throughout his public career. He tied Alexander Hamilton's Jewish background to the establishment of the American banking system in the interests of the rich[2] (Kazin 1995, 130). Coughlin became increasingly anti-Semitic in his broadcasts by the late 1930s—silver became "Gentile silver" as opposed to Jewish gold—and he was eventually forced off the air by the Catholic Church. During World War II, Coughlin's national magazine was shut down under threat of prosecution for sedition. But well before that, Coughlin's monetary notions entered the Ham and Eggs movement through the appearance in the pension movement of Gertrude Coogan, Coughlin's former economic adviser.

Coogan complained she got no credit or royalties from her advice to Coughlin and presumably hoped to avoid that mistake with Ham and Eggs. It was, after all, only a short hop from her proposal to pay veterans' bonuses with new currency to paying old-age pensions with stamp scrip. However, her falling out with the Ham and Eggs movement limited her potential for cashing in on the lucrative pension scheme, and she went off on her own to other causes. These included opposition to the Bretton Woods international monetary agreement of 1944 and opposition toward postwar American financial aid to (evil) Britain.

The EPIC Campaign

California was the home of Upton Sinclair's End Poverty in California (EPIC) campaign for governor in 1934, which contained monetarist elements. Until 1934, California politics had been dominated by the Republican Party, whose members outnumbered Democrats 4 to 1. The incumbent governor, Frank Merriam, a rather colorless individual nicknamed "Old Baldy," had assumed the governorship after his predecessor—"Sunny Jim" Rolph—died in office early in 1934. With the state in the grip of the Great Depression, and with the national Democratic sweep under Roosevelt in 1932, Merriam appeared vulnerable in the 1934 gubernatorial election (Greg Mitchell 1992, 31). He was a conservative individual, something of a blank upon which different observers projected different personal traits. One author asserted that Merriam was a one-time "kleagle" in the Ku Klux Klan (Cray 1997, 73). But an appointee of Merriam's characterized him as "a very fine human being" (Earl Warren Oral History Project 1977, Schottland, 8). In any event, Upton Sinclair became his Democratic opponent.

Sinclair was an eccentric author with socialist sympathies. Although he temporarily broke with the Socialist Party owing to its opposition to American entry into World War I, he ran unsuccessfully for Congress in 1920 on the Socialist ticket (Zanger 1974). Sinclair campaigned several times as a Socialist for other offices: for U.S. senator in 1922 and for California governor in 1926 and 1930. (Thus, running as a Socialist he had already faced the Rolph–Merriam ticket in 1930.) Sinclair was most famous for his exposé of the meatpacking industry in the book *The Jungle*. But he had written many other books, often self-published, on such pet beliefs as "mental radio" (telepathy) and weird diets.

Still, despite his oddities, Sinclair had friends among the artistic and intellectual community at home and abroad. He had helped finance famed Soviet director Sergei Eisenstein in the making of a film in Mexico. (Sinclair apparently cut off financing after receiving a telegram from Stalin indicating lack of support for the project.) He was able to persuade Albert Einstein, who spent some time at Cal Tech, to write an introduction to the German edition of his book on mental radio. Einstein also wished Sinclair well when he learned of his campaign for governor (Greg Mitchell 1992, 174–76, 302–3).

Sinclair decided to run for governor as a Democrat after being summoned to a meeting in 1933 at a Santa Monica hotel by a local Democratic Party activist, Gilbert Stevenson. Stevenson later went on to write anti-Semitic tracts dealing with monetary and other matters (Singer 1974, 375–76). Sinclair was reportedly dismayed subsequently to discover this facet of Stevenson (Schlesinger 1960, 112). But at the time of the meeting, Stevenson made a persuasive case to Sinclair that he should run for governor as a Democrat. Stevenson had personal reasons to feel disenchantment with the prevailing economic system; he had lost control of the prestigious Miramar Hotel in Santa Monica—still in operation today—thanks to the Depression (Schwartz 1998, 249). Responding to Stevenson's suggestion that he run for governor, Sinclair proceeded to outline for the attendees a program to pull California out of the Great Depression.

To run as a Democrat, Sinclair had to abandon his friends in the Socialist Party, many of whom regarded his switch as a traitorous act. Socialist leader Norman Thomas condemned Sinclair's EPIC program as an "impossible" plan during the campaign (Katcher 1967, 77). Indeed, Sinclair's action killed off any hopes the Socialists had for becoming a force in state politics. Many voters, who might have gone for the Socialists, went instead for Sinclair and remained Democrats thereafter (Leader 1980; Greg Mitchell 1992, 72–74).

Having made the switch, Sinclair wrote a short pamphlet predicting his victory—*I, Governor of California and How I Ended Poverty*—and outlining his steps as governor. The pamphlet immediately went into mass circulation and led to the formation of numerous EPIC clubs throughout the state. Sinclair's candidacy overwhelmed the party regulars. In the primary, he bested traditional Democrat George Creel, securing Sinclair the nomination with Sheridan Downey running on the same ticket for lieutenant governor. The two candidates were quickly termed "Uppy and Downey." Significantly, Creel—who had links with the Roosevelt administration—received more votes in the primary than did Sinclair *outside Los Angeles County*. Thus, EPIC was a Los Angeles affair (Leader 1972, 137).

Essentially, the EPIC plan called for the unemployed to take over idle factories and farms as cooperatives. Cooperatives and communes of various types, it might be noted, had a long history in California prior to EPIC (Schwartz 1998, 177). The EPIC cooperative takeovers would be financed by scrip to be issued by a new California Authority for Money. Various cooperative movements already operated in California under names such as "reciprocal economy." The notion was that if unemployed people and resources were engaged in cooperative barter, they could hoist themselves out of the Depression (Whiteman and Lewis 1936, 146–87).

Creating scrip to stimulate business was not a California invention, but the idea was eagerly received in the state. It lived on after the EPIC campaign under such names as "Tradex," a quasi-bank system founded in 1932 through which credits were exchanged among participants (Lindsay 1960, 88; Whiteman and Lewis 1936, 188–202). And, in fact, there had been many experiments in Los Angeles with cooperatives, scrip exchanges, and other forms of self-help beginning in the early years of the Great Depression. Some of these cooperatives were sponsored by communists as a way of organizing the unemployed. But cooperatives had a still longer history in southern California, going back to the Llano del Rio Co-operative Colony of the World War I era. Sinclair had contacts with some of the figures that had been involved in that earlier experiment (Greenstein, Lennon, and Rolfe 1992).

The leaders of Depression-era self-help groups apparently made sure their members were registered to vote. One report put the registration rate for group members in Los Angeles at 94 percent (Leader 1972, 113–20, 181–83, 253). Voting propensities mattered, of course, to politicians. Thus, it should be no surprise that the Los Angeles County board of supervisors created a county department to foster cooperative enterprises (Ford 1961, 11–12).

A number of the later Ham and Eggs activists, notably Robert Noble and Sherman Bainbridge, apparently had links to the Tradex movement. Presumably, they learned about scrip money schemes through this involvement. Indeed, Tradex described its scrip as a "commodity dollar," a phrase identified with Irving Fisher upon whose writings Ham and Eggs stamp-money was later to be based[3] (Whiteman and Lewis 1936, 199).

In Upton Sinclair's EPIC version, the scrip issued by the state would be "backed" by funds raised through sales of $300 million of bonds to the federal government. Evidently, Sinclair thought that the Roosevelt administration had promised to buy such bonds, based on a vague conversation with a New Deal official (Singer 1974, 379–80). In any event, with the source of funds no longer a problem, all persons over sixty "in need" would receive a monthly pension of $50. Idle farms would be bought by the California Authority for Land; idle factories by the California Authority for Production.

The EPIC campaign led to a massive increase in Democratic registration, effectively making the party competitive in state politics thereafter. It put Republicans into a panic, as they saw their control of state government potentially at an end. As a defensive move, Earl Warren, then Republican district attorney of Alameda County, was commissioned to draft up amendments to the state constitution for the ballot. The amendments were designed to protect incumbent Republican appointees with new civil service protections should Sinclair win (Katcher 1967, 76). In Los Angeles County in particular, the Democrats went from being a minority party to being dominant, at least as measured by registration (Leader 1972, 143). Yet the Democratic Party's old-line regulars were not happy to be displaced by the EPIC newcomers. Nor was the Roosevelt administration anxious to see Sinclair win, for fear of having the New Deal tarred as aligned with radicalism. Unaware of FDR's disdain for EPIC, Sinclair attempted unsuccessfully to obtain Roosevelt's endorsement. He thought he had had more success with Father Coughlin, who—Sinclair said—had endorsed EPIC after a meeting of the two over a Sunday supper (Schlesinger 1960, 116; Whiteman and Lewis 1936, 221; Greg Mitchell 1992, 127). Unfortunately for EPIC, Father Coughlin subsequently repudiated the reported endorsement, embarrassing Sinclair (Starr 1996, 151).

Sinclair apparently did not understand the significance of the elderly vote to his campaign. The elderly had been attracted to his $50 per month pension proposal, even though it did not match Townsend's $200. After all, there was no Townsend Plan option on the state ballot. However, Sinclair opposed the Townsend pension plan. In contrast, his running mate, Downey—a more astute politician—later became a major Townsend supporter. Sinclair opposed the transactions tax basis of the Townsend Plan as regressive (Earl Warren Oral History 1976a, Clifton interview, 4). He soft-pedaled his own $50 pension proposal, hoping in vain to win Roosevelt's endorsement by instead supporting Social Security, then under consideration in Congress (Putnam 1970, 39). And Sinclair probably believed that once his EPIC plan was in place in California, restored prosperity would take care of the needs of the elderly along with everyone else's.

The failure of Sinclair to court the Townsendites allowed incumbent Merriam to move into the pension void. It was costless for Merriam to endorse the Townsend Plan as it was a national program with no state action required. If there was a cost, it was a reported $12,000 rumored to have been promised—although reportedly not ever delivered—to the Townsend organization by the Republicans (Whiteman and Lewis 1936,

219; Fitzgerald 1951, 19). All Merriam had to do was say he was for Townsend and that he sure hoped Congress would enact the plan. At least some Democrats in the state legislature learned this lesson from Merriam. Assemblyman Sam Yorty—an anti-Sinclair Democrat who eventually became mayor of Los Angeles in the 1960s—also endorsed the Townsend Plan (Ainsworth 1966, 88).

Sinclair's candidacy, and the likelihood that he could win against Merriam, panicked the state's business establishment. A massive campaign was mounted to defeat Sinclair, featuring precedent-setting use of an advertising agency in politics to sell the otherwise unappealing Merriam. Negative advertising and publicity became the core of the effort.

The campaign focused so much on Sinclair's failings, and so little on Merriam's virtues, that Merriam himself complained to its sponsors (Gottlieb and Wolt 1977, 208–9). But he was told to follow the script and he did. Included in the anti-Sinclair campaign were false newsreels shown in California movie theaters. Among other elements of these newsreels were fake shots of unemployed bums flocking to California on freight trains to cash in on expected government largesse under EPIC.[4]

In contrast, King Vidor's classic film *Our Daily Bread*, which portrayed the worker and farmer cooperative notion in a sympathetic light, was kept out of Los Angeles theaters until 1935, well after the EPIC campaign. (It had been designated by the *New York Times* as one of the ten best films of 1934.) As the Vidor film demonstrated, not all of Hollywood was against Sinclair. He had at least the support of Charlie Chaplin, who spoke to the crowd at EPIC rallies (Leader 1972, 139; Greg Mitchell 1992, 559, 578).

In the end, Merriam won by 1.1 million votes to Sinclair's 876,000. Merriam even carried Los Angeles County, although by a lesser margin than the rest of the state (Leader 1972, 142). The vote was amazingly close, given the all-out campaign mounted against Sinclair. (Downey, running for lieutenant governor, received 200,000 votes more than did Sinclair, but still lost by a slight margin.) Democratic party regulars, for example, endorsed Merriam—forsaking their official candidate—in a negotiated arrangement that had Merriam make some supportive remarks about the New Deal. And there was a third-party "Progressive"— Raymond Haight—also on the ballot, who garnered over 300,000 votes.

Haight, as had Merriam, costlessly endorsed the Townsend Plan as something Congress—not the state—should implement (Putnam 1970, 41). Initially, Dr. Townsend supported Haight but then switched to Merriam when the latter endorsed the Townsend Plan (Fitzgerald 1951, 18). Had Sinclair been willing to rise above principle and court the Townsendites, and had there been no significant third-party candidate, he might well have won.[5]

After the election, the EPIC clubs and movement remained intact, and eventually Sinclair made various stabs at reconciling with the Townsendites. In a move that foreshadowed the strategy of George McLain, EPIC pushed for raising state relief payments to the elderly to $50 a month. It subsequently endorsed a successful compromise effort in the legislature to raise payments to a maximum of $35 and cut the eligibility age to sixty-five from seventy. Sinclair asked Congressman John McGroarty, who had submitted Townsend bills in Congress, to modify the proposal to provide an income and inheritance tax base (rather than Townsend's transaction tax). At one point Sinclair sought to outdo Townsend by proposing $400 per month as a pension. None of these gestures, however, produced a formal alliance between EPIC supporters and Townsendites (Putnam 1970, 42–46).

Despite Sinclair's personal opposition to the Ham and Eggs proposal, some EPIC clubs later drifted into the Ham and Eggs movement, partly due to Sinclair's abortive courtship of Townsend (Grenier 1974, 334). Sherman J. Bainbridge, who later became a key Ham and Eggs personality, was a member of the EPIC board of directors in 1935. He persuaded the board to require that all EPIC propaganda carry a line endorsing a $200 pension to attract Townsendites (Putnam 1970, 46). It was only a step from one pension scheme to another.

Academic Monetarism and New Deal Policies

Notions about fiddling with the currency as a Great Depression remedy were not confined to the political and academic fringes by any means. Irving Fisher, the Yale professor whose stamp-money ideas were adopted by the Ham and Eggers, supported a "commodity dollar" rather than a gold dollar. Prices of a broad range of goods should be stabilized using modern index numbers after sufficient "reflation" to undo the deflation that accompanied the onset of the Depression. Fisher was a well-respected expert on index numbers as well as money. And he had earlier combined the two interests in formulating the quantity theory of money. The theory suggested that in the long run the money supply determined the price level (Fisher 1922/1963).

In 1935, Fisher put out his reflation/stabilization plan in a book dedicated to President Roosevelt. As was the case with many reformers,

Fisher apparently thought that the president was following his advice or, at least, might be convinced to do so. When the gold standard was initially abandoned by the United States, Fisher saw the move as a step in the right direction, despite the acknowledged opposition of many orthodox economists of the day. Indeed, Fisher admitted his own move away from orthodoxy. He reported that at the time of William Jennings Bryan's free silver campaign, he opposed Bryan in favor of "sound money." By 1935, however, Fisher reported that "had the campaign occurred at the present time, I would not have been so strenuous an opponent of Mr. Bryan" (Fisher 1935, 375). It was not that Fisher bought the free silver rationale of the Populists. Rather, he thought that in the depression of the 1890s, as in the Great Depression of the 1930s, a monetary expansion would have provided the needed reflation.

Fisher (1936) also supported "100% money," a system under which banks could not create money but would instead have to hold reserves against 100 percent of their deposits. In this he was supported by several prominent economists at the University of Chicago. The Chicago Plan basically would have created two types of banks. Checking banks would have had to hold reserves against 100 percent of their deposits. With 100 percent reserves, these banks would not have been a source of loans. Thus, the money supply (currency plus demand deposits) would not be subject to contraction due to loan defaults. Savings banks would hold long-term accounts and would make loans. But these long-term accounts were not considered "money" by the proponents of 100 percent reserves. Versions of these proposals were debated in Congress although never enacted (Phillips 1995). And the Roosevelt administration never endorsed 100 percent money, relying instead on various other banking reforms.

Unlike Fisher and his compatriots, George F. Warren, a professor of agriculture at Cornell (who had coauthored a well-known book on money, prices, and gold) did obtain the ear of President Roosevelt. Warren's basic idea was that raising the price of gold would cause all other prices to rise proportionally (Warren and Pearson 1935, 144). Such a rise—if it occurred—would accomplish the kind of reflation Fisher was seeking. But it flew in the face of Fisher's quantity theory, which predicted that without a change in the money supply, a gold price change would not have much effect.

And, indeed, Irving Fisher turned out to be correct. Roosevelt's gold price increase had little direct impact on the overall American price level, an interesting proof that money and gold were not the same thing, even under a gold standard. On the other hand, George Warren's advice amounted to a major devaluation of the dollar relative to other currencies. As a result, internationally traded commodity prices rose substantially in dollar terms. All of this experimentation with money was highly visible to the public and was made more so by FDR's references to money, gold, and banking in his radio fireside chats. Furthermore, to avoid windfalls to holders of gold when the gold price was officially raised, publicly held gold was called in at the old official price. Americans were thereafter forbidden by law to hold gold (until this prohibition was repealed decades later). And there was also official diddling with silver. (See below.) Thus, many Americans were affected by these monetary manipulations. Even if they had no gold or silver bullion, ordinary citizens would have seen changes in the physical appearance of the national currency, reflecting the manipulations.

The Roosevelt administration was split between inflationists/reflationists and orthodox sound-money types. Democrats in Congress had a strong inflationist bent left over from free silver days, especially among those representatives and senators from rural areas. All sorts of proposals were made ranging from free silver to the issuance of greenbacks from a Coughlin-type nationalized central bank. Seeking alliances, congressional proponents of monetary expansion would sometimes tie their proposals to specific expenditures such as public works for the unemployed or veterans' bonuses or pensions (Reeve 1943, 28–30, 87–90, 98, 118).

Alternatively, arguments were made that silver prices should be raised for reasons other than monetary expansion. For example, China—which was on a silver standard—was said to have cheap labor due to low silver prices. In turn, the cheap labor imports from China were accused of undercutting U.S. industry (ibid. 254). One result was that the silver industry was subsidized by the Roosevelt administration even though a true silver standard was not implemented. By bidding up the world price of silver, the administration managed to provoke complaints from China, which experienced a large silver outflow to the United States and resultant deflation (ibid. 106).

But not all in the Democratic Party agreed with the ad hoc monetary policy of the New Deal. Al Smith, the 1928 Democratic candidate for president and—like Roosevelt—a former governor of New York State, denounced departures from gold as fostering "baloney dollars" (Schlesinger 1959, 245). Nonetheless, the official policies with regard to money certainly contributed to an atmosphere in which previously unusual proposals about the currency were not necessarily seen as odd or radical.

Los Angeles, in particular, may have been partial to paper money. A travel guide from the 1920s reported that Californians as a rule preferred metallic to paper money. But those from northern California referred to paper as "Los Angeles money." So perhaps it should not be surprising that proposals for retirement "warrants" originated in Los Angeles (King 1997).

Underconsumption and Planning

Various underconsumption theories developed, or became popular, during the Great Depression. Closely associated were theories that the Depression was caused by insufficient income going to consumers. Marxists, of course, pioneered in the notion of contradictions in capitalism that would cause periodic crises. But the idea was also paradoxically popular among some in the business and political establishment. President Herbert Hoover urged employers not to cut wages when the Depression began, relying on this approach. For a time, some major employers heeded his advice although the Depression eventually overwhelmed the wage structure. When the New Deal was initiated, the idea was again put forward. Under the National Industrial Recovery Act of 1933 and later the pro-union Wagner Act of 1935, upward pressure on wages was taken as a Good Thing, which would stimulate consumption. That argument appears explicitly in the Wagner Act's preamble (Daniel Mitchell 1986; Kaufman 1996). The notion was that unions would raise wages and stimulate the economy through increased consumption by workers.

Huey Long and Gerald L.K. Smith

Huey Long built a political career in Louisiana attacking the state's business establishment, especially oil companies. His first elective victory put him on the state Railroad Commission. This position gave Long regulatory authority over oil pipelines and a platform for a first unsuccessful run for governor. Nonetheless, he pioneered in the use of radio as a campaign medium in the early 1920s during that race. And in his second attempt in 1928, he succeeded in becoming the youngest governor in Louisiana history.

As governor, Long created a powerful political machine that could produce public works, patronage, and programs popular with the electorate. He overcame an impeachment attempt in 1929, cementing his control of the state. When Long decided to step out on the national stage, running for the U.S. Senate in 1930, he saw to it that a puppet governor was installed in his home state. In effect, Long held the two offices—senator and de facto governor—at the same time.

Initially, Long was able to develop a national following of "Share-Our-Wealth" clubs without much of a program. "I haven't any program or philosophy. I just take things as they come," he declared (Schlesinger 1960, 50–52). His main appeal was in being for a redistribution of wealth and in being a colorful character. According to Long, the Great Depression arose "because a handful of men in the United States own all the money" (Mann 1992, 22). That approach was enough for his supporters. Long adopted the nickname "Kingfish" from a character in the popular *Amos and Andy* radio program. He also lifted a campaign slogan from William Jennings Bryan, the free-silver populist: "Every man a king" (Bennett 1969, 124).

But eventually, as the Ham and Eggs folks also discovered, it became necessary to have an explicit program; slogans and vague ideas ultimately need to be turned into a plan. Long had backed the Roosevelt presidential candidacy in 1932, but he then opposed Roosevelt's National Industrial Recovery Act as promoting monopolies and soon attacked FDR directly. Long's competing program involved heavy progressive taxation of income and wealth, one-time bonuses of $5,000 to every family as a "homestead allowance" combined with a $2,000 guaranteed annual income, reduced working hours, "adequate" pensions for those sixty years old and over, and other components.[6]

Long apparently planned to make a third-party run for the presidency in 1936, believing he could take enough votes from Roosevelt to give the election to the Republicans. He had been buoyed in this belief by Upton Sinclair's victory in the Democratic gubernatorial primary in 1934 (Greg Mitchell 1992, 26). Long calculated that after four years of Republican control and mismanagement, the country would turn in despair to the Kingfish in 1940 (Mann 1992, 31). Members of the Roosevelt administration found this strategy quite plausible and were quite concerned about a Long third-party effort. Meanwhile, as Upton Sinclair had done with regard to the California governorship, Long wrote a book predicting his election and describing his deeds after becoming president.

But Huey Long never got to make his presidential run. He was assassinated in 1935. Although there is still debate about the circumstances of the murder, the assassin was the son of a Louisiana judge. The judge had been gerrymandered into an election district in which he was likely to be defeated in the next election, perhaps providing a motive for his son's action. Long's wife was appointed to serve out his U.S. Senate term, but she did not have the political ability to take control of the Share-Our-Wealth movement. Huey and his brother, Earl, who later became Louisiana governor, had been estranged because of Earl's public charges that Huey had taken a bribe. So Earl was not the heir-apparent. Huey's son, Russell, who later became a senator (and pushed Employee Stock Ownership Plans as a wealth-sharing technique in the 1970s and 1980s), was not a feasible candidate. Russell was only a teenager at the time of the assassination.

With the family unable to take charge of the Long legacy, the notion of a presidential run lived on in the twisted care of Gerald L.K. Smith. Smith was a preacher linked to the Long enterprise. As a high schooler, Smith had won an elocution contest reciting William Jennings Bryan's "Cross of Gold" speech. Smith took control of some of the Share-Our-Wealth movement despite efforts to block him by other Long associates. He ingratiated himself with Francis Townsend by escorting him from a hostile congressional hearing at which Townsend had refused to testify. Eventually, an alliance of Coughlin, Smith, and a wavering Townsend resulted in the Union Party and the candidacy of William ("Liberty Bill") Lemke, a North Dakota congressman, for the presidency in 1936.

Lemke was a quasi-Republican who had nonetheless supported FDR initially. He began his political career in the Non-Partisan League, a group with populist and agrarian elements fighting against railroads, financiers, and grain elevator operators. Lemke backed bills for free silver and other currency expansion while in Congress. And he supported a moratorium on farmers' debts. But Lemke was never quite in control of his own presidential campaign; Coughlin and Smith tended to dominate with Townsend increasingly left in the background.

Smith was a rabid anti-Semite and made a Union Party convention speech condemning "Franklin D. Jews-Evelt."[7] The Union Party's official platform was Coughlinite, calling for a new central bank to replace the Federal Reserve and new currency to buy back the national debt. The platform combined this monetarism with Long-ish demands for limits on annual income and inheritance. Economic security for the aged was promised. But the Townsend Plan was not actually in the platform, and Lemke was personally slow in endorsing the plan.

This omission of the Townsend Plan may have been Father Coughlin's influence; before the Union Party alliance, Coughlin had once called the Townsend Plan "economic insanity" (Bennett 1969, 183). At one point, Coughlin appeared to support the "Lundeen bill." The Lundeen proposal, an alternative to the Townsend Plan, would have taxed the rich to provide pensions (Whiteman and Lewis 1936, 137). Lundeen was a comprehensive unemployment relief bill that included old age as a category of inability to work. Because of its high benefits—the unemployment benefit was essentially 100 percent of the wage—it was estimated to cost almost as much as the Townsend Plan[8] (Paul Douglas 1936, 74–83). Indeed, critics of both Townsend and Lundeen linked the two plans together as examples of wildly unworkable proposals (Quadagno 1988, 109). Social Security—which was actually a radical departure from past federal policy—thus became the "moderate" pension proposal before Congress.

Townsend's connection with Long's (and now Smith's) "Share-Our-Wealth" movement was as tenuous as his link to Coughlin. The "cofounder" of the Townsend movement, Robert Earl Clements, had had an amiable chat with Huey Long before the latter's death. But no meeting of the minds resulted (U.S. Congress, House of Representatives 1936, 330). As had Upton Sinclair in 1934, Smith and Coughlin neglected the pensionite vote, which in turn cost their party votes.

As a result of the Union Party's weak support for the Townsend Plan, Townsend's supporters were not mobilized to obtain the petitions necessary to put Lemke on the ballot in California and some other states. Thus, Lemke was not available as a choice to California voters for president except as a write-in candidate. In the end, Townsend—as a California resident—said that even though he supported Lemke, he would vote for Republican Alf Landon so as not to waste his vote on a write-in candidate. Moreover, the California Democratic Party, under the leadership of then-chairman Culbert Olson, had apparently planted infiltrators in the Townsend clubs. Their task was to hold onto Townsendite votes for Roosevelt (Bennett 1969, 221).

Lemke was no Huey Long when it came to campaigning. His only major endorsement—if it can be called that—was by "General" Jacob S. Coxey. Coxey—in a foreshadowing of the 1932 Bonus Marchers—had led an "army" to Washington in 1893 demanding unemployment relief and money creation for public works.[9] As were the later leaders of the 1932 Bonus March, Coxey was arrested and became a folk hero. But such an endorsement, combined with the lukewarm support of Townsend, could not dent Roosevelt's popularity. Lemke—who was no substitute for Huey Long as a vote getter—received fewer than 900,000 votes, 2 percent of the national total, and sank into oblivion. Gerald L.K. Smith appeared subsequently as a speaker at abortive rallies aimed at reviving the Ham and Eggs movement in 1946 (Zimmerman 1980, 92; Lindsay 1960, 89). Townsend tried to start his own political party in California in the late 1930s, but it never amounted to much, even in Los Angeles (Leader 1972, 150).

Social Credit

The Social Credit movement, which originated in Britain, had strong elements of underconsumptionist thinking. This movement spread to other countries, including Canada, where the home-grown Social Credit Party elected a government of Alberta province in 1935. As propounded by its British founder, Major C.H. Douglas, the Social Credit movement was based on the notion that there was an inherent imbalance between the value of production and the value of income received for consumption. It should be noted that at the time this doctrine was conceived, national income accounting was in its infancy. Accounting identities such as income equals product were not well understood. Nor was input-output analysis available—which shows how the value of final products can be disaggregated into the payments to factors of production down the chain of the stages of production.

In any event, Major Douglas wrote in an opaque style on economic matters—seemingly a requisite for obtaining a following of True Believers. He sprinkled his works with anti-Semitic references including favorable comments about the fraudulent "Protocols of the Learned Elders of Zion."[10] Such conspiratorial references appear also to have been part of the general formula for gathering acolytes during the 1930s and before.

Not surprisingly, Social Credit also had a monetary component. It was this element that attracted famed poet Ezra Pound—who had earlier supported the EPIC plan's proposed issuance of scrip[11] (Singer 1974, 395; Greg Mitchell 1992, 137–38). (Pound somehow saw in Fascist Italy a country having Social Credit virtues—views that led to his hospitalization and incarceration in a mental institution following World War II.) Major Douglas quoted William Jennings Bryan's famous "Cross of Gold" speech in his preface to the revised edition of his principal text (C.H. Douglas 1937, vi). And it was in part this populist aspect of Social

Credit that appealed to the agrarian Alberta electorate. Many Albertans had been schooled in Bryan's free silver notions coming north across the U.S.–Canadian border in an earlier period.

Father Coughlin met with Major Douglas during a swing of the latter through North America to meet with his Canadian and American followers. Douglas was given the opportunity to speak on radio coast-to-coast while in the United States (Finlay 1972, 135). During the EPIC campaign for governor of California in 1934, Republican candidate Frank Merriam endorsed Social Credit as a national (not state) policy. But he persisted in referring to it as "social credits" (Schlesinger 1960, 120; Whiteman and Lewis 1936, 219). As in the case of the Townsend Plan, Merriam was happy to endorse any proposal that would pull votes from Upton Sinclair but which required no real action on his own part.

Major Douglas proposed to solve the underconsumption problem—which he summarized in his "A+B Theorem"—by having the government calculate the value of potential production. Then it would distribute sufficient money to allow consumption of this amount. As with other such movements of the day, Social Credit tended to confound money and income. Thus, supplying income and creating money were seen as much the same thing. Rather than just making payments to the elderly (although some in the British movement began with old-age pensions as a cause [Finlay 1972, 138]), the government under Social Credit would make payments to *everyone*. Still, Major Douglas suggested to the Albertans that the dividend could be graduated, with the elderly getting the largest bonuses (Mallory 1954, 66).

The Alberta Social Credit regime was never pure enough for Major Douglas, a fact that led to schisms and turmoil in the Alberta provincial movement. Douglas and his "true" disciples doubted a province could implement the complete program; it required central government action in their view. In contrast, Alberta's version of Social Credit was based on the assumption that the province could implement the program.

Alberta's impure version of Social Credit was developed by the charismatic William Aberhart, a high school principal and preacher with strong fundamentalist and antievolutionist beliefs and a fascination with the book of Revelation. He began airing religious broadcasts in the mid-1920s through his Calgary Prophetic Bible Institute. A fast learner, Aberhart quickly came to understand the power of radio to influence listeners (and to raise money).

During the Great Depression, Aberhart's religious broadcasts began to take on an economic character. He was reportedly deeply shaken by the Depression-related suicide of a student in his high school. A fellow educator, who had been trying to interest Aberhart in Social Credit, used the suicide event to persuade him that the doctrine was the solution to the prevailing distress. Social Credit became the economic message of choice on Aberhart's broadcasts. Gradually, economics replaced religion on his programs. In particular, a "Man from Mars" broadcast series became popular. The plot involved a Martian who arrived on Earth to research economic conditions in Alberta. Social Credit would be explained to the visitor and the Martian would demand to know why dumb Earthlings were refusing to implement this obvious solution. (When the program was performed before a live audience, the Martian for no apparent reason wore an Arab headdress.)

In addition to the broadcasts, pamphlets and newspapers began to be issued by the Alberta Social Credit movement. Aberhart started touring the province making dramatic speeches favoring Social Credit. The pamphlets proposed a scheme quite similar to Ham and Eggs—including scrip or "credits" that would supplement ordinary Canadian money. However, in its "final" (but never implemented) version, the bonuses would be paid to everyone, not just the elderly, in keeping with Major Douglas's proposal. Existing political parties in Alberta would not adopt the program, and so to implement the plan, a new political party was formed. It ultimately won control of the Alberta government in 1935, and Aberhart became provincial prime minister (Irving 1959).

The Alberta Social Credit government unsuccessfully attempted to pay a "social dividend" of $25 a month to each citizen in the form of "Alberta credit"—that is, provincial scrip (Mallory 1954, 69–70). These efforts were observed south of the Canadian border. Father Coughlin made favorable statements about Social Credit after receiving the Albertan prime minister (Reeve 1943, 104; Irving 1959, 102). The Social Credit government—which lasted until 1971—actively promoted international banking conspiracy theories of a Coughlinesque variety. Even after the death of Prime Minister Aberhart in 1943, the provincial government issued reports denouncing the Bretton Woods international monetary institutions. It viewed international finance as a conspiracy in league with socialists to centralize government and weaken provincial power. And, of course, Alberta's Social Credit plans *were* blocked by the central Canadian government. As the saying goes, even paranoid people have enemies.

The political turmoil in Alberta may have put a damper on enthusiasm for Social Credit in the United States. Major Douglas's on-again/off-again relationship with the Alberta government was not good publicity. Nonetheless, congressional hearings were held on a Social Credit bill in 1936. The Ham and Eggs literature touted the Alberta experience as proof that the Ham and Eggs plan could work in California. But President Roosevelt cited the Alberta experience as an example of why Ham and Eggs would not work.[12] Still, the "pump-priming" component of the New Deal (giving people income to spend to stimulate the economy) had at least superficial similarities with Social Credit. So, too, did Keynesian "multiplier" notions that were beginning to filter into the United States from Britain.[13]

The Utopian Society and Technocracy

Although it is impossible to trace all the connections between different groups and schools of thought, much of the Social Credit doctrine appears in the beliefs of the Utopian Society. It was the Utopians (along with Plenocracy) with which Sherman Bainbridge and Roy Owens of Ham and Eggs were initially affiliated. The Utopian Society of America (with acronym "USA") originated in Los Angeles but had branches (and rump groups) in other parts of the country. It claimed to be following the principles of Edward Bellamy, author of *Looking Backward*, an 1888 novel about an improved socialist society in the year 2000.[14] The novel created a social movement when it appeared, with Bellamy-inspired clubs scattered around the country at the time.

Despite its proclaimed tie to Bellamy, the Utopian Society was created in 1933 and had no formal link to the older movement. But the claim of older wisdom apparently was helpful to the Utopian Society. One of its promoters, W.G. Rousseau, claimed to be a descendant of Swiss/French philosopher Jean-Jacques Rousseau, for example (Leader 1972, 125). Another had been involved in the Julian oil scandal, an infamous southern California stock-rigging scheme of the 1920s (Cleland 1947, 133–34, 210–11, 219). The Utopian Society viewed a maldistribution of income and an "unscientific monetary system" as the root of the Great Depression. The monetary system was unscientific because it was based on precious metals rather than productive capacity. Utopians also had elements of the EPIC campaign's link to "Technocracy," and promoted "production for consumption," a slogan similar to EPIC's "production for use."

With Technocracy being touted as the cure for the Depression by the *Los Angeles Daily News* and its publisher, such thinking was becoming more mainstream. Its seeming foundation in science and engineering attracted individuals who did not want to consider themselves "radicals." Sam Yorty, for example, the anti-EPIC Democrat who was elected to the California State Assembly and eventually became mayor of Los Angeles, began his political thinking in Technocracy. Yorty argued that "those who stamp a label of Socialism on Technocracy are merely dodging and befogging the real issue" (Ainsworth 1966, 62; Bollens and Geyer 1973, 3–5).

Technocracy's true believers—known as "technates"—argued that "the scarcity of goods [was] being progressively destroyed by the application of science." Only the "Mysticism of Money" was maintaining the scarcity. Prices should be set in energy units (ergs) "independent of supply and demand" and goods would be exchanged for labor in terms of some kind of energy equivalent of work (Loeb 1933, 7, 27, 34–35, 40). Money would be replaced by energy certificates, handed out equally to all citizens. Working life would be between ages twenty-five and forty-five (Katcher 1967, 73). In a throwback to the principles of scientific management, there was asserted to be a single correct technical solution to all economic problems.[15] Finding the solution awaited only the application of expertise.

> How best to produce and distribute the products of man's efforts is an engineering problem for each detail of which there is always a right answer. (Loeb 1933, 76)

The source of these engineering solutions would be found in government-established monopolies—one for each industry. Each would be run by a chairman who would serve the public good. Such service would be guaranteed because, with all material needs satisfied by Technocracy, the chairman would have no reason to be greedy (Loeb 1973, 77–78). A board of engineers would oversee the monopolies. As a side benefit, all war would be abolished as the state, by being able to mobilize energy effectively, could deter any aggressor (ibid., 96–97).

Technocracy did not originate in California. Some of its early adherents included famed electrical engineer Charles Steinmetz, economist/sociologist Thorstein Veblen, and other well-known figures of the day. However, it had a strong base in California, a headquarters in Pismo

Beach, and adherents at Cal Tech (Whiteman and Lewis 1936, 8; Furst 1949, 5; Cleland 1947, 218). As is often the case with such movements, Technocracy had a tendency to splinter; a group known as the "Continentals," which claimed it had a more humanistic interpretation of Technocracy than those of the original technates, developed in the Los Angeles area (Leader 1972, 123).

Such splinters did not matter to the Ham and Eggers, who were as happy to attract Technocracy followers to their cause as anyone else. In the major Ham and Eggs book, a quote from Howard Scott, director of Technocracy, Inc., appears prominently on the first page of text. The quote warns that once per capita energy consumption reaches 30 percent above current levels, "the social operation of the United States will become increasingly critical." The book also cites numerous technological advances that were about to happen and would presumably put people out of work. Among these is a warning that "Henry Ford proposes to build his car almost entirely from soy beans and other vegetable products," thus decimating the steel industry (California Pension Plan 1938, 11, 22).

The publisher of the *Los Angeles Daily News*, Manchester Boddy—with his enthusiasm for Technocracy—was also supportive of the Utopian Society. Boddy was a man of mercurial political tastes—hard to characterize on a right/left spectrum. He opposed Upton Sinclair and backed Frank Merriam in the EPIC campaign, despite EPIC's affinity for technocratic planning[16] (Gottlieb and Wolt 1977, 234). And he was a man of many interests; Boddy's unique botanical estate later became the Descanso Gardens, a major park now owned by Los Angeles County (Ford 1961, 166). But despite Boddy's support for Technocracy and Utopianism, the publishers of other papers were less broad-minded. They saw the Utopian Society as a home of "red radicalism" (Rosenstone 1970, 296–98).

Some of the charges of radicalism may have been due to the admiration the followers of Technocracy had for the planning process in the Soviet Union. The Soviet attempt to rationalize production in five-year plans seemed a Technocrat's dream (Loeb 1933, 204–5). Utopians, with their Technocracy orientation, may have been tarred with the same brush. Apart from what the Soviets were doing, the early New Deal—under the National Industrial Recovery Act—had also sought to turn industries into cartels and to rationalize production.[17] Thus, those who saw the New Deal as overly leftist would be likely to harbor the same views about Technocrats and Utopians.

Some of the charges of radicalism may also have been due to the Utopian Society's racial tolerance. It had prominent black officials and reportedly gave Augustus Hawkins a start in state politics (Whiteman and Lewis 1936, 56–57). Hawkins was eventually elected to Congress and is best remembered for an attempt to mandate federal policy to achieve full employment in the 1970s, the Humphrey–Hawkins Act. To this day, the chair of the Federal Reserve is obligated to make a Humphrey–Hawkins report to Congress—an unknowing tribute to California Utopianism.

Unlike many other social movements, however, the Utopian Society functioned as a secret order, with odd rituals and oaths. Members and clubs were given numbers to keep identities secret (ibid. 34–35). The organization's recruitment tool was a play that began with actors representing fifth-century pilgrims and proceeded to the modern era. At the end of the play, the entranced audience was asked to send petitions supporting Utopian Society goals to FDR. Apart from the play, the Utopian Society used as its theme the song "Ah, Sweet Mystery of Life, at Last I've Found You" (Ford 1961, 8).

Various factions got hold of the organization (and its treasury) over the years, but for a while it was big enough to hold mass meetings in the Hollywood Bowl. And it had a regular radio program on station KMTR, the same station on which Robert Noble touted Ham and Eggs (Leader 1972, 129). Included in the Utopian Society's platform was the need "to provide a full measure of comfort and security for the aged" (Van Dalsem 1942, 22). Thus, the station's listeners could hear pensionite messages from various perspectives.

The Bonus Marchers

While some in the 1930s needed to dress up proposals for payments to the deserving (or to everyone) in elaborate economic theories, others felt free to make simpler demands. The earliest manifestation of this tendency was the "Bonus March" of 1932. Demands of the veterans who marched on Washington, D.C., were simple enough: Cash now!

Veterans of World War I had been promised a bonus as part of a law enacted in 1924 over the veto of President Calvin Coolidge. The bonus varied in magnitude depending on the type of military service performed. Those veterans who were owed more than $50 were not paid in cash but rather in certificates maturing in 1945. Pursuant to 1931 legislation, only

50 percent of the face value of these certificates could be borrowed in advance. Effectively, the bonus marchers wanted the rest, about $2.4 billion, paid immediately. They descended on Washington in 1932 to press their claims on Congress and President Hoover as the so-called Bonus Expeditionary Force. Included among the marchers was a contingent from distant Los Angeles (Leader 1972, 187).

Ultimately, the Bonus Marchers were dispersed by Army troops, commanded by General Douglas MacArthur, in a violent confrontation. The episode left a black mark on the Hoover administration and a cloud over MacArthur. Nothing could have been worse than the sight—captured on newsreels of the day—of veterans attacked by the army in which they had served. A smaller repeat of the Bonus March under the Roosevelt administration was co-opted by the new president with offers of relief jobs to the marchers (Bartlett 1937; Watkins 1993, 98–107). The bonus issue simmered in Congress in the years following the march. Eventually, a bonus bill was enacted—over a presidential veto—in 1936 (Leader 1972, 190).

Ironically, the Bonus March might never have occurred had World War I veterans been given a pension similar to that received by Civil War (and Spanish-American War) veterans. Pensions for veterans (and dependents) of those wars had been seen in the period immediately after World War I as too expensive a practice to repeat. As noted in chapter 1, many reformers may have viewed the Civil War pension episode as an unfortunate exercise of corrupt patronage (Orloff 1993, 233–37). So instead of pensions, World War I veterans were offered cheap contributory life insurance and annuity plans, so-called war risk insurance. Most veterans did not take advantage of these plans, for they required personal payments (Epstein 1968, 527–31; Epstein 1928, 184–85). The offer of the 1924 bonus in addition to war-risk insurance can be seen as an attempt by Congress to compensate for lack of pensions that previous veterans had received.

In any event, the notion of mistreated World War I veterans was very much part of the national consciousness. One symptom of this feeling can be seen in the movie *Goldiggers of 1933*, a Depression-oriented musical. The film's final number—"Remember My Forgotten Man"— shows World War I "doughboys" marching off to war, suffering during the war, then coming back to cheering crowds. But in 1933 they are on breadlines and sleeping in doorways despite having done their patriotic duty. Such sentiments helped keep the veterans' bonus issue alive.

Spreading Work: Exclusion

Notions of spreading work around inevitably become popular during periods of limited employment opportunity. In the 1990s, for example, this idea found favor in Germany and France, both countries that were experiencing high unemployment. Limiting the workweek, as in those countries, is only one way of spreading work. Another way is to limit the employment of those who do not "need" it, or should not have it, so that the more deserving might have jobs. Such efforts are often seen with regard to foreign immigrant workers, both legal and illegal. But in the 1930s, the targets were also married women (who—it was argued—should give up jobs so that male breadwinners and single women could have them) and children.

Perhaps the most explicit example of the tendency to exclude the undeserving came in the form of the Los Angeles "bum blockade" of 1936 (Ford 1961, 13–14; Domanick 1994, 59–63). Unemployed transients were coming to the city, sometime by freight train, sometimes by hitchhiking. Los Angeles mayors had been decrying the problem since 1930.

Today Los Angeles is famous (or infamous) for its vast freeway network. But in the 1930s, a columnist in the *Los Angeles Times* claimed that having good roads into the city would be its undoing by providing a conduit for unemployed migrants. He claimed that the Roman Empire had collapsed because it, too, had built good roads (quoted in Leader 1972, 200). And during the EPIC campaign, a major charge by Upton Sinclair's opponents was that his recovery plan would attract the unemployed from other states.

The upshot of this concern about in-migration was the stationing of Los Angeles city police on the California borders with Oregon (!), Nevada, and New Mexico. Those migrants with no "visible means of support" were offered a choice of leaving the state or serving a thirty- to eighty-day jail term at hard labor for vagrancy. Not surprisingly, the blockade engendered great controversy within the state and nationally. In the city itself, the *Los Angeles Times* was a major supporter of the blockade and its architect, Police Chief James Davis (Gottlieb and Wolt 1977, 220).

The obvious illegality and unconstitutionality of the blockade was challenged by the American Civil Liberties Union (ACLU) on behalf of a Los Angeles resident, John Langan. After finishing a job in Arizona, Mr. Langan—described variously as a "mining man" and "former motion picture director"—found himself temporarily blocked by the police from returning to California. However, Langan after returning home had an encounter with police officer Earle Kynette of later car bombing and Ham and Eggs fame. After this encounter, Langan withdrew his lawsuit. Kynette was apparently very persuasive. He was so convincing, in fact, that Langan eventually wrote a letter to the chief of police recommending Kynette for promotion. But despite the failure of the ACLU suit to proceed, the "bum blockade" was withdrawn after about two months of mounting pressure (Leader 1972, 194–218; Henstell 1984, 21).

Spreading Work: Standards

The power of the federal government to set labor standards had been limited by court decisions prior to the Great Depression. Many states, however, had laws limiting child labor, requiring school attendance, and restricting the working hours of female employees. The intent behind such laws varied. Some proponents wanted to protect women and children from harsh labor conditions; others wanted to protect adult male workers from female and child job competition.

The National Industrial Recovery Act (NIRA) of 1933 sought to make industry into cartels, partly to reflate prices and partly to restore business "confidence" by eliminating cut-throat competition. Firms were encouraged to sign industry codes of conduct regulating pricing, market shares, and labor standards. Under these codes, various minimum wages were set, limits on child labor were established, a forty-hour workweek was established as the norm, and sex-based wage differentials (lower wages for women) were discouraged. All of these measures had work-spreading aspects, directly or indirectly.

In 1935, however, the constitutionality of the NIRA was tested at the U.S. Supreme Court. As was other early New Deal legislation, the NIRA was found to overstep the Court's narrow view of federal government power to regulate interstate commerce. The Roosevelt administration was unsuccessful in obtaining congressional authority to "pack" the Supreme Court with new, friendlier justices. But the controversy seemed to move the court to a wider interpretation of federal authority. One beneficiary of this broader definition of federal power was the Fair Labor Standards Act of 1938 (FLSA).

The FLSA went through various phases as a proposal before Congress (Irving Bernstein 1985, 116–45). An early version of the bill would have had a government board setting various industry-by-industry standards, a revival of the NIRA approach. By this time, however, Congress had become more conservative. It was leery about giving a new administrative board substantial economic discretion. In the final compromise version, which took effect a few weeks before the first Ham and Eggs proposition was on the ballot, general (across-the-board) legislated standards were adopted.

These standards included a minimum wage, limits on child labor, and a requirement to pay time and a half for overtime work. The initial minimum wage was 25 cents per hour with subsequent increases provided. Overtime was set to cut in after 44 hours in 1938, scaling back to 40 hours in 1940. Discouragement of overtime and child work was seen as a job-spreading/job-creating measure.

No specific provisions were made for female workers, although the same minimum wage applied to all covered employees, regardless of sex. There was no general prohibition on lower wages for women than men in the FLSA. But at the very bottom of the wage scale, the same minimum wage rate would have to apply.

Of course, the Ham and Eggs plan was not a labor standards proposal. It contained no regulation of hours or minimum wages. But it provided such a large pension for those fifty years old and over—*on the condition of not working*—that many older workers would have left employment. And with many older workers induced to exit the workforce, opportunities for younger workers would presumably be created. In that respect, there was a work-spreading element in Ham and Eggs similar to actual federal policy. And, as will be seen in the next chapter, work spreading was a conscious element in the Townsend pension plan, a predecessor to Ham and Eggs. For that matter, the original Social Security Act of 1935 dealt with *both* pensions and unemployment insurance. The linkage—that old-age pensions would remove the elderly from competition with the younger unemployed—was evident (Quadagno 1988, 19).

Making Connections in Later Eras

On their face, money creation, the fairness of income distribution, and work spreading are not directly related to pensions. Certainly, current discussions of pensions—whether private or Social Security—are not usually placed in those contexts. In particular, fiddling with the currency is not much discussed at all in modern times. And it is not a political winner when it is discussed.

For example, when Steve Forbes made his unsuccessful bid for the Republican presidential nomination in 1996, his proposals to bring back the gold standard seemed oddball. Forbes's handlers generally downplayed this aspect of their candidate—such issues no longer appeal to a large audience—and focused instead on his flat-tax plan. The same thing happened to Jack Kemp, the 1996 Republican vice presidential candidate (and gold standard supporter).

Gadfly supply-side economist Arthur Laffer had also pushed for a return to gold during the Reagan campaign of 1980. Congress required that a "Gold Commission" be set up to study the issue. But the monetary question was quietly shelved with a study and report soon after Ronald Reagan became president. The Reagan administration could see no political gains from pursuing such an arcane issue and stacked the Gold Commission mainly with individuals opposed to gold. Occasionally, academic economists still publish articles about monetary schemes to stabilize the price of a basket of commodities, but these discussions now seem mainly for internal amusement within the profession.

Apart from the Reagan and Forbes/Kemp flurries, gold, silver, currency, and Federal Reserve conspiracies are now mainly the stuff of right-wing groups and militias. Such fringe groups—in true Ham and Eggs fashion—sometimes finance their activities with fraudulent checks on the grounds that the currency in circulation isn't "real." Absent "real" money, the groups feel free to create their own. The location of some of these extremist groups, places like Montana and Idaho, is a dim reflection of the Populist free silver movement that once flourished in those mining regions. But it is doubtful the modern-day militias and less-violent extremists realize that the doctrines they spout have a long history in American politics.

Income distribution *has* been discussed in recent years, notably the rise in wage and income inequality since the 1970s. The issue has been raised by both the political left and right. California State Senator Tom Hayden, a Democrat and one of the "Chicago 7" defendants, for example, raised issues of "social justice" in his unsuccessful bid to become mayor of Los Angeles in 1997. Hayden noted in a newspaper interview at the time of his mayoral bid that he had been raised in Father Coughlin's parish as a child. He reportedly was influenced by the priest's doctrines of Social Justice (Newton 1997). Hayden has also shown traces of Coughlin's monetarism, condemning a rival candidate in an earlier race for working at the International Monetary Fund (IMF) and—still earlier—calling for consumer representation on the Federal Reserve.

At the other end of the spectrum, there is conservative columnist Pat Buchanan. In his bid for the Republican nomination for the presidency in 1992 and 1996, Buchanan decried the impact of international capitalism (and particularly the North American Free Trade Agreement [NAFTA]) on worker's wages. Unlike Hayden, however, Buchanan has dabbled in Coughlinesque anti-Semitism.

The sources of the rise in wage and income inequality are much debated among academics, but mainstream politicians, including President Bill Clinton, have tended to pose remedies involving education and training if they acknowledge the issue. Inequality is not depicted as a cause of economic depression, partly because there has been no depression. Of course, there have been business cycle fluctuations since the 1970s. However, the role of the government in dealing with these undulations of the economy is now discussed in terms of conventional monetary and fiscal policy.

Politicians' careers are still sensitive to poor macroeconomic performance; George Bush is widely viewed as having lost to Bill Clinton because of his seeming unconcern for the recession of 1990–1991 and a sluggish recovery thereafter. However, it is not fashionable for politicians to do more than recite economic figures knowledgeably and appear to be in command of the facts. Staffs of experts are now charged with preparing technical reports and plans that candidates can disown if controversy develops.

To the extent that the work-spreading legislation of the 1930s has been a recent topic of discussion, it has been in terms of making labor policy "family-friendly." Various proposals have been made to allow workers to be able to elect "comp time" off rather than overtime pay for hours above 40 per week. But the notion of creating more jobs by reducing the workweek has been confined mainly to European countries with high chronic unemployment.

The creators of Ham and Eggs took strands of doctrines and currents of thinking that were popular in their era and linked them to a demographically driven pension plan scheme. When the baby boomers retire in the twenty-first century, those political entrepreneurs who take up their cause will have to be equally creative, fashioning proposals—whatever these might be—from doctrines and plans in vogue at that time.

The 2030s will undoubtedly be characterized by different concerns and styles of expression than the 1930s.

Once a political entrepreneur has developed a program and has achieved some success with it, the political marketplace reacts like the commercial marketplace. Other politicians may jump on the bandwagon. Or competitors may arise with variants of the original. Chapter 6 will present speculation on what such doctrines might be at the time the boomers retire. But there are still some historical lessons to analyze first from the era of Ham and Eggs.

As will be seen in the next chapter, the Ham and Eggers had in fact created a variant of an already-popular pension model, the Townsend Plan. Their main contribution was to convert the national Townsend Plan to the state level and to substitute stamp-money for the Townsend Plan's tax-based financing mechanism. Indeed, the major official Ham and Eggs book invited Townsendites to join the Ham and Eggs cause at the state level while awaiting the national plan (California Pension Plan 1938, 65–66).

Both Townsend and Ham and Eggs shared the claim that in fact there would be no net cost to the government. Indeed, they asserted that there would be a more-than-offsetting stimulatory benefit to the economy. Such claims of no cost are inevitably popular in any era. The supply siders of the early 1980s, for example, demonstrated this point by promising that tax cuts would add to—not subtract from—government revenue and help balance the federal budget. Political entrepreneurs who appeal to the baby boomers in the twenty-first century may well make claims of no-cost remedies, too.

Chapter 4

Townsend Versus
Social Security

> Senator, let me ask you, what creates income?
> Nothing in the world but demand. Now, let us have demand, an
> abundant demand, and we shall
> vastly increase the national income.

Dr. Francis E. Townsend (hearing, U.S. Congress, Senate, 1935, 1025)

In 1936, a congressional investigation was launched into "Old-Age Pension Plans and Organizations." Despite its plural title, the investigation was focused on only one plan, the Townsend Plan. It was focused on only one group, Old-Age Revolving Pensions, Ltd., the Townsend organization. A special "Select Committee" of Congress was established to conduct this investigation. Its chair, Congressman C. Jasper Bell of Missouri, was reportedly chosen because he was considered to have a safe seat controlled by the Kansas City Pendergast machine. With such a seat, Bell would not have to fear electoral reprisal from the elderly Townsendites, or so the reasoning went within the Roosevelt administration (Bennett 1969, 178–79). Prior to the hearings, a radio debate was held between an Oklahoma congressman and a representative of the Townsend organization. Instead of debating the merits of the Townsend Plan, however, the congressman—setting the stage for the hearings—attacked the Townsend organization as a money-making scheme (Whiteman and Lewis 1936, 118).

An interesting question raised by this episode is why such effort and stealth was required to deal with an elderly Long Beach, California, physician and his followers. The Roosevelt administration already had won its battle for Social Security, which had been passed by Congress in the previous year. Pension issues—and therefore competing pension proposals—were no longer on the New Deal agenda. So why the investigation of Dr. Francis E. Townsend? According to one historian, the answer to this puzzle is very simple:

> The Bell Committee's purpose was almost wholly political in nature; its objective was the discrediting of the (Townsend) movement and the humiliation of its leader. It aimed to destroy the Townsend organization's effectiveness as a political force in the 1936 elections. (Bennett 1969, 179)

At the time, Roosevelt was not at all sure of the outcome of the forthcoming 1936 election. The blank check given him by Congress in 1933 was no longer available, now that the economy—although still mired in aftermath of the 1929–33 slide—was no longer in free fall. Roosevelt had opposition from conservatives within his own party and from Republicans. Moreover, Senator Huey Long could well be a candidate for president on a third-party ticket. And Long might receive enough votes to throw the election to the Republicans. Finally, some contemporary observers saw an incipient Fascist danger in the blind enthusiasm of the Townsendites. They compared Dr. Townsend to Hitler, as far-fetched as that seems in retrospect (Whiteman and Lewis 1936, 265–67).

Roosevelt's economic policy was under continuous attack. Particularly controversial was his decision to go off the gold standard in 1933 and then return with a devalued dollar in 1934. The currency decision entailed invalidating various "gold clauses" in private and official contracts—a matter that ultimately went to the Supreme Court and was narrowly decided in Roosevelt's favor. However, the New Deal gold policy was denounced in a speech by former President Herbert Hoover, who remained a figure of significance in Republican politics. Responding to a letter from a supporter, Roosevelt said: "[Hoover's view] may be a factor in 1936 but I am inclined to think at present that more serious opposition may come from the Dr. Townsends, the Huey Longs, etc."[1] Plainly, the Townsend Plan, and its originator, was on the president's mind.

In short, the eventual Roosevelt landslide in the fall 1936 election was not foreseen earlier that year. And the political climate seemed very unstable. The constant political polling that characterizes the contemporary scene did not exist. What information was available to the Roosevelt administration as a gauge of public opinion was largely anecdotal.

Sources of information included such things as a letter from a major trade union official worried that workers might be attracted to the Townsend Plan, postal reports on the volume of mail going to the Townsend organization, the special election of a Republican congressman from Michigan on a Townsendite platform, warnings that Republicans were "flirting" with Townsend, and warnings that California Townsendites would try to infiltrate the Democratic National Convention.[2] It was certainly *not* foreseen that 71 percent of those voters favoring the Townsend Plan would in fact vote for Roosevelt in the election, despite Dr. Townsend's admonitions (Cantril 1941, 209). Those Townsendite voters were clearly not aware of the degree to which the Roosevelt administration had instigated the Bell hearings. They wrote to the president asking him to halt the Bell investigation (Figure 4.1, p. 97). Surely they did not know of the enlistment of the postal authorities by the administration to get the goods on Dr. Townsend.[3]

Indeed, the attempt to find some dirt on the Townsend operation went back to 1934 at least. Edwin E. Witte, executive director of the administration's Committee on Economic Security, tried to enlist the FBI in this endeavor. Witte's committee, the planning task force for the administration's Social Security proposals, requested an FBI investigation in November 1934. One of Witte's complaints was that Townsend publications made it appear that Roosevelt supported their plan.[4] The FBI closed the case after concluding that nothing Townsend had done warranted federal prosecution. However, Congressman Bell requested the FBI to supply him with any criminal records it had on selected Townsend officials including Dr. Townsend himself.[5] FBI director J. Edgar Hoover furnished files for certain individuals, but he indicated uncertainty as to whether the individuals for which files were found were the same people in whom Bell had an interest.[6] A later effort by Congressman Bell to obtain information directly from local FBI agents (rather than going through Hoover) was rebuffed.[7]

Pardon Me?

After Dr. Townsend's initial testimony to the Bell committee, he walked out of the hearings in the arms of Gerald L.K. Smith. The walkout prompted a contempt-of-Congress citation, conviction on this charge after a trial, and a jail sentence.[8] Requests to Roosevelt for a pardon for Townsend poured in from Townsendites and some members of Congress. Townsend himself was content to be a martyr and would not request a pardon, the normal procedure. When he was about to report to jail, however, an *unsolicited* pardon from FDR miraculously appeared leading to grateful letters from relieved Townsendites (Figure 4.2, p. 98).

According to an official press release, the president had been persuaded to issue the pardon by a telegram from a now-benevolent Congressman Bell. In it, Bell argued that the Townsend walkout had been planned by "men of stronger will and intelligence" than the doctor possessed and that Townsend should not be held responsible.[9] Of course, by the time the pardon issue arose, the 1936 election had passed and the political danger from Townsendite activities had receded. Townsend's link up with Father Coughlin and Gerald L.K. Smith in the Union Party campaign for the presidency had fizzled.[10]

As Townsend gleefully reported in his autobiography, the presidential pardon had been issued so quickly that the White House had failed to make a carbon copy and later requested he send the original back to duplicate for the files (Townsend 1941, 212). Still, his walkouts from investigations were not always so successful. Townsend also strolled out of a court proceeding investigating the funding of his Cleveland organization. After a short car chase, however, he was hauled back to court by a law enforcement officer (Whiteman and Lewis 1936, 144–45).

Origins of the Townsend Plan

All of this effort to destroy Townsend and his plan may seem a bit excessive in retrospect for a proposal that, some say, had its origins in a humorous magazine article. The article was written not by Townsend but by advertising executive Bruce Barton. Writing in *Vanity Fair* in 1931 as the Depression intensified, Barton proposed as a joke that "every man and woman in the United States be retired from work at the age of forty-five on a pension amounting to one-half of his or her average earnings in the preceding five years." Barton went on to explain that the problem with the modern economy was underconsumption. "My remedy," he wrote, "is simple and Fundamental. Create a special automatic class of Consumers." Barton went on, "Let young men do the work, and old men loaf," a statement eerily similar to the official slogan of the Townsend program: "Age for leisure; youth for work."

Townsend, of course, would not acknowledge any relationship between Barton's joke and his own later plan (Bennett 1969, 152). And in any event, there were other such plans (not intended as jokes) around at the time to copy. For example, as the Bell committee gleefully pointed out, a similar program was copyrighted in 1931 by a dentist named C. Stewart McCord, said to be inspired by Technocracy (Whiteman and Lewis 1936, 66; U.S. Congress, House of Representatives 1936, 757–64; Cantril 1941, 171, note 4). But the fact was that well before the Great Depression, removing the elderly from competition with younger workers was seen by some reformers as a way of raising wages (Quadagno 1988, 100).

Moreover, pension plans for the elderly had been proposed in Congress well before the Great Depression. One bill in 1911, for example, proposed a means-tested pension of $4 per week for those sixty years old and over (without specifying a funding mechanism). Pension bills were submitted periodically during the 1920s. Perhaps the earliest in the line of congressional efforts to set up a general pension system was a bill of 1909, endorsed by the American Federation of Labor. At the time, there were doubts whether a national pension plan would be constitutional. But veterans' pensions clearly were legal; Civil War veterans and their dependents were receiving them. So the bill proposed creating an "Old Age Home Guard" for those sixty-five years and over. Members of the Guard would be paid $120 per year for unspecified "military" duties (Squier 1912, 339–47; Epstein 1968, 532–33; Epstein 1928, 259–62; Skocpol 1992, 212–17).

Even if federal authority to establish a national pension plan was questioned, there was little doubt that states could do so. By 1933, seventeen states had some kind of pension system. These plans typically demanded long residence in the state to establish eligibility and required that some or all of the cost be funded at the county level. As noted in chapter 1, California had adopted the first "mandatory" plan in 1929, requiring the counties to offer old-age assistance partly financed by the state. Another eight states provided that counties could optionally create such plans (Epstein 1968, 534–35).

In short, Townsend had many sources from which to compile a plan. But rather than acknowledge any plagiarism (or even inspiration) from a preexisting source, Townsend had his own, more poignant, story of how his particular proposal was conceived. Townsend's version was that he had looked out his window and had seen old women foraging in his garbage pails for food. His fury at the injustice of the sight inspired him to come up with his particular plan.

Specifically, the women-in-the-garbage incident led Townsend to decide, he later reported, that all citizens sixty years old and over should

receive $200 each month from the federal government. The $200 figure, double Robert Noble's later $25 per week in the initial version of
Ham and Eggs, was deliberately set high, Townsend later explained.
The idea was that with such a high number, no one would likely come
up with a plan with a still larger pension.

Despite his assertion, Townsend's earliest version of the plan set the
figure at $150, not $200.[11] (In reproducing this version in his autobiography, Townsend retroactively rewrote history and changed this figure
to $200 to accord with the later version [Gaydowski 1970b, 382, note 4;
Townsend 1943, 138].) And in 1941, Townsend claimed the plan was
never $200—only *up to* $200 with a then-current estimate of $50
(Townsend 1941, 6, 8). The only condition for receipt of the pension
was to be that beneficiaries refrain from working (the work-spreading
notion) and that they promise to consume the entire pension in one month
(the underconsumption notion).

Townsend's pension would be financed by a 2 percent turnover or
"transactions" tax. But it would actually be costless, according to the
Townsendites, for the plan would stimulate the economy by far more
than the pension expenditure, a multiplier they called the "velocity effect" (Bennett 1969, 151–52). In one original version, the plan would
have had the government create $2 billion in new currency to start the
"revolving" feature of the plan (Neuberger and Loe 1973, 58). The revolving terminology was meant to suggest that, once started, the plan
would be paying for itself with the transaction tax amply refilling government coffers due to the multiplier effect.

With a $2 billion jump-start via new currency, this version of the
Townsend Plan had a money creation element, although that component
was lost as the transactions tax became the central element of finance and
controversy. The language of the official Townsend literature spoke of the
velocity of money (a notion that was part of Irving Fisher's quantity theory
of money). It pointed to excess bank reserves as potential fuel for economic recovery. Thus, monetarism was part of the Townsend Plan at some
stages, and the notion of forced expenditure foreshadowed the stamp-
money spending–incentive element of the later Ham and Eggs scheme.

Dangerous Alternative Views

Townsend literature warned the faithful to beware of criticisms of the fea-
sibility of the plan from "stock-market operators" as well as "college pro-

fessors, economists, and newspaper writers" (Brinton 1936). Indeed, critics were not in short supply. The Tax Policy League declared that the Townsend Plan would "crush business (and) bankrupt the country." The League listed among its supporters Prof. Paul H. Douglas of the University of Chicago, later president of the American Economic Association and senator from Illinois. League literature fretted about the poor grandma who, instead of spending all of her pension in a month, innocently gave her grandson a $5 bill for his savings. Would she be targeted by a government "army of snoopers and ferrets" (Walker 1936)? President Roosevelt himself kept officially quiet about the Townsend Plan. But in a letter to a young nephew, he declared it would be an economic disaster.[12] Presumably, these presidential views were shared with others as well.

As for Townsend himself, his views on government were hard to classify on the traditional left-right spectrum. On the one hand, he refused to endorse Upton Sinclair's EPIC campaign because it "opposes the profit system" (Townsend 1941, 170). On the other hand, as a young physician in Belle Fourche, South Dakota, he conceived himself a socialist and wrote a socialist column for the local newspaper. Townsend involved himself in politics early on, running for Belle Fourche city council and winning his seat by one vote (Gaydowski 1970a). At the peak of his pension movement, Townsend made the mistake of inviting Socialist Party leader Norman Thomas to speak to his followers. To the booing audience, Thomas pronounced the Townsend Plan to be a "quack remedy," a particularly unkind description of a scheme created by a physician (Bennett 1969, 9).

Much later in life, Townsend endorsed the left-wing candidacy of Henry Wallace for the presidency on a third-party ticket in 1948 (ibid. 290). Wallace was pushing a pension plan to pay $100 per month to those over sixty. In a letter to the Independent Progressive Party (which eventually was the vehicle for the Wallace candidacy in California), Townsend expressed his disenchantment with Republicans and Democrats alike. But he also noted that "many of our staunch Townsendites are not in accord with my views" and thus made the endorsement personal rather than on behalf of his organization.[13]

Wallace's national Progressive Party refused to grant more than a general endorsement of Townsend's role in raising the plight of the elderly. In the end, only the candidate of the tiny Vegetarian Party actually advocated *the* Townsend Plan in 1948 (Holtzman 1975, 184). Townsend himself attended the convention of the left-leaning CIO union federation, ostensibly as a reporter for his own newspaper.[14] And the FBI received complaints from citizens during the early Cold War era that Townsend was a communist.[15] Yet despite Townsend's seeming leftist leanings, Townsend often appeared to be more at home with Republicans, perhaps because of the hostility his program drew from the Roosevelt administration.

Whatever his original core beliefs, after some personal misfortunes, Townsend found himself as an assistant health officer for the Long Beach, California, health department. When he was laid off in 1933 at age sixty-six, his interest in pensions (and his own lack of one) clearly focused his mind on the financial problems of retirees and the state of the national economy. Exactly how he formulated his plan is unclear. The sight of old ladies rummaging through garbage does not automatically lead to a particular remedy. So Townsend's creation story is at best incomplete.

The inspiration could have been the humorous Bruce Barton article in *Vanity Fair* or the serious McCord proposal or some other. It could also have been derived from the Social Credit movement with its notion of a government dividend to provide sufficient consumption power. At times, Townsend was attracted to Social Credit and similar movements. He reportedly had to be steered away from such other proposals and kept focused on the Townsend Plan as his own movement evolved (Neuberger and Loe 1973, 93).

Townsend initially outlined his ideas in letters to the *Long Beach Press Telegram*. Apart from his own residence in the city, Long Beach was at the time what California historian Kevin Starr dubbed "the geriatric capital of United States" (Starr 1997, 11–12). And Townsend soon involved a local real estate salesman, Robert Earl Clements, in working out the details. The two men became partners in the Townsend enterprise (with Clements officially the "cofounder"). This partnership lasted until a later falling out shortly before Clements's damning testimony to the Bell committee.

Clements had more business acumen than Townsend and could foresee the revenues from elderly supporters that the plan might produce. But he did have the unfortunate custom of referring to the Townsend movement as a "racket" (Schlesinger 1960, 39). Such sloppy habits were to haunt the movement when the Bell investigation took place (U.S. Congress, House of Representatives 1936, 585, 593).

As Townsend clubs formed, the new movement began to wield political influence. A San Diego legislator was recalled in 1934 for criticizing the Townsend Plan (Bennett 1969, 173). Merchants in San Diego complained that Townsendites were demanding credit at their stores in advance of their soon-to-be-enacted pensions. This pressure was intensified by the election of Democratic congressman, John Steven McGroarty, on a Townsendite platform in 1934 (Neuberger and Loe 1973, 69–70).

McGroarty was a former *Los Angeles Times* writer. He had led a campaign by the newspaper in the 1920s to revive Los Angeles' Olvera Street, the old Mexican plaza that remains a major tourist attraction to this day (Gottlieb and Wolt 1977, 155). In 1933, the California legislature named him the state's "poet laureate" for his California-oriented plays and poems. Once elected to Congress, McGroarty went on to introduce the first Townsend bills in the House of Representatives.

But Republicans could also benefit from the Townsendite vote. As was earlier noted, a Republican congressman from Michigan was elected on a Townsendite (and prohibitionist) platform (Whiteman and Lewis 1936, 108). Closer to its California home, Townsendites provided a boost to the Republican anti-EPIC campaign. Needing support against Democrat Upton Sinclair and his EPIC campaign, Republican Governor Frank Merriam endorsed the Townsend Plan. After the election, Merriam pushed a recommendation to Congress through the California state legislature favoring the Townsend Plan. But he explicitly recommended there be no change in California's own state plan of Old Age Assistance (Merriam 1935). The Townsend voters were initially interested in seeing their plan enacted at the federal level, not in incremental improvements to existing state programs. So Merriam could have the pension vote without providing the pensions.

Despite the endorsement of Merriam by Townsend over the EPIC slate of Sinclair and Sheridan Downey in 1934, Downey subsequently announced his support for the Townsend program. Indeed, he proposed repealing the newly passed Social Security system and its replacement by the Townsend scheme. Downey married this proposal with support for Father Coughlin's demand for a nationalized central bank. Coughlin's bank would "safeguard the proposed Townsend Plan," Downey argued[16] (Downey 1936, 20–21, 44). Downey's variant of the Townsend Plan would have had the central bank buy bonds issued to finance the pensions. That is, he wanted a national plan financed by money creation, a foreshadowing of Ham and Eggs at the state level.

After being elected to the U.S. Senate on a Ham and Eggs platform in 1938, Downey continued his support for pensions, warning that a new depression was imminent unless saving was reduced through Townsend-style pensions (Downey 1939). By the end of the decade, he was able to cite the pessimism of Harvard professor Alvin Hansen, an early Keynesian, in support of the danger of excessive saving (Downey 1940, 31). Thus, yet another doctrine had been drawn upon to support the pension proposal.[17]

The Economics of the Townsend Plan

Despite the political support it engendered, the economics of the Townsend Plan were soft. In 1935, for example, when the Townsend Plan competed as a proposal in Congress with Social Security, nominal Gross Domestic Product (GDP) per capita was about $570 per annum. Had there been no Depression, of course, the figure would have been higher, perhaps $785 in 1935 prices.[18] Hence, a pension income of $200 per month ($2,400 per year and $4,800 per couple) was a great deal of money. To put the amount in anecdotal perspective, years later famed baby doctor and best-selling author Benjamin Spock recalled his attempts to establish a pediatrics practice during the Depression. "It took me three years before I earned as much as $100 a month *gross*," he reported.[19]

In fact, the amount of the proposed pension was so large that the Townsendites published budgets for their members to prove that the monthly spending obligation could be met (Brinton 1936, 24; Neuberger and Loe 1973, 72–73). Even so, these budgets included refrigerators, washing machines, and radios bought on an eighteen-month installment plan. Presumably the elderly would be turning over their durable appliances every year and a half unless they could come up with other forms of expenditure.

The potential elderly recipients of the Townsend pension amounted to just under a tenth of the U.S. population in 1935. Thus, there would have had to be a transfer from the other nine-tenths of a sum just short of 30 percent of non-Depression GDP to finance the Townsend Plan, if everyone aged sixty and over received it. That is, even if the plan were assumed to restore prosperity, it would still involve a huge transfer of income. Naturally, the transfer as a percentage of GDP at the depressed economic levels of 1935 would have been much higher, about 40 percent of GDP. Even if it is assumed that GDP could be somewhat higher than just a "non-Depression" level and that some of the elderly would turn the pension down because of other income sources, the hypothetical transfer involved would remain very large.[20]

Given its large proposed expenditure, the exact financing of the Townsend Plan becomes important. Townsend's turnover or transactions tax was set at 2 percent, a seemingly small number if the words "turnover" or "transactions" are interpreted to mean a sales tax. In fact, they were intended to mean a tax on each market transaction, *including intermediate transactions*. That is, the tax would be levied on the coal sold to the steel mill and again on the steel sold to the automobile plant and again on the sale of the automobile to the consumer. Basically, the tax would be imposed if cash changed hands at any stage of processing and sale.

As critics soon pointed out, such a pyramid tax would create incentives for vertical consolidation to avoid the levy (National Industrial Conference Board 1936, 25). That is, the tax system would create an incentive for the automobile company to own its own steel mills and its own coal mines. Such consolidation would erode the Townsend tax base, aside from its distortionary impact on industrial organization. In any event, the tax would raise prices by orders of magnitude more than the small 2 percent figure suggested. An economist apparently supported by the Townsend organization testified before Congress that there could be a 24 percent price increase for a 2 percent tax on all gross transactions and "transfers."[21] And like a sales or value added tax, the transactions levy would be regressive.

There was also the issue of whether a transfer from the nonelderly to the elderly would have much of a stimulative effect. The Townsend reasoning was that the transfer would move income from savers to nonsavers (as the pension had to be completely spent each month). Although estimates of the marginal propensity to save in the 1930s are not available, average personal saving propensities were quite low and sometimes negative during the Great Depression. Given the Hard Times, people were living hand-to-mouth and spending what income they had. Thus, taxing nine-tenths of the population who were already experiencing economic difficulties and transferring the income to the remaining nonsaving tenth would be unlikely to have much of a multiplier effect. The consumption loss of one group would be replaced by the consumption gain of another.

Despite this logic, once the original Social Security plan was adopted, the Townsend Plan might have been seen more stimulatory (or less of an economic drag) than the federal program. As originally enacted, Social Security was to be a funded defined benefit pension. That meant there would be a considerable buildup of reserves in its trust fund before pensions would be paid. The early Keynesian economists of that era put part of the blame for the recession-within-the-Depression of 1937–1938 on the forced saving of the Social Security tax. They favored something closer to a pay-as-you-go system with benefits paid out of incoming revenue (or perhaps financed via deficit spending). Townsend's program was pay-as-you-go, and in 1939, when Social Security was modified and pushed toward the pay-as-you-go model, the Townsend agitation may have played some role in congressional policy (Sass 1997, 98).

Attracting the Elderly

The Townsend Plan may not have had much potential for an economic multiplier, but it did have a political multiplier effect in attracting elderly followers. A 1939 poll, summarized in Table 4.1, revealed the obvious. Those who most favored the Townsend Plan were elderly and/or poor. Money flowed in from Townsend clubs around the country. As letters flooded Congress in support of the Townsend program (as opposed to the New Deal administration's Social Security proposal), angry senators began to grill Townsend and Robert Earl Clements about their organization's finances (U.S. Congress, Senate 1935, 1015–70). Indeed, these hearings may have been the impetus for the later Bell committee investigation.

It is apparent that there were really two worlds in collision in 1935. On the one hand, there were those planners in the Roosevelt administration, combined with reformers of various stripes and respectable academics, who were putting together Social Security with the assistance of congressional allies. On the other hand, there were the Townsendites and their congressional allies with a rival proposal. The paradox was that the administration's proposal for federal assistance for the aged was being condemned by the elderly electorate. As one commentary of the period put it:

> Here was President Roosevelt, ready and eager to launch a system of paying every old person thirty dollars a month. No president in history had done anything except give lip service to so advanced a proposal. Now Mr. Roosevelt actually was suggesting that it become law. And millions of people west of the Mississippi were ridiculing and condemning his proposal! The Townsend club members were well aware that thirty dollars was exactly one hundred and seventy dollars less than what Dr. Townsend planned to give them. (Neuberger and Loe 1973, 85)

Table 4.1

Public Attitudes Toward the Townsend Plan: 1939 (%)

Group	Favor plan	Oppose plan	No opinion
Age			
Under age 30	31	53	16
30–50	34	53	13
50–60	37	54	9
Over age 60	46	46	8
Economic status			
Above average	17	76	7
Average	28	59	13
Poor	49	42	9
On Relief or Old			
Age Assistance	69	26	5

Source: American Institute of Public Opinion reproduced in Cantril, p. 192.

In fact, the Townsend Plan $200 figure was not as solid as its supporters thought. Congressman McGroarty introduced a second version of the plan in a new bill that provided that the pension could not *exceed* $200 (i.e., it could be less, depending on funding).[22] The new bill, with its compromise contingent amount, caused splits within the Townsend organization, as well as a split between Townsend and McGroarty. And ultimately it was Social Security that emerged victorious from Congress. Yet as various historians and political figures have noted, the Townsend agitation "was a potent political force in the passage of Social Security" (Bernstein 1985, 66; see also the citations in Gaydowski 1970a, 197–98). Voting for Social Security was the only alternative for many in Congress who did not want to support the Townsend Plan. To vote against both was to be antielderly. The then-radical Social Security proposal was inadvertently transformed by Townsend into the "moderate" option.

The Congressional Investigation

Viewed in historical perspective, the transcript of the Bell investigation into the Townsend Plan is startling. Were such an investigation to have been conducted in the age of television, Dr. Townsend would probably have emerged as a hero, despite the unfavorable information revealed. The investigation was so clearly aimed at destroying Townsend that his walkout from the congressional hearing would have evoked nationwide cheers, had it been televised. One can only imagine the impact of the scene would have had on the modern-day "Six O'Clock News." Unfortunately for Dr. Townsend, the electronic technology for such a national forum did not then exist.

The flavor of the questioning can be found in committee accusations that Dr. Townsend was a closet atheist or communist. He was questioned as to whether he belonged to a church (no) and whether he believed in God (yes). The committee's line of questioning in this regard may have been triggered by the tendency of Townsend club meetings to take on a religious aura with singing of "Onward Pension Soldiers" and "Glory, Glory, Hallelujah; Our Plan Is Marching On" (Roosevelt 1936, 13–14). In addition, various clergymen had become Townsend supporters. To such supporters, Townsend-as-accused-atheist was not likely to be appealing.

In any event, the Bell committee pointed out that elderly atheists and communists who received the Townsend pension might spend their funds in promoting their reprehensible causes. Not mentioned was the fact that atheists and communists who received Social Security payments—which Congress had previously enacted—could also spend their money to further their beliefs. But the Bell committee did hear from a Daughter of the American Revolution, a former Townsend club official, who testified that she had come to realize that the Townsend Plan was communistic (U.S. Congress, House of Representatives 1936, 580, 681, 752, 765–67, 895). Such testimony was treated seriously by the Bell committee.

Disparaging editorial comments and interjections by Bell committee members were frequent:

> *Committee Counsel James B. Sullivan:* The headline of "Wolves in sheep's clothing" is on the address made on Sunday, February 2, 1936, "Blood money attacks Townsend plan" by Edward J. Margett, which was given over stations KFRC, KHJ, KGB, KDB, KMJ, KFBK, KGW, and KERM.
> *Congressman Joseph A. Gavagan:* "It is too bad they did not have a station called KNUT." (U.S. Congress, House of Representatives 1936, 116–17)

The damage to Townsend was primarily indirect. There was Robert Earl Clements's reported description of the movements as a "racket" (ibid. 585, 593). There was a Townsendite reverend who—the Bell committee let it be known—wrote letters too obscene to be reprinted in the published hearings (Whiteman and Lewis 1936, 124–25). And there was the matter of the above-mentioned Ed Margett.[23]

Margett was a high Townsend movement official who had previously been indicted (but not convicted) for assorted crimes such as pimping and bootlegging. Townsend insisted on keeping Margett on the payroll even when reports of his unsavory background surfaced, on the grounds that Margett had been "cleared" (U.S. Congress, House of Representatives 1936, 102–15, 695, 911–67). Margett was said to have described himself as "cleaning up" financially in the Townsend movement, yet another unfavorable quote with which Townsend had to deal (ibid. 909). However, Mr. Margett went into hiding when the Bell committee called him to testify, and he did not emerge until after the hearings were over (Whiteman and Lewis 1936, 129–30).

Probably the greatest damage done to Townsend himself was the revelation of the large sums that the movement produced through contributions, dues, and sales of literature. Townsend and Robert Clements owned Prosperity Publishing Company, which put out the *Townsend Weekly*, the official newspaper of the movement. It was primarily through this company, rather than through the clubs themselves, that money was channeled to Townsend and Clements. There was revenue from direct sales of the newspaper and other publications as well as newspaper advertising income from questionable patent medicines such as "Kuhn's Famous Remedy" and "Juvenus" to cure "weak glands" (U.S. Congress, House of Representatives 1936, 183–84).

As Clements's testimony wore on, the income he reported receiving tended to rise under committee grilling. The committee inquired about various items on his expense account down to whether it was proper for him to have charged certain laundry bills (ibid. 89). But it was the raw income received that was most damaging. Townsend eventually bought out Clements's share in the publishing venture after the two had their falling out. Clements received $25,000 for his shares on top of a dividend from those shares of another $25,000. In addition, he received a regular salary for his work, bringing the total "take" during his affiliation with the Townsend movement to something like $75,000 (ibid. 316–17). For the vast majority of Townsend supporters, particularly when weighed against 1936 prices and income levels, such amounts would have seemed huge.

Townsend was also embarrassed by the testimony of Robert R. Doane, an economist the movement had apparently supported during earlier hearings on Social Security and the Townsend bills. Questions had been raised at the time concerning who was paying Doane and whether he

Figure 4.1 **Sample Letter from Townsendites to President Roosevelt Protesting the Bell Hearings**

West Sacramento Calif. May 25ᵗʰ-36

President Roosevelt

> *We the members of Townsend Club No 11 West Sacramento, do respect-*
> *fully ask that you use the power invested in you as President of our United States,*
> *to stop this disgraceful and un-American "Bell Investigation" so-called, and*
> *stop the persecution of our beloved leader Dr. F.E. Townsend, and by the exer-*
> *cise of your high authority to thus exalt yourself in the esteem of your citizens*
> *whose rights you have sworn to protect.*

> *We represent two hundred (200) voters in our small club.*

Respectfully Submitted,

President Dr. D B. Boyd
Secy. Mrs. C Simpson

Source: Official file 1542 (Townsend), Franklin D. Roosevelt Library.

---

was in effect a double agent. University of Wisconsin economist and Social Security expert Edwin E. Witte believed that Doane in fact worked for "big business" interests desirous of embarrassing President Roosevelt and undermining support for Social Security.[24]

In any event, when brought before the Bell committee, Doane fell over himself to please its members hostile to the Townsend Plan. He now testified that the Townsend Plan could not possibly work because of an insufficiency of revenues that the transactions tax could provide. Moreover, he testified that both Clements and Townsend knew the plan was deficient in this regard (U.S. Congress, House of Representatives 1936, 229–308, 409). Doane also stated that the Townsend Plan would lead to rationing, although how this result would come about was not made clear:

> *Chairman C. Jasper Bell:* When you say we would have to have a ra-
> tioned economy, you mean a forced economy; do you not?
> *Dr. Doane:* Oh, yes.
> *Chairman Bell:* Forced at the point of a bayonet; is not that right? . . .
> *Congressman J. William Ditter:* Well, it would be the collective sys-
> tem of the Communists; would it not?

Figure 4.2 **Sample Letter Thanking the President for Pardoning Dr. Townsend After His Conviction for Contempt of Congress**

April 22, 1938
820 Brook
Dallas, Tex.

Honorable President
Franklin D. Roosevelt

Dear Friend
    I do thank you that God pardoned Dr. Townsend through you it was a loveable thing to do. Of course you know God has inspired Dr Townsend to bring "his God's" supply to his people. Didn't you see that perseverence that Dr Townsend has, that is the power of God. Of course, I do not need to tell you, for you know it already. This plan will be the law of our land. Our God will put it in operation some day, God will put the desire in our present President's heart if it is your place to use the plan but if it is not your place to put if in operation, the desire will be felt in th heart of some future President. For all power belongs to God we are his ideas doing his will.
    I do thank you again for your kind deeds and wish Gods guidance for you and yours.

Your Friend and well wisher

Mrs Annie Self

Source: Official file 1542 (Townsend), Franklin D. Roosevelt Library.

    Dr. Doane: There would have to be some central authority directing all this.
    Congressman Ditter: There would have to be commissars, similar to commissars in the Soviet Union?
    Dr. Doane: We could not do it under our present constitutional form of government.

    Some of the testimony produced by the committee revolved around whether the Townsend movement had broken any laws by engaging in political activity such as endorsing candidates. Such testimony, however, could not have been very hurtful to Townsend. His supporters were obviously engaging in political activity in trying to have their program enacted. Politics was precisely what they wanted to do. But there was also testimony that Townsend had referred to his supporters as "old fossils [who] don't know what it is all about" (ibid. 586, 593). Townsend was never given the chance specifically to deny the remark, but its appearance in the public record could not have helped him with his elderly constituency.

Townsend and the President

Townsend's "relationship" with President Roosevelt—if it can be called that given its one-way nature—was a peculiar one. He desperately wanted his plan to be a central part of the New Deal. From the plan's earliest days, Townsend and his supporters constantly wrote to FDR. Initially, it was to obtain an interview with the president so that Townsend could "explain" his plan. Then it was to stop the Bell hearings. Later it was to grant Townsend a pardon. Townsend wrote to Roosevelt in 1937 congratulating him on his reelection and again requesting an interview.[25] No such interview was ever granted.

Generally, Townsend appeared to be naïve about the forces arrayed against him. After a conversation with a senator from Florida in which Townsend asserted that his plan, by ending poverty, would reduce crime, the senator referred him to the FBI as a crime expert. Townsend then took a tour of the FBI building, presumably without knowledge of the various attempts to use the FBI to discredit his group. He confided to the agent giving the tour that if the FBI would support the Townsend Plan, he would see to it that the bureau's budget would be increased once the Townsendites had political power.[26]

In 1940, Townsend tried a new tactic to win Roosevelt's attention. He sent a letter to the president inviting him to speak to the annual Townsend convention about the growing national defense effort.[27] Townsend may have thought that an invitation to speak on a nonpension issue would entice the president, particularly in an election year. The letter sparked discussion within the administration about how to respond; public support for military affairs prior to the attack on Pearl Harbor was weak. However, Roosevelt was not about to lend any credence to the Townsend Plan; he would not even send a representative to the convention.

In the end, the president simply answered Townsend's invitation with his own letter describing the defense effort. But the Townsend/defense issue did not die. Again in 1941, but before Pearl Harbor, the administration received a recommendation from an official charged with the West Coast defense effort that Roosevelt—or at least the vice president—should meet with Townsend. Such a meeting, it was suggested, would increase public support for defense preparations.[28] But, as before, no meeting was arranged.

Townsend's futile efforts to achieve presidential recognition suggest he never understood the degree to which Roosevelt regarded him as a crackpot. Nor did he fully comprehend the extent of the efforts by the administration to discredit him. He may also not have understood the indirect impact his movement had in pushing Congress to enact the Social Security plan he had scorned as inadequate.

The Townsend organization continued on, proposing federal legislation, after FDR died. As a California Congressman, Richard Nixon apparently provided some support to such a bill. But as vice president in the late 1950s, his staff rebuffed efforts by the Townsend people to win support for legislation providing benefits for anyone over sixty of $130 to $140 a week. By that time, Townsend and his organization had largely faded into political oblivion.[29] And the elderly in California were no longer disproportionately represented in the state's population.

Lessons to Be Learned

The Townsend experience provides two types of lessons. For pension supporters of the period, the outline of the Townsend proposal provided guidance for the design of, and created support for, subsequent pension schemes. And for the future it illustrates how a popular cause can be pulled together from existing doctrines and social trends in the face of favorable demographics.

Lessons for the Period

The defeat of the Townsend Plan and the Bell committee investigation clearly indicated that the federal outlook for the Townsend proposal was not promising. Still, Townsend bills continued to be dropped into the congressional hopper. But after the 1935 peak in agitation, the possibility of anything happening as a result of these bills markedly declined.

Nonetheless, the federal defeat also raised the possibility of pension activity at the state level. The Bell committee itself received testimony about a rump Townsend group's efforts in Colorado to put a pension initiative on the ballot (U.S. Congress, House of Representatives 1936, 462–63). And, of course, the unsuccessful state-level Ham and Eggs movement was soon to follow in California.

Colorado's experience is instructive. Like California, it had a dispro-

Figure 4.3 **Percentage of the Population Aged Sixty-five and Over: United States, California, and Colorado**

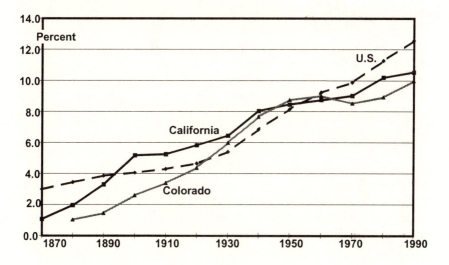

Note: Data for Colorado not available for 1870.

portionate number of elderly residents in the 1930s, as shown in Figure 4.3. And the Colorado experience foreshadowed the shift by George McLain in California during the 1940s toward an emphasis on Old Age Assistance and away from pensions for everyone. O. Otto Moore, an attorney and political figure initially affiliated with the Colorado Townsendites, became disillusioned with the Townsend approach. He had himself been involved in congressional testimony for Townsend and reported himself as appalled by the lack of economic sophistication of the Townsend hierarchy. One incident he recounted had Dr. Townsend opening a contribution envelope and simply stuffing a $5 bill into his pocket (Whiteman and Lewis 1936, 123).

Moore became convinced that the plan Townsend wanted to be enacted was unworkable. He set about enhancing the already-existing Colorado old-age welfare system instead. As in other states, such systems became eligible for federal subsidy under the Social Security Act of 1935. The new source of funds made working at the state level more attractive and feasible.

Given their new state-level focus, Moore and his associates—through the "National" Annuity League—put on the 1936 Colorado ballot an amendment to the state's constitution. The amendment set the minimum monthly payment to eligible elderly at $45 a month, well below the Townsend and Ham and Eggs levels. Still, $45 was a significant sum compared with most states' relief payments to the elderly. Moreover, the plan earmarked much of state and local sales and other taxes for a pension fund to finance the $45 benefit. Colorado voters passed this amendment, setting in motion a protracted political battle that went on for years in the state. Strong in opposition were state and local officials and politicians who found much of their discretionary spending diverted into a mandatory use.

Initially, the Colorado legislature refused to establish a pension fund despite the voters' mandate. Court battles ensued, eventually forcing establishment of a fund. Pension benefits began to be paid but for less than $45, producing more litigation and several unsuccessful repeal efforts by plan opponents. It was not until the final years of World War II that the full $45 level was actually reached. By that time, of course, inflation had reduced the real value of the nominal sum, and prosperity had added to the tax revenues needed to pay for it. Still, elderly recipients actually received "jackpot" bonuses when the pension fund received monies beyond the levels needed for the basic benefit. And an attempt to repeal the jackpot element of the plan was also rejected by Colorado voters (Moore 1947; Leonard 1993, 84). In the early 1950s, Colorado had the highest average monthly Old Age Assistance (OAA) grant in the nation ($73). California followed as second highest with $69 (Bond et al. 1954, 241).

The Colorado experience showed that there were advantages to be obtained at the state level for pension advocates. First, efforts could be targeted at states with large elderly populations or where the pension movement—for whatever reason—was particularly strong. Second, it was doubtful that the resources would exist at the state level for a full-scale Bell-type investigation of movement finances. As an example, no official investigation of the Ham and Eggs movement in California was ever made (although there were some legislative inquiries concerning George McLain's later movement).

Despite the advantages of working at the state level, Townsend himself was slow to absorb the fact that there was not going to be a federal plan. Initially, he—and the national Townsend office—opposed state-level action. Such activity, it was argued, would interfere with efforts to push for a federal program. Some of this opposition may have been due to simple rivalry with former Townsendites such as O. Otto Moore, who had gone their own way with more moderate schemes.

Whatever the reason, Townsend and his associates campaigned for a federal constitutional amendment to require the government to enact a Townsend-style pension. Given the lack of enthusiasm in Congress for the plan itself, it remains a mystery why Townsend thought Congress would ever adopt such an amendment. Perhaps Dr. Townsend felt that his pardon from Roosevelt indicated he had more influence in Washington than was actually the case.

Townsend campaigned personally *against* an Oregon plan in 1938 and a North Dakota proposal in 1939. He also opposed a 1939 Florida plan that had been introduced into the legislature. The only state action that was acceptable to Townsend was the passage of legislative recommendations to Congress to enact the federal Townsend Plan. Quite a number of these were passed (Holtzman 1975, 192). As California Governor Frank Merriam had already demonstrated, such state-level endorsements of a national plan were costless to politicians.

For those activists who wanted to work for actual pension plans at the state level, there was another lesson that could be learned. When the economics of the Townsend Plan were attacked, the criticism was primarily on the basis of the transactions tax. Would it be too burdensome to the young? Could it raise enough money? Would it boost prices? Would it foster industrial concentration?

The lesson was that if the tax were removed as a central element, a potential controversy would be blunted. In this light, it is easy to see the appeal of Robert Noble's Ham and Eggs plan with its stamp-currency scheme. The stamp-currency was not an explicit tax and seemed to promise bountiful resources for the elderly at no cost to anyone else. Stamp-money was manna from Heaven. Taxes had to be collected on Earth.

With the prospects of federal action nil, Dr. Townsend finally had a change of heart with regard to state action. He teamed up with Sherman Bainbridge, by then exiled from the Ham and Eggs movement for opposing the Allen brothers, to lead a western states campaign. Townsendites in California put a plan on the state ballot in 1944, five years after the second Ham and Eggs initiative had failed. But they went back to the unpopular tax idea—proposing a 3 percent income tax to finance the pension. And they scaled the pension back from $200 per month to $60 for everyone sixty years old and over who promised not to work and to spend all their pension money, a variant of the "Sixty-Sixty" Plan.

To provide a sweetener for those California voters leery of a new income tax, the Townsendites also proposed to repeal sales taxes. With a wartime demand boom characterizing the economy, the argument of the 1930s that the plan would stimulate the economy seemed out of place. Instead, the proposal was said to guarantee subsequent *postwar* prosperity and to open jobs for veterans returning after the war as the elderly retired. But opponents pointed to the advances in old-age assistance pensions in California, now subsidized by the federal government. In the official ballot pamphlet the opponents—led by Ham and Eggs veteran George McLain—declared that

> Townsend Movement leaders have failed to get their plan through Congress, and are now endeavoring to foist their proposals on the voters of California. (California, Secretary of State 1944)

McLain clearly wanted no competition for the title of Mr. Pension of California, which he was rapidly achieving. In the end, the 1944 California Townsend proposal received a third of the vote, about the same proportion as the second Ham and Eggs initiative (but substantially less than the 45 percent received by the first). Plans on state ballots in Washington, Oregon, and Arizona were also defeated. But the Townsendites later had some indirect successes. As in California under George McLain, the pension issue gradually shifted toward improvements in Old Age Assistance, the federally subsidized program. Townsendite pension agitation indirectly led to improvements in such programs in various states, albeit under other leadership (Holtzman 1975, 191–98).

Lessons for the Future

As in the case of Ham and Eggs, the ingredients for the Townsend Plan were taken from various ideas, doctrines, and social currents prevalent at the time. Although Dr. Townsend may have gotten his sums wrong, his plan was more in line with the New Deal's spirit than the Roosevelt administration would have cared to admit. Townsend made a direct connection between his pension and moving the economy out of the Great Depression. But there was also a connection between Roosevelt's interest in Social Security—the administration's pension proposal—and the president's macroeconomic thinking.

I PRODUCE · I DEFEND

Emblem of Upton Sinclairs's "End Poverty in California" (EPIC) campaign for governor in 1934. As originally put forward, EPIC included a pension element. Sinclair's dropping of that element and his opposition to the Townsend Plan cost him critical votes.

Emblem of Old Age Revolving Pensions, Ltd., the official name of the Townsend organization. Critics claimed its slogan—Youth for Work, Age for Leisure—had been taken from a tongue-in-cheek article that had appeared in a national magazine.

TOWNSEND AT THE HELM

"God deliver us from further guidance by professional economists! By following their advice and leadership—which has enriched those they serve—the common people have been deprived of their heritage. The time has arrived when the citizenry must take charge of their government and repudiate the philosophy of want and hunger in a land of wealth and abundance."

DR. FRANCIS E. TOWNSEND.

Dr. Francis E. Townsend as depicted in a Townsendite pamphlet.

Los Angeles Examiner photograph of the Ham and Eggs Board, November 1938. Standing fourth from left: Lawrence W. Allen. Seated from left to right: Willis Allen, Sherman J. Bainbridge, Roy G. Owens. Courtesy of *University of Southern California* on behalf of the USC Library Department of Special Collections.

Top, left to right: California Governor Frank F. Merriam who endorsed the Townsend Plan and beat the EPIC campaign in 1934; Governor Culbert L. Olson, who beat Merriam in 1938 and who was seen as a traitor to the Ham and Eggs movement; Governor Earl Warren, who defeated Olson in 1942 with pensionite support. Bottom row, left to right: California State Assemblyman William B. Hornblower, who worked with the Fraternal Order of Eagles on behalf of old age assistance; U.S. Senator from California Sheridan Downey, endorser of Ham and Eggs and a supporter of the Townsend Plan in the Senate.

Los Angeles Police Captain Earle Kynette reading a copy of the
U.S. Constitution as the Grand Jury considers charges in connection
with the car bombing of a private detective. Kynette was later
convicted and sent to prison for the bombing. Courtesy of *Herald
Examiner* Collection, Los Angeles Public Library. Used with
permission.

"THE ROOSEVELT STORY" Produced by TOLA PRODUCTIONS, Inc.
Permission is hereby granted for reproduction by newspapers, magazines, trade publications and exhibitors' displays — Made in U. S. A.

President Franklin D. Roosevelt feared the potential impact of a third-party campaign involving the Townsendites and others in the presidential election of 1936.

The new Social Security system, enacted by Congress in 1935, required registration of and record keeping for millions of Americans.

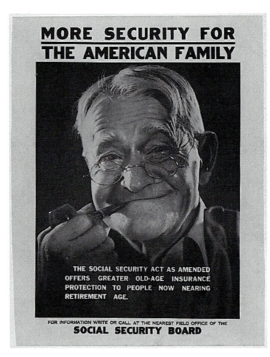

Posters such as these popularized the new Social Security system.

Roosevelt believed that lack of confidence was what was keeping the economy depressed. The famous line from his first inaugural address—"the only thing we have to fear is fear itself"—was in fact an economic doctrine. Providing protections to consumers through measures such as Social Security, to business (through the National Industrial Recovery Act cartelization), and to farmers (through various price support programs) would boost confidence and hence spending and investment. Or so Roosevelt seemed to think.

The enemies of the New Deal also saw the connection between Townsend's plan and official administration policy. For example, an anti-Townsend analysis of the time by the National Industrial Conference Board stated:

> Those who regard the Townsend scheme as dangerous and delusive should remember that it is only a logical extension of the same assumptions upon which almost all public policies in the United States are based at the present time. Its widespread acceptance is a natural and inevitable consequence of the forces of mass emotion which have been set in motion and stimulated into political activity by the systematic propagation of these same assumptions in securing support of similar schemes through the exploitation of popular ignorance, envy, and prejudice during the past three years. (National Industrial Conference Board 1936, vii)

The difference between Townsend, Ham and Eggs, EPIC, Share-Our-Wealth, and other off-center movements of the period and that of the New Deal was that Roosevelt was more cautious and had "respectable" analysts to work on his proposals. He tried to avoid proposals that seemed radical and, where they were in fact radical (as Social Security certainly was!), to put them in nonthreatening formats. Thus, the Social Security system was set up to look like one of the (relative rare) private pension plans then in existence, with a trust fund and defined benefits based on past wage earnings. In the initial stages of the development of the Social Security plan, Roosevelt wrote that:

> The system ought to be operated through the post offices. Just simple and natural—nothing elaborate or alarming about it. (quoted in Bernstein 1985, 50)

Indeed, the initial distribution of individual Social Security numbers was carried out through the Post Office until Social Security offices could be established. In the end, the basic design of Social Security was heavily influenced by the (few) liberal-minded businessmen who worked with the Roosevelt administration's planners (Jacoby 1997, 209–14; Orloff 1993, 288–89).

When the baby boom begins to retire in the twenty-first century, it is not clear that a Roosevelt-type "simple and natural" solution to its financing problems will exist. But there surely will be someone to take the leadership in harnessing the political energies that will be released should the elderly boomers feel frustrated. There might also be those waiting to capitalize on frustrations of younger voters who may feel excessively burdened. And these political entrepreneurs of, say, the 2030s may not be confronted with as moderating an influence as Roosevelt had in the 1930s. Chapter 6 will return to that issue. But it is necessary first to examine in more depth developments in California in the prosperous 1940s.

Chapter 5

Gerontocracy's Last Stand: Earl Warren and Uncle George

> The county board of supervisors and many state official make it very hard on old people. If we can send millions abroad all the time to help them a forin people better give a little more for a respectful living for old pioneers that made this country what it is today. And you young people better help. You will be old someday.

> *Follower of George McLain (Pinner et al. 1959, 77)*

Both the Ham and Eggs movement and the Townsend movement had their origins in the Great Depression of the 1930s. California contributed its elderly demographics, which gave these movements their home. But does history suggest that movements of dissatisfied elderly could occur in conditions of general economic prosperity rather than economic depression? When American baby boomers retire in the twenty-first century, there is no reason to believe that they will do so in economic circumstances as dire as those of the 1930s. Thus, if lessons are to be drawn from the past about the future, it is necessary to examine elderly politics in conditions of prosperity as well as depression.

As noted in chapter 1, California did have a pre-Depression history of political agitation on behalf of the elderly. Pushed by the Fraternal Order of Eagles (FOE), the state adopted the nation's most liberal system of "outdoor relief" (cash payments instead of poorhouses) for the elderly on the eve of the Great Depression. Under this system, the state mandated that counties provide outdoor relief but agreed to share in the costs.

During the 1940s, prosperity returned to California. The development of wartime defense industry in the state sucked in job-seeking newcomers at a remarkable rate. From 1940 to 1950, the state's population rose by over 50 percent! Particularly during World War II itself, the jump in population that came with the booming state economy created a housing shortage and a host of other social problems. Although many observers feared that the Great Depression would return when the war-related spending ended, California made a remarkably smooth adjustment. The state continued on a path of economic and population growth after the war that generally exceeded the national average.

It was not until the 1950s that the influx of young wartime and postwar job seekers brought the state's age profile below the national average, producing the youth culture for which California is now famous. Thus, in the prosperous 1940s, California's demographics still retained an elderly tilt. And during most of this period, the governorship was in the hands of Earl Warren. Knowledge of how this middle-of-the-road, Republican governor dealt with the pensionites provides clues about the way future mainstream politicians will deal with the boomers when they become an elderly constituency. In essence, Warren appeased them as much as possible while holding on to other elements of his political constituency. Appeasement worked at times; at other times—as I shall discuss below—the elderly constituency could spin out of control.

Documenting Earl Warren

Because of Earl Warren's later national prominence as Chief Justice of the U.S. Supreme Court as well as chairman of the "Warren Commission," which investigated the assassination of President Kennedy, numerous biographies have profiled his career (Cray 1997; Huston 1966; Katcher 1967; Pollack 1979; Severn 1968; Weaver 1967; White 1982). Warren himself was at work on an autobiography when he died in 1974. It was edited and published posthumously (Warren 1977).

As chief justice, Warren presided over key decisions desegregating the public schools and other public institutions, extending various rights to criminal defendants, and applying the principle of "one man, one vote" to electoral boundaries. These decisions led to Warren's veneration as a saint by those of a liberal political persuasion. At the same time those on the extreme right demanded his scalp. An old joke says that kids growing up in southern California could easily have believed that

Warren's middle name was Earl and that his first name was "Impeach," so ubiquitous were the "Impeach Earl Warren" signs.

In fact, Warren's national profile began to form while he was still California's governor and even before. In 1948, most notably, he ran for vice president with the seemingly unbeatable Thomas Dewey of New York. But it turned out to be a losing venture, which nonetheless produced a campaign biography aimed at a national audience (Stone 1948). It was often said at the time that had Warren been the presidential candidate, and Dewey the candidate for vice president, the Republicans might well have won.

By following middle-of-the-road politics, Warren could appeal to the Democrats who were in a majority by the time he ran for statewide office. Harry Truman said of Warren, "He's a Democrat and doesn't know it" (Weaver 1967, 55). And, referring to Warren, the Democratic California attorney general told Franklin Roosevelt in 1943: "Everything we have in California is better than it is anywhere else. Even our Republicans are better than the Republicans anywhere else" (ibid. 101).

The Warren era in California politics—although less well known than his period on the Supreme Court—left a profound mark on the state. Doctoral dissertations in political science have analyzed Warren's approach to politics and style of administration (Bell 1956; Melvin Bernstein 1970). The University of California at Berkeley undertook a major oral history project on the Warren years in the 1970s, interviewing everyone from key political figures of the Warren era to his schoolboy postman. Finally, the California State Archives have preserved an amazingly complete set of records, down to the numerous penny postcards Warren received from the public. Not surprisingly, the Warren archives contain one of the best collections of pensionite literature available; Warren could not afford to ignore that potent constituency. What emerges from all of this writing, research, and preservation is a governor quite different from his two predecessors: Culbert Olson and Frank Merriam.

Olson, Warren's immediate predecessor as governor, was an EPIC campaign Democrat. He was elected to the California legislature during Upton Sinclair's losing bid for the top office against incumbent Governor Merriam in 1934. Olson's election as the first Democratic governor after decades of Republican dominance marked a flirtation by the electorate with New Deal influences and—by California standards of the period—radicalism. Olson was willing at least to appear supportive of the Ham and Eggs proposition in 1938 when he ran for governor, although he was privately relieved when it lost. His subsequent waffling—and then overt opposition to the second version of the Ham and Eggs ballot proposition in 1939—left him branded as a traitor by the pensionites.

Frank Merriam basically endorsed anything his handlers told him to support in the 1934 gubernatorial election—including the Townsend Plan. From the viewpoint of the state's business community, anyone—even the nonentity that Merriam appeared to be—was preferable to Upton Sinclair and his EPIC economic program. Endorsing the national Townsend Plan was in any event costless for Merriam as it was a federal, not a state, proposal.

But by the time Earl Warren was a candidate for California governor in 1942, all the peculiarities occasioned by the Great Depression were gone. California's electorate was not in a mood to lead the nation toward seemingly radical or utopian economic policies. But it still contained a large elderly constituency who wanted pensions. So how did politician Warren intersect with the pensionites? The record suggests that he regarded the pension issue as very important to his gubernatorial candidacy. And once having made commitments to the pensionites, he did not want to be seen as another Culbert Olson (i.e., as having betrayed them after being elected).

Warren's Early Background

Earl Warren was born to parents of Scandinavian origin in Los Angeles in 1891. His father, a railroad worker, had taken part in the famous Pullman strike of 1895 and for a time was blacklisted[1] (Huston 1966, 20–21; Severn 1968, 4). But he moved the family to Bakersfield and eventually found employment as a railroad worker again. The Warren household was strict; no drinking or gambling allowed, an orientation that seemed to color Warren's later political career (Severn 1968, 14). Although his parents placed emphasis on education, Warren was an indifferent student in high school, more interested in football than academics (Earl Warren Oral History Project 1971, Ashe and Henley, 28–30).

Despite a lack of academic achievement, Warren nonetheless went on to college at the University of California's Boalt Hall law school, an unusual move for a boy from Bakersfield in that period. At Boalt he was again not a notable scholar and was warned at one point by the law school dean that he might not graduate (Huston 1966, 29–30). Although he engaged in some high jinks in college, by the time he graduated from Boalt, Warren had emerged as a straight arrow who would not take a drink while Prohibition was in effect (Cray 1997, 48; Warren 1977, 37). He felt himself enough of a patriot during World War I to enlist in the military, although he never saw overseas action (Huston 1966, 31). Despite the lack of combat, the military experience was a sobering one; twelve members of his company died, not from war injuries but from the infamous 1918 flu epidemic (White 1982, 23).

Warren did not immediately enter politics. Indeed, there is no evidence that a political career was on his mind when he graduated from law school. However, being in Berkeley awakened an interest in the progressive Republican thinking of the era. In particular, Warren was an admirer of Hiram Johnson, who was elected California governor in 1910 and—in an unprecedented response by the voters—reelected on a platform of good government and reform. Notably, Johnson and his progressives brought to California such components of direct democracy as the initiative and recall. These new institutions tended to weaken the established political parties and to put more emphasis on individual candidates (Cresap 1954, 11–18). Thus, when Warren did turn his sights on statewide office, his campaigns were always officially "bipartisan" and focused on Warren-the-man rather than on the Republican Party.

Warren's first legal experience was in the private sector. But through a friend who had been elected to the state legislature, he eventually found work on the staff of a legislative committee (Huston 1966, 35–36). Later, Warren worked in the office of the district attorney of Alameda County, which contained the city of Oakland. When the incumbent district attorney resigned, Warren took the position. He began to accumulate credentials as a crime and corruption fighter in the county. Under Warren, the district attorney's office attracted national attention; Columbia professor and New Deal "braintruster" Raymond Moley dubbed Warren's regime as the "best in the nation" (Cray 1997, 68).

Warren had to run for office to remain district attorney. It was during this time that he became active in Republican politics. He attended the 1928 Republican National Convention as an alternate delegate and was a full delegate to 1932 convention (Pollack 1979, 53). By 1934, Warren was chair of the California Republican Party. In that position, he fought Upton Sinclair's EPIC campaign for the governorship in what he termed "a crusade of Americans against Radicalism and Socialism." Warren branded EPIC as "a foreign philosophy of government, half Socialistic and half Communistic" (Cray 1997, 75; Weaver 1967, 60). Apart from the campaign rhetoric, Warren genuinely disliked seemingly radical schemes and theories. At the time, he put the New Deal, with its economic planning and monetary manipulations, into that distasteful category.

As his career progressed, Warren began to accumulate credentials that would assist in his later electoral efforts. Clearly, being identified with fighting crime and corruption was a popular position. Sending corrupt city officials to jail—which he did as district attorney—did not hurt his reputation, either. Nor did his successful efforts to have the legislature adopt various anticrime bills. Then as now, being tough on crime was a winning platform for a politician.

In 1925, Warren married a young widow with a child and eventually had five more children with her, producing an especially photogenic family. He became friends with Joseph Knowland, influential publisher of the *Oakland Tribune*, who assisted in his career at various stages. Warren also did radio commentary on the high-profile Lindbergh kidnapping trial, a move that helped make his name known in the state (Cray 1997, 69–71). In a Lincolnesque move that could be told and retold, Warren helped reelect a dying member of the California Assembly. Then—because it was late at night and the streetcars were not running—he walked miles to tell his frail friend of the victory (Stone 1948, 33–34).

The 1934 anti-EPIC campaign had a side effect that benefited Warren, who by this time clearly had high political ambitions. Republicans feared that Upton Sinclair might win the governorship and that state patronage might fall into the hands of the Democrats. They pushed through the legislature various civil service protections to limit the damage to their existing appointees. Warren included proposals upgrading the authority (and salary) of the state's attorney general in these bills. With the position upgraded, Warren had inserted the next rung in his political ladder, a move some observers saw as "preparing a good job for himself" (Huston 1966, 50–51; Severn 1968, 66–67).

Not all Warren's actions as district attorney made friends. A major challenge for Warren was the Point Lobos murder, also known as the "ship murder case." A maritime supervisor had been killed after apparently shortchanging a worker. Warren ultimately convicted several union officials of the murder. Warren's tactics included holding a suspect incommunicado for an extended period in a location unknown to his lawyers until a confession was obtained. Because of the political sympathies of some of the participants, Warren apparently viewed his actions as an anticommunist crusade. The result was antipathy toward Warren from many—not all—in the growing union movement of the period, particularly those in the left-leaning CIO (Cray 1997, 81–90; Pollack 1979, 56–57).

Running for Attorney General

In 1938, Earl Warren was ready to make his move for statewide office, specifically the upgraded position of state attorney general. Only two years before, at the 1936 Republican National Convention, Warren had led a slate of delegates apparently linked to Herbert Hoover against a rival slate committed to Frank Merriam as a favorite son.[2] But now, Warren—a committed Republican by any measure—announced he would conduct a "bipartisan" campaign. He would take advantage of California's cross-filing laws, and run in both the Republican and Democratic primaries. This bipartisan stance was to mark all of Warren's subsequent California campaigns. Only in his 1948 vice presidential bid could he not take the bipartisan position.

In the 1938 Republican primary, Warren had relatively smooth sailing. His campaign was marred only by a personal tragedy when his father—by then a reclusive Bakersfield landlord—was found bludgeoned to death in his home, a murder that was never solved. But on the Democratic side, not surprisingly, Warren faced significant opposition.

One of Warren's six rivals in the 1938 Democratic primary was Carl Kegley, an attorney employed by the Ham and Eggs movement who was fighting against efforts in court to have the "Thirty Dollars Every Thursday" initiative removed from the state ballot.[3] The other attorneys with Kegley representing Ham and Eggs were Sheridan Downey, the eventually successful Democratic candidate for U.S. senator; John W. Preston, also a senatorial hopeful; and Representative John Dockweiler, hoping to receive the Democratic nomination for governor.

Kegley had actually been a Republican until 1930. He was a graduate of both the University of California—where he had been a heavyweight boxer—and Stanford. Initially, his campaign made no mention of pension issues or Ham and Eggs. Kegley hoped instead to attach himself to Franklin Roosevelt's popularity. He accused Warren of referring to the president as "a pirate."[4] Kegley promised "to eradicate special privilege" and pointed to a song he had written for Roosevelt:

> On with Roosevelt! On with Roosevelt! Win in 1938. Now the time is
> here and election's near, we have pledged the Golden State. We give you
> California. It's the grandest State of all! We're loyal to our leader and
> we're ready for the call.[5]

As the primary date approached, however, Kegley came to realize
he had a problem. There were five other Democrats on the ballot (including California Assembly Speaker William Mosley Jones) and
crime-fighter Warren was the best-known name. Thus, Kegley recognized that he had better rely on more than his questionable songwriting
talents. In short, Kegley's best option was to exploit his Ham and Eggs
connections to the hilt if he hoped to win. A communist newspaper
reported that it had it on "reliable authority" that Earl Warren had told
supporters that the Ham and Eggs plan was unconstitutional because
of its currency creation element.[6] Meanwhile, Ham and Eggers were
being whipped to a frenzy by the (ultimately unsuccessful) case to
force California's secretary of state to ban the pension initiative.

Passionate Ham and Eggs enthusiasts assembled before the state
Supreme Court building singing "Glory, Glory, Hallelujah." Meanwhile,
Ham and Eggs opponents argued before the court that the initiative
petition contained an inadequate description. And the California State
Employees Association protested that state workers did not want to be
paid in funny money. Although the suit to remove Ham and Eggs was
rejected by the California high court, the episode raised the specter of
future legal challenges should the proposition pass. The state attorney
general would then be charged with defending the Ham and Eggs plan.
Surely, Ham and Eggs voters would want someone in that office committed to their program, Kegley argued. As a defense attorney for the
Ham and Eggs proposition, he was clearly the man for the job.

In this charged atmosphere, Kegley himself became the target
of controversy. Reports appeared in the press that Kegley had been
suspended for three years from practice before a federal district
court for "misconduct." He had been charged with having privately
uncovered an individual who had stolen some "Liberty Bonds"
(World War I era federal bonds) and then offering to be the culprit's
lawyer.

Kegley clearly needed more allies given this unpleasant disclosure,
and Ham and Eggers were rallied to his cause. His political propaganda declared:

To Each and Every Member and Friend of the California State Pension Plan:

It is the greatest privilege of my life to serve more than a million of you in the capacity of your Chief Counsel for the defense of the Retirement Life Payments Act. I will ardently and vigorously defend your fundamental rights as citizens to go to the polls and vote for the Retirement Life Payments Act into the basic law of this state.

Furthermore, I intend to work for its adoption on Nov. 8.

When elected Attorney General, I will diligently and vigorously use all the power and authority vested in me by the State of California and will employ every available resource to further defend and ward off any and all attacks which may be brought against the Retirement Life Payments Act.

Moreover, I will cooperate with your Administrator to make the Retirement Life Payments Act function and work successfully.

Gratefully,
Carl S. Kegley[7]

Technically, Ham and Eggs leader Lawrence Allen was also on the Democratic primary ballot as a candidate for state attorney general.[8] Nonetheless, the Ham and Eggers claimed to have a poll showing Kegley would win the primary. But the actual outcome of the August primary was different. The whiff of scandal and the split among the (true) Democrats on the Democratic primary ballot hurt Kegley. Earl Warren won both the Republican and Democratic primaries, with Kegley coming in second among the Democrats. Warren also won the nomination of a third "Progressive" Party.[9] Given this result, Warren had every reason to believe he would be running unopposed in the November election. But it was not to be.

Carl Kegley continued to run after the primary as a write-in candidate with Ham and Eggs backing. He hoped that a combination of Ham and Eggs enthusiasm and of anger by regular Democrats that Warren had purloined their party's nomination would provide him with a chance at an upset victory. Indeed, Democratic National Chairman James A. Farley spoke to Californians on the radio urging a write-in vote for Kegley.

Kegley, in a radio address of his own, held up the specter of Warren as attorney general failing to defend the Ham and Eggs plan in postelection court battles if it passed. He cited an alleged forthcoming challenge from someone in Denver who claimed to have copyrighted the plan. Warren took the position that he could not comment in detail on the Ham and Eggs proposal because—if elected—he would have to evaluate it should there be any court challenges.

On other matters, Kegley criticized "Oil Warren" for accepting a contribution from petroleum interests. More incongruously, he charged that Warren—if elected attorney general—would not go after gambling interests aggressively. In the Los Angeles mayoral recall campaign, Kegley—along with Ham and Eggs leaders Willis and Lawrence Allen— backed incumbent Mayor Frank Shaw. As was noted in chapter 2, Shaw's corrupt government had become entangled indirectly in the Ham and Eggs campaign.[10] In short, the campaign was continuing and becoming more complicated despite Warren's "bipartisan" listing on both the Democratic and Republican ballots.

Warren now faced an electoral dilemma. Should he rely on the fact that Kegley—the "unseen foe" as Warren termed him—was not on the ballot and thus not bother to campaign vigorously? Should he mount an aggressive anti-Kegley effort, branding him "the tail to the kite" of Ham and Eggs? Or should he claim that Kegley was seeking Ham and Eggs support even though the Warren campaign had reports that Kegley had indicated in private a lack of enthusiasm for the Ham and Eggs proposition?

Eventually, Warren decided on a strategy of continued campaigning without mentioning Kegley by name. After all, putting Kegley's name in the press would only make it easier for voters to write in the Kegley name on Election Day. To a political supporter Warren wrote:

> I agree that I should have some publicity in the newspapers, but I do not believe we should advertise Kegley through our releases.[11]

Instead, numerous earlier supporters received letters from Warren thanking them for their earlier efforts in the primary and asking them to continue the campaign:

> There is but one remaining obstacle, and this is the "thirty dollars a week write-in" campaign to elect one of the defeated candidates. I do not yet know what proportions it will take, but if those who were interested in my cause in the primaries will vote for me again in November, I do not believe it can be successful.[12]

Warren so studiously avoided actually naming Kegley that in his autobiography, he misspelled Kegley's first name as "Karl" (Warren 1977, 124). Undoubtedly, he could find nothing in his own campaign materials in which he had ever written out Kegley's full name! Still, despite having adopted a strategy of ignoring Kegley, Warren was clearly concerned. In a letter to the California state treasurer, a Warren supporter, he worried that "if the'Ham and Eggs' plan runs wild it may be a distinct threat" to his candidacy.[13]

In any event, Warren's no-name strategy worked. On Election Day, he received 1.5 million votes and Kegley a little over 460,000. Still, for Kegley to obtain that many votes as a write-in candidate was a tribute to the power of the Ham and Eggs proposition which itself received 1.1 million votes (45 percent). When Earl Warren later ran for governor, he took this electoral lesson to heart. As for the partisan outcome in 1938, Warren was the only statewide Republican to win office.

Warren as Attorney General

Having won the attorney general position, Earl Warren could sidestep the pension issue and leave newly elected Democratic Governor Culbert Olson to wrestle with it. Warren continued his popular crime and corruption fighting. Olson, meanwhile, as outlined in chapter 2, found himself labeled as a traitor to the Ham and Eggs movement when he failed to call a special Ham and Eggs election in the spring of 1939. Worse, Olson then opposed the 1939 version of the plan when it appeared on the fall state ballot. Warren's eye was clearly on the governorship while these events were unfolding.

During the unsuccessful Ham and Eggs attempt to recall Olson after the 1939 election, Warren's name was raised as a potential candidate should the recall go forward (Earl Warren Oral History Project 1976a, Clifton, 29). And as the governor's term continued, Warren and Olson became more and more antagonistic on many issues. They feuded over Olson's pardoning of radicals, including those involved in Warren's earlier "ship murder" prosecution. Warren succeeded in blocking an Olson appointment to the state Supreme Court. And as World War II threatened and then directly involved the United States, Warren and Olson fought over California's defense preparedness.

In a peculiar way, the war led to a confrontation between Attorney General Earl Warren and Ham and Eggs founder Robert Noble, although not over the pension issue. Noble, it will be recalled, had cooked up the Ham and Eggs scheme originally described as "$25 Every Monday." But he had been ousted in a coup by the Allen brothers at the behest of Captain Earle Kynette of the Los Angeles Police Department. And the Allens then converted the scheme to "$30 Every Thursday" to evade

Noble's lock on the original slogan. Nevertheless, Noble continued his pension agitation with what followers he had among dissident Ham and Eggers. He ran for governor in 1938 as a minor party candidate (attacking Carl Kegley along the way). Noble's electoral platform was that he was the one true gubernatorial candidate committed to the Ham and Eggs program. But his election effort earned Noble few votes; the Allens had successfully marginalized him among the pensionites.

Noble next surfaced as a neo-Nazi, if not an outright one. Just prior to the war, isolationism—often tinged with anti-Semitism—was a major current in American politics. Famed aviator Charles Lindbergh made a highly publicized speech cautioning Americans to avoid being drawn into the war by the Jews and the British. After Japan's attack on Pearl Harbor, however, most isolationists either recanted or—as Lindbergh did—simply kept quiet. Not Noble. In fact, he became increasingly vocal.

Operating within a pro-Nazi group, the "Friends of Progress," Noble unleashed a barrage of propaganda. Citing the Lindbergh speech, Noble announced that he had impeached Roosevelt in a "People's Congress" and would now try him in a "People's Senate." Among Noble's partners in this endeavor was a former director of the local American Civil Liberties Union (ACLU) in Los Angeles. Both were arrested by the FBI and then released in late 1941. But by mid-1942, both were rearrested, convicted of sedition, and imprisoned (American Legion 1942; Schwartz 1998, 348–49; Bennett 1969, 247). Other charges against Noble included income tax evasion and stealing coins from a pay phone (Fitzgerald 1951, 35).

There were in fact both federal and state charges of sedition brought against Noble. Noble was so brazen that it was impossible to ignore his pro-Nazi activities that were being reported to Attorney General Warren.[14] Warren, acting for the state, instructed his assistant attorney general to file a felony complaint against Noble and his partners for failing to register their group as a subversive organization and for libeling General Douglas MacArthur.[15] What apparently appealed to Noble about the Nazis was that the German government gave loans to all newlyweds, a distant echo of Ham and Eggs. Evidently, government payouts to newlyweds were as attractive as government pensions for the elderly for Noble. And Ham and Eggs also had a monetary conspiracy element. Thus, Noble saw the Bank of England as part of a conspiracy with Jews and New Dealers to push the United States into war with the "enlightened Nazis."

Noble also had kind words for Germany's ally, Japan, which—he said—had improved economic conditions in conquered Manchuria. He also asserted that Hawaii was not properly incorporated into the United States and therefore the Japanese attack on Pearl Harbor was not an attack on the United States at all. Also reminiscent of Ham and Eggs was the continuous fund raising for the Friends of Progress at the various public gatherings at which Noble's views were expressed. Despite these documented activities, Noble's state conviction was ultimately reversed at the end of the war, in part with the support of the ACLU, which defended his right to voice unpopular views.[16]

There is no direct evidence that Warren overtly linked Noble to his earlier Ham and Eggs activity during the prosecution. But there is a good chance that Warren knew of the Ham and Eggs connection. After all, Warren's first statewide campaign against Carl Kegley in 1938 coincided with the initial Ham and Eggs proposition. The fact that Noble was on the gubernatorial ballot that year as the self-declared Ham and Eggs candidate, albeit on a minor party ticket, might also have been brought to Warren's attention. If Warren did know about the Ham and Eggs link, this knowledge could not have made seeking the electoral support of the inheritors of the Noble pension movement an attractive prospect for Warren. But seek their support he did.

The 1942 Campaign for Governor

Earl Warren did not lack in what would today be called "self-esteem." He was not introspective and tended to accept whatever verities he had been taught. And he was often able to see his actions as consistent with those verities, even when to outsiders the contradictions seem apparent. Thus, Warren could declare himself a "bipartisan" candidate—because he cross-filed in both Republican and Democratic primaries—and yet be deeply involved in Republican politics. Warren's actions in convicting gamblers and the defendants in the "ship murder" case seem out of step with his later Supreme Court decisions on defendants' rights. Yet Warren could declare in his autobiography that his views on law enforcement never changed (Warren 1977, 117). His opposition as governor to efforts at apportioning legislative districts according to population conflicted with his later "one-man, one vote" position.[17] In that one instance, however, he admitted in retrospect to motives of "political expediency" (Pollack 1979, 209–10).

Finally, there is the issue that arose when he was state attorney general and that seemed to conflict totally with his later racial desegregation decisions on the U.S. Supreme Court: relocation of Japanese Americans and Japanese immigrants during World War II. Warren quasi-apologized for his actions in his autobiography (which was not published before his death), and reportedly broke down in tears when interviewed in the early 1970s for the Berkeley Oral History project on the subject. But he never came to grips with the political aspects of his actions on relocation (Warren 1977, 149; White 1982, 77). In his autobiography, Warren attributed these actions to a combination of impulsive behavior and "the cruelty of war." There was more to it, however.

The fact is that Warren's push to relocate California's Japanese-origin population was politically popular and a tool to use against Culbert Olson in the 1942 gubernatorial election. It was what today would be called a "wedge issue," particularly as Olson showed some reluctance concerning the mass relocation and internment. (Olson came up with arguments that Japanese farmers might be needed for the wartime harvest and therefore should be left in place.) Warren's harsher position remained a popular stand throughout the war, even as the prospect of his first re-election in 1946 approached. Thus, just as Warren's position on apportionment as governor was, in retrospect, a matter of political expediency, so, too, was his approach to Japanese internment.

This simple explanation of his actions not only eluded Warren as he wrote his autobiography at the end of his life; it also escaped his various biographers. Yet it gives a clue toward how he would behave with regard to the pension issue. If he wanted to obtain pensionite votes, he would have to be politically expedient, as he had been on the issue of Japanese relocation. As a union leader of that era later remarked:

> I think Warren knew where he wanted to go. I think Warren wanted to be governor of the state of California, and every move he made . . . was aimed at that. And I think he would have used any means to reach it.[18]

In the 1938 campaign for state attorney general, Earl Warren had actually obtained support from a group of Japanese. They put ads in Japanese-language newspapers stating that Warren was "too big a man to stir up racial prejudice" (Cray 1997, 92). However, even in that earlier campaign, Warren raised the issue of evasion of the anti-Oriental "Alien Land Law" and promised to end such circumventing by "cooley [*sic*] labor." California's anti-Oriental racism was always close to the surface and state politics reflected that fact.

By 1942, the Warren appeal on the Japanese issue was more openly racist than in 1938. Caucasians of German and Italian ancestry could be tested for their loyalty, he stated, "but when we deal with the Japanese we are in an entirely different field" (Weaver 1967, 107). The fact that no disloyal acts by Japanese had been uncovered was itself suspicious, according to Warren. It just showed that they must be planning something big and were merely lying low. Japanese-origin individuals owned land near defense facilities, suggesting espionage as a motive to Warren. (Warren produced maps of this pattern of Japanese land ownership that he regarded as suspicious.) Those Japanese born in the United States, and therefore American citizens, were of "more potential danger" than were the foreign-born Japanese.

After relocation took place, the rhetoric continued from now-Governor Warren. When there began to be talk of returning those relocated back to their California homes in 1943, Warren opposed the proposal, saying that "if the Japs are released, no one will be able to tell a saboteur from any other Jap" (ibid. 109). Even when locked up, controls on the Japanese should be tight, Warren argued. He complained that the Japanese inmates of the Tule Lake relocation camp were being allowed to make long-distance telephone calls (Katcher 1967, 149).

Most biographers have sought to explain and excuse Warren's behavior as the result of the general climate in which he was raised.[19] California, they noted, had a long history of anti-Oriental prejudice. Phone subscribers of Asian ancestry were not listed by name in the Bakersfield telephone directory when Warren was a boy there. Progressive Governor Hiram Walker, whom Warren idolized, had presided over the Alien Land Law much to the chagrin of the Wilson administration,[20] which wanted good relations with Japan (with which the United States became allied during World War I). In this view, Warren was unthinkingly echoing the sentiments of other Californians of his era.

But while all of this background is true, it simply meant that politicians could foster their election prospects by tapping local prejudices. And in the 1942 gubernatorial election, just as anti-Japanese sentiment could be so-tapped, so, too, could pensionite agitation. The question for a Republican such as Warren was a pragmatic one: How could the pensionites be wooed without antagonizing Republican voters who certainly would not want openly to truck with folks like the Ham and Eggers?

With pensionite agitation focused on the state rather than the national scene, just endorsing Townsend, as Frank Merriam had done, was not a viable option. Fortunately for Warren, incumbent Governor Olson—traitor to the Ham and Eggs cause—made this pensionite wooing much easier than it might otherwise have been. Just not being Olson was a major plus for candidate Warren from the pensionite perspective. Any promises to do something about the pension issue added considerable allure, even if the promises were vague. Warren thus initially adopted an "I'm-not-Olson/vague-pension-promise" approach. He also used the more respectable Fraternal Order of Eagles (FOE) for a speech of June 21, 1942—rather than the Ham and Eggs and Townsend groups—to launch his appeal to the pensionites. The FOE had an established history of respectable agitation on behalf of the elderly in the 1920s. In short, the Ham and Eggers had already helped undermine the incumbent Olson. They needed Warren as much as he needed them. And Warren could get their support without endorsing odd monetary plans or Townsend-like transaction tax proposals.

To the Eagles, Warren declared:

> Your organization has pioneered the old age movement. . . . You have done more to aid the aged than any other organization. . . . I know something of the long, hard, uphill fight that you have made for a sound, sensible, liberal pension system that would provide a decent standard of living. . . . And I also know something of the bitter disappointment which you experienced when the present Governor of California, last year, signed a restrictive pension act which wiped out many of the liberal features of the 1937 pension law. . . . If an old man, anxious to feel that he is playing some small part in the war effort, raises a "Victory Garden" and sells $5 worth of vegetables to his neighbors, that amount is deducted from his pension check. . . . If he raises a few chickens and sells a few eggs, even the small sum he receives . . . is deducted. . . . If a lodge donates dues to an elderly member to keep him in good standing, so that he will be assured of a decent burial, even the amount of dues is taken out of his pension check. That to me is about the most prideless imposition that could be foisted on splendid old people who have helped to build this State. . . .
>
> Formerly, under the bill which was enacted at the 1937 session of the Legislature, and which was sponsored by your organization, a beneficiary under the old age pension act was permitted to earn and keep up to $15 a month. And when the present Governor of California permitted that provision to be canceled out, without even making a fight for the old people whom he had promised so much, it was a slap in the face to thousands of self-reliant, self-respecting elder citizens.

I intend to state my views on the pension issue both clearly and emphatically; for to me nothing is more reprehensible than playing politics with the hopes and security of the tens of thousands of deserving old people who must look to government for aid in their later years. We have had far too much political hypocrisy in . . . recent years. We have had far too many extravagant promises—and far too many broken pledges. We have been plagued by extreme proposals which jeopardized not only the pension movement, but the very solvency of State Government. We have had candidates who were willing to ride into office with the backing of such movements—and who then welched on their pre-election bargains. But in all the turmoil . . . the Eagles Lodge remained sane on the pension issue—and continued its fight for gradual improvement of the existing system. . . .

I believe we should stop thinking of an old age pension as a dole which we grant to the needy. I believe every elder citizen, when he reaches the age fixed in the statute, should have the right to retire on an annuity, or a pension. I don't believe he should have to be in need to secure it. I don't believe he should be forced to relinquish any outside income he may have or any property he may have acquired. I don't believe he should be forced first to look to his children for support. I believe in an old age pension as a matter of right, as something we earn in our productive years by our contributions to the upbuilding of the community. And if I am elected Governor of California, I shall my utmost to see that that principle is embodied in our pension law.[21]

How should this speech be translated? Read literally, Warren was calling for a radical departure from the existing state pension system. There was to be no means testing, an idea embodied in the relatively new federal Social Security system but not in any state old-age assistance program. Indeed, if California had proposed to administer a nonmeans tested state pension, it would have been cut off from the federal subsidy provided under the Social Security Act. While the basic federal Social Security pension plan was not means-tested, state old-age assistance was definitely required to be means-tested "welfare."

Still, all Warren had actually promised to do was his "utmost" and—given federal law—his utmost could not produce the plan he described. There was no danger of such any such plan being enacted in California. In contrast, as the campaign wore on, Warren promised to recommend that the state take over the full cost of old-age pensions, eliminating the counties' share. This was something on which, in principle, he could deliver.[22] But, as will be seen, when a proposition including such fully-state paid pensions was actually adopted by the voters in 1948, Warren favored its repeal.

The FOE speech makes indirect reference to the (unnamed) Ham and Eggs plan, which, Warren said, would have threatened state solvency. But it indirectly condemns incumbent Governor Olson for using the Ham and Eggs movement to be elected and then opposing the revised Ham and Eggs proposal in 1939. And the speech uses the Eagles as the model organization that helps the elderly, but does so through gradual improvement. The indirect reference to Olson's treachery was a direct appeal to the Ham and Eggers. The use of the Eagles convention as a forum was an appeal to moderate voters.

To understand the FOE speech more fully, and later Warren campaign actions on pensions, it is helpful to know the dilemma Warren faced in the spring of 1942. Warren's campaign was clearly sensitive to pensionite concerns. An internal memo from a special agent in the attorney general's office concerning a proposed pension initiative found its way into Warren's campaign files. The agent reported that the sponsor of the initiative claimed to have welded Townsendites and Ham and Eggers into a single force that would back the new initiative. This initiative was a revival of an old idea from the early 1900s of creating a "home guard" in which the elderly would "serve." They would be paid for this service, in this case at a rate of $60 a month.

More important than the proposal, which never made its way onto the ballot, was the assessment that the pensionites could be united in an effort to defeat Olson if the initiative succeeded.[23] The line between official business of the attorney general's office and pension politics in the governor's race was being blurred. But a poll taken for the Republicans at about that time showed Olson ahead of Warren statewide and in every area of the state except the Bay Area (where Warren was best known).[24] Aggressive moves would be required to reverse this outcome. Pensionite votes would be needed if Warren were to defeat Olson.

But abstract possibilities of uniting pensionites behind Warren had to be turned into concrete strategy. And Warren faced an immediate dilemma. He had received an invitation directly from Dr. Francis Townsend to speak to a regional Townsend convention in Long Beach (home of the Townsend movement) in late May. The problem for Warren was that he could not possibly speak to the Townsend folks without upsetting his conservative Republican constituents. Franklin Roosevelt had refused earlier to speak to a Townsend convention about nonpension issues, as noted in the previous chapter. Both politicians understood that speaking to such a convention was tantamount to endorsing the Townsend Plan regardless of what was actually said. And Dr. Townsend understood that point, too.

The difference between Roosevelt and Warren was that Roosevelt did not need Townsendite support after 1936, while Warren had good reason to think he did need it in 1942. If Warren turned down the invitation and did nothing more, it would have appeared as a slap in the face to pensionite voters. Time was needed to come up with a plan; Dr. Townsend would have to be stalled. Thus, a week after Townsend sent his invitation, Warren's assistant, Helen MacGregor, wrote back to Townsend saying Warren was away from the office (as if the state attorney general could not be reached!) and would respond upon returning. This move bought some time for formulating a strategic response to Townsend's invitation.

A draft letter was initially prepared from Warren to Townsend in which Warren would decline to speak on the grounds that he had not had enough time to study the pension issue. But that draft—which would suggest ignorance of a key California concern—was rejected. Instead, on May 19, 1942, Warren wrote back to Townsend saying that he could not attend the convention because there were various pension initiatives that might be on the ballot. According to the letter, as attorney general, Warren might be called upon to deal with "legal problems" these possible ballot measures had raised.[25]

But the Warren strategy of putting off Townsend was soon imperiled. Governor Olson did not feel *he* should not speak to the Townsendites and did so in late May. There Olson expressed his belief that pensions should be federally funded, still a Townsend position at the time. Olson supported the Sixty-Sixty plan, $60 per month for those aged sixty and over.[26] Warren's silence on pensions could not be sustained.

An internal campaign memo written shortly before the Eagles speech appears to underlie what later became the strategy of Warren's pensionite election bid. In it an argument is made that Warren could not ignore the pension issue. If he remained silent, the Townsend and Ham and Eggs people would cast a protest vote for some third candidate, and Governor Olson would be reelected. Warren should therefore take some affirmative stance on the pension issue. Specifically, it is suggested, Warren should state that the existing $40 per month state pension is inadequate. And he should promise—if elected—to form a pension "Committee of 25" with five representatives of Townsend, five of Ham and Eggs, five from capital, five from labor, and five representing white-collar workers. The committee would be charged with recommending a new state pension plan for California and the method for raising the money to fund it.[27]

Apparently, despite the memo, at that point in the campaign Warren was reluctant to be so specific about pensions. But he did accept the idea that he had to make a statement on the issue. The Warren camp decided to make use of William Hornblower, the former state legislator who had pushed the Eagles' pension agenda in the 1920s and early 1930s. Officials of Campaigns Inc., the Republican consulting firm that had handled the anti-EPIC campaign, got in touch with Hornblower just before the FOE convention. Hornblower reported that the Eagles were upset about the federal rule on state pensions with its tight limits on outside income. The Victory Garden and the raising-of-chickens stories were surfaced. Hornblower believed that Olson could have done more to have the feds relax their rules on outside income.[28] Campaigns Inc.—which had run the anti-EPIC campaign in 1934—prepared a digest for Warren of the earlier "Recall Olson" effort with reference to Olson's betrayal of the Ham and Eggers. Warren's speech was then developed from these materials.

Warren's FOE speech was effective in putting Governor Olson back on the defensive concerning pensions. Within a couple of weeks, the Eagles issued a press release that picked up Warren's don't-penalize-Victory-Gardens theme. Although the FOE would not endorse candidates, their past president came out for Warren.[29] And Roy Owens, the "economist-engineer" for Ham and Eggs proclaimed that "Earl Warren's statement on pensions is by far the most statesmanlike pronouncement yet made by any public official in America."[30] In a radio address shortly after the FOE convention,[31] Olson found himself having to defend California's tightening of the outside income standard to meet federal rules.

But putting Governor Olson on the defensive was not enough. Warren publicly sent a telegram to Congressman Ward Johnson of Long Beach, the home base of Dr. Townsend, congratulating him for sponsoring a bill in Congress relaxing the outside income rules.[32] Thus, Warren was doing something (symbolically) about the federal restrictions while Olson was left to protest that he was just complying with the rules. Seeing the peril of his position, Olson managed to obtain a liberalized interpretation of the rules from the Roosevelt administration. But the Ham and Eggers simply charged that this switch in the rules was merely a political assist from the national Democrats for a desperate Olson.[33]

Figure 5.1 Sample Letter Received by Earl Warren from Ham and Eggs Warren Supporter and Response from Warren

---

Oct. 19ᵗʰ 1942

Hon., Earl Warren
Attorney General of California
Sacramento, Calif.

Dear Sir:

    Because of your Attitude towards the Payroll Guarantee Association, believe most of the "Ham & Eggers" will support you for Governor.

Am sure 8 at El Monte, 4 Ontario, 4 Fontana, Several San Bernadino, all "Ham & Eggers" will vote for you.

Sincerely Yours,

George H. Whitehead
516 Lexington Ave,
El Monte, Calif.

P.S. Voted for Mr. Olsen when he was elected, <u>but</u> no <u>more</u>.

           —————————

Mr. George H. Whitehead
516 Lexington Ave,
El Monte, Calif.

Dear Mr. Whitehead:

    Thank you for your kind letter and for the interest you are taking in my campaign, particularly in connection with the views I have expressed on Old Age Pensions. I shall always try to merit your confidence.

Sincerely yours,

Earl Warren

Source: Earl Warren papers, California State Archives, F3640: 456.

As the gubernatorial campaign wore on, Olson emphasized his endorsement of the Sixty-Sixty plan. Warren supporters did not directly attack Sixty-Sixty, since it obviously appealed to the pensionites. But the Warren campaign charged that because Olson had once betrayed Ham and Eggs, if elected again he would surely betray Sixty-Sixty.[34] Thus, Warren for the moment could avoid specifics about his views on pensions and just concentrate on Olson-as-betrayer (Figure 5.1).

Despite the attacks, Governor Olson was not about to give up on obtaining support from rank-and-file Ham and Eggers. In a radio address, he called on Ham and Eggers to vote for him because he was committed to a "just and workable pension system." Ham and Eggers should understand that he opposed their plan only because it was unworkable.[35] Olson charged that the Allen brothers had demanded $50,000 from him after the primary to obtain their support—which he refused. But, Olson said, he had "excellent reasons to believe that following the August primary election the Ham and Egg leaders were entertained long and lavishly" by Warren campaign officials.[36] Indeed, an Olson campaign official charged that the Allens had gotten $25,000 from the Republicans (Burke 1953, 221; Fitzgerald 1951, 48).

With the gubernatorial campaign nearing its conclusion, Warren modified his pension strategy. The early strategy memo—which Warren mainly rejected in the spring—had called for a governor's pension committee that would contain representatives of the various pensionite groups. The memo's author wrote to Warren in early September saying pointedly that if his advice had been followed, Warren could have won both the Democratic and the Republican primaries. Better reconsider the pension committee idea, the letter advised.[37] And Warren did.

In early October 1942, Warren pledged—if elected—to create such a committee with representatives from various groups including the Townsendites and the Ham and Eggs people. The committee would have forty days to come up with a recommendation for pension reform that Warren would then submit to the state legislature. If the legislature failed to pass the recommended plan, Warren pledged to call a special election on pension issues "as soon as hostilities of the present war have ceased."

The pension committee pledge was indeed what Warren needed to rally the pensionites behind him. Each group could see themselves obtaining official recognition from the governor through committee membership. They could bask in a state-sponsored public spotlight. Such an opportunity was something they had never received from Governor Olson during his four years in office. And when the ballots were all counted, Olson was out and Warren was in. In his inaugural address, Warren stated:

> It is my conviction that our pension system should not be based upon the requirement of pauperism. I want it to be based on social right. I believe, as most of you believe, that the ultimate solution of the pension problem will come through advances made on a national scale. Yet, we should not permit this thought to delay our own efforts to build and maintain a pension structure within the limits of our ability to pay.[38]

After the official inauguration ceremony, Olson and Warren rode down in the same elevator in the capital. Olson said, "Well, I hope you have a better term in office than I did. Mine was four years of hell." Warren said, "Hmphh. Well it depends on how you handle it" (Earl Warren Oral History Project 1976a, Clifton, 14). And one of the first things Warren had to handle was putting together his promised pension committee. Having criticized Olson for betraying his pensionite followers during Olson's term in office, Warren could not begin own his term with a second betrayal. There would have to be a pension committee and it would have to contain representatives of the Ham and Eggers and the Townsend people. As it turned out, however, the most significant committee member was a representative of neither group, one George McLain.

The Rise of "Uncle George" McLain

Who was George McLain? In 1942, he was a pensionite with his own, relatively new, group. McLain's father, a paving contractor, had lost his business in the Great Depression and was forced to apply for a county pension at age eighty. According to George McLain, it was the undignified treatment of his father by county bureaucrats that brought him to the pension cause. If so, it took him awhile to arrive there.

Junior McLain, who had been employed by his father's paving business, also applied for relief. He ended up working on a county building project. With his consciousness raised by Hard Times, young George quickly saw the connection between social movements and politics. In 1932, for example, he was a spokesperson for the Los Angeles Unemployed Voters Association at a city council meeting. The association was a group he had organized a year earlier, and it generally pushed for public works projects and self-help cooperative exchange programs such as the "Tradex" plan. A year later McLain ran for mayor of Los Angeles using Unemployed Voters Association as a support base, but he failed to make a significant showing. It was clear that representing the unemployed was not going to advance McLain's career any further.

However, there were other causes available. McLain joined up with EPIC and achieved minor status in that movement. He made an unsuccessful election bid for membership on the Los Angeles board of education. In 1936, the year of the "bum blockade" in which Los Angeles police officers briefly closed the state borders to job seekers, McLain formed a group called "Natives of California, Inc." Its purpose was to "restore the Government of California to the natives of the State, and keep it there." But the new organization went nowhere, and after two more unsuccessful electoral attempts, McLain joined Ham and Eggs in 1938. With the second defeat of Ham and Eggs in 1939, McLain split off from that movement, taking along a short-lived splinter group known as the "Militant Body" (Leader 1972, 177; Pinner, Jacobs, and Selznick 1959, 26–34).

There were more unsuccessful bids for political office by McLain. But not easily discouraged, McLain was learning political skills. He knew how to form alliances with other politicians. For example, McLain had been tapped by Culbert Olson to sabotage the Allen brothers' abortive effort to recall the governor after the defeat of Ham and Eggs in 1939. McLain originally received money from Olson indirectly to assist with Olson's 1942 bid for reelection as governor. But when it seemed more likely that Olson would lose, McLain moved over to Earl Warren's campaign. Warren's preelection pledge to create a pension committee whetted McLain's appetite. McLain declared on the eve of the election that

> Olson is the party responsible for ignoring [the] abuses that recipients of old-age assistance are enduring daily.[39]

As soon as the election results were in, McLain wrote to Warren:

> I trust that you will favor me as a member of [the pension] committee representing a large section of old-age pensioners. You may be interested to know that I am very familiar with the Federal and State laws relative to old age Security, and I have been the first pension leader to have been able to unite the leaders of other pension groups . . . to support a sane and sensible measure to liberalize the present Old Age Security Act of the State of California.[40]

The letter went on to drop names of Democratic and Republican politicians with whom McLain claimed to have connections, as did a later communication in December.[41] Among the names dropped were Raymond Haight, a Warren supporter who had been the third-party "Progressive" candidate for governor during the 1934 EPIC campaign. Haight, however, wrote to Governor-elect Warren in late December reporting that McLain was *not* favored by the other pension groups.[42]

And all McLain received back from the governor-elect was a form letter indicating "the matter you mentioned has been carefully noted and will be called to [Warren's] attention at the earliest opportunity."[43] Such a distant response undoubtedly made McLain uneasy. The future of his pensionite career depended on obtaining a seat on the governor's committee.

McLain was not the only one becoming nervous. A veritable campaign among the pension groups was taking place for membership on Warren's promised committee. Willis Allen and Roy Owens of Ham and Eggs sent a telegram in early January 1943 asking to meet with the new governor. Warren's assistant secretary wrote back that the governor was willing to have a meeting. Meanwhile, McLain met with William T. Sweigert, a key Warren aide, indicating a desire to be on the State Welfare Board, as well as the pension committee. With Raymond Haight viewed as a Warren insider, Roy Owens wrote an ingratiating letter to him suggesting that Haight should chair the committee. In early February, the Payroll Guarantee Association (the Ham and Eggs group) was asked to name its representative to the new committee. Evidently, Warren was not prepared to pick among the Ham and Eggs characters himself.

When word reached McLain that the rival Ham and Eggers had been invited to select a representative, he asked his radio listeners to write to Governor Warren and demand a seat for himself. The letters poured in (Figure 5.2). Meanwhile, Myrtle Williams, who worked with McLain as his group's "secretary treasurer" (more about her later), sent a telegram to Warren aide Sweigert complaining about the neglect of McLain. It was unfair, she said, to include the Ham and Eggers without also inviting McLain's group:

> Because of the lack of recognition from the governor's office we are having a difficult time convincing our membership that Mr. Warren appreciated their support. We trust that our demonstrated faith and loyalty will soon be rewarded. [44]

In fact, McLain had already been chosen, and a telegram to that effect was sent the next day. McLain, of course, immediately accepted the invitation to become a member of what was officially called the "Citizen's Statewide Committee on Old Age Pensions." The seventeen-man committee was chaired by a banker and had four representatives from the legislature (two Republicans, two Democrats), two union representatives (one from the AFL, one from the rival CIO), two farm representatives, a

Chamber of Commerce representative, representatives of the counties (which administered state old age assistance), with the rest of the membership from pension-oriented organizations.

The respectable Fraternal Order of Eagles (FOE) was represented by William Hornblower, the former legislator who had carried FOE pension bills in the 1920s and early 1930s. He had earlier written to Warren that the pension plans being batted about just prior to the Statewide Committee's formation would be financially ruinous to the state. The Townsend folks received two representatives, one their third-party candidate for governor in 1942. An anti-Townsend group, which supported expanding conventional Social Security—the General Welfare Federation of America—also had a representative. Ham and Eggs was represented by Roy Owens. And finally, there was George McLain, representing his own group that he had taken over from something called the "American Citizens' Pension Association." The original group had favored national pensions, but McLain converted it to a California-level organization that he termed the "Citizen's Committee for Old Age Pensions."

In announcing his new pension committee, Governor Warren declared that "old-age security is our most fundamental problem." The committee should, he said, "be able to eliminate those political considerations which have so often confused discussions of pension matters." But Warren also said that the existing state pension cap of $40 per month was inadequate. Thus, the committee was clearly expected to come up with a higher figure. With $40 viewed as too low, and the $60 of the Sixty-Sixty plan viewed by Hornblower and others as too high, it could easily have been guessed that $50 would be the compromise.

The Pension Report

Once established, the new Citizen's Statewide Committee held public hearings. Lawrence Allen testified on behalf of Ham and Eggs. His latest plan was to give anyone "frozen out of industry in this machine age"— regardless of age—$20 per week to be paid out of "Stabilization Exchange Checks." If the plan were adopted, he explained "very conceivably it could be the vehicle that would carry Earl Warren straight to the White House in 1944."[45]

Notes on the meeting indicate that the White House remark touched off such loud cheers from Allen's supporters "that the chairman had to rap

Figure 5.2 **Sample Letters from McLain Supporters to Earl Warren**

2-19-1943
Honorable Gov of Calif
Sacramento

Dear Gov. I am writing to you at the request of Broadcast Wanting all old Calif.
to write and tell you how hones Mr. McLain is, in my opinion. Now this is rather
confusing to me as I never have heard that Mr. McLanes characterr was brought
in to question and it seems that my opinion would be of very lettle use to Mr.
Mclane in His efforts in behalf of the Old People That is one of the Politicions
methods of getting apointments Now Dear Gov I voted for you on your Past
Record and am glad to say that so far I had no reason to change my mind or
regret my choice Though I am 87 years Old and have been a Democrat all my life
And I am for Old Age Pensions as us Old People Pioneers surely deserve some
Reward for the many hardships and women and men had to endure so that our
Posterity might enjoy luxuryes that surrounds them now Hoping that you will
asist the Pension movement and thanking you in advance.
Respt.
J A Dalameter
Compton

Feb. 17, 43
Mr. Ear Warren, Governor
Sacramento Calif

Dear Sir - Tho we do not know Mr. Geo. McClain personally we do hear of his
unselfish Sacrific for the poor and oppressed even in his earlier life and now we
heave been hearing him on his daily 5:45 PM broadcast, and we are incouraged
by his untiring effort to bring about a decent pension for the "as he puts it"
neglected aged people which everyone does, or should realize is badly needed
and why any one could write you trying to hinder such a cause, can only be
ungodly & selfish. So we are appealing to you our much appreciated Governor;
to please give Mr. Geo. McClain your whole-hearted support, in his nerve straining
effort to help the poor, old, & sick folks, which too, will relieve them of the awful
dread of depending on their children for help who as usual under normal times
have all they can do to support & educate their children. Trusting that you will
give him your support, we are all very sincerely yours.

Mr. & Mrs. R.S. Gibson
Los Angeles

Source: Earl Warren papers, California State Archives, F3640: 4041 and 4044.

repeatedly for order."[46] However, the speech was notable for two elements. First, it drifted away from pensions and the elderly base of the Ham and Eggs movement toward something resembling Canadian Social Credit. Second, it focused on unemployment at a time when—thanks to the war economy—joblessness was fast becoming a distant memory. In short, Lawrence Allen's statement ensured that nothing that came from the Ham and Eggs people would be taken seriously by the committee.

Dr. Townsend also appeared at the meeting, but he spoke in favor of federal legislation as proposed by California's Townsendite senator, Sheridan Downey. Townsend, it will be recalled from the previous chapter, had not yet turned to state legislation, as he would in an unsuccessful campaign for a Townsendite California ballot proposition in 1944. Townsend was still convinced that any pension plan should be federal.[47] With Ham and Eggs drifting away from its constituency and ignoring the changed economic climate, and with Townsend disinterested in state legislation, those who focused on Warren's charge to recommend changes in the existing state plan had an edge.

The McLain proposal fell into that category. Basically, the McLain group advocated the Sixty-Sixty plan (which Culbert Olson and the Democrats had supported). It asked also for an end to the state requirement that children contribute support for their aged parents. And—noteworthy for its future portents—it proposed that the state, not the counties, should administer the system.

If anyone emerged as the hero of the day, it was Earl Warren. The minutes indicate that the Los Angeles pension committee hearings were "packed to the window sills" and that "people were standing in the corridor, out on the porch, and down on the steps outside the building." Furthermore, "one of the chief characteristics of the meeting was that almost every speaker made some reference to Governor Warren, and in every instance the applause was enthusiastic and in some cases almost violent."[48]

The committee made its official report to the governor at the end of March 1943, six weeks after its creation. In simple terms, the pensionites—with the exception of William Hornblower of the Eagles—supported Sixty-Sixty in a minority dissent. (Vernon Kilpatrick, a Democratic assemblyman from Los Angeles, joined with the pensionite minority.) The minority report made vague references to the need to consider various tax or "self-liquidating credit" plans for financing, reflecting the Townsend and Ham and Eggs signatories.[49] The majority favored $50 per month with no reduction in age below the existing sixty-five. (Had the state lowered the age below sixty-five, payments to those younger would not have received any federal subsidy.) The labor representatives signed the majority report but indicated it was a matter of political pragmatism; a majority in favor of $50 would lead to legislative enactment of the pension increase. Anything beyond that figure would go nowhere.

This political insight proved to be correct; most of the committee's recommendations were soon adopted by the California legislature. The labor representatives also wanted the committee to remain in existence after it reported, a wish that was not granted.[50] There was no desire in the Warren administration to keep the public spotlight on the pension issue once it had been dealt with by the pension committee. Warren, of course, received the credit from those pension recipients pleased by the $10 increase (and the blame from those who wanted a $20 increment). Overall, however, the report and its enactment were both regarded by Warren as models for bipartisan citizens' involvement in solving state problems.

Apart from the raise in the pension cap to $50, the pension committee report recommended an increase in the allowance for real property, an increase in the allowance for personal property, continued relatives' contributions but with a more liberal schedule, retention of county (rather than state) administration, and an increased share of the state in the total aid provided. All of these recommendations were included by the state legislature in the enacted plan except the increase in the real property allowance (Richard Harvey 1959, 149) (Figure 5.3).

Of course, this incremental approach was not enough for the Ham and Eggers. Roy Owens accused the majority of "a perpetuation of the 'pauper's oath of need' theory." Taxes to pay for pensions would not expand purchasing power as such transfers simply redistribute income, he declared, in a slam at the rival, tax-oriented Townsendites. The state should create a "stabilization account," a variant of the currency creation scheme of the previous Ham and Eggs initiatives. Pensions would be paid in "stabilization checks." Unless this scheme was enacted, there would be "an early end of private enterprise through the insidious entrance of State Socialism,"[51] Owens argued.

While criticizing the majority report, even the Ham and Eggers were reluctant to attack Warren personally, particularly with state pensions about to rise at his behest. But a Warren supporter noted that whatever goodwill existed should not be expected to last, and recommended that

Figure 5.3 **Letters to Governor Warren After His Pension Committee Reported**

> *July 4, 1943*
> *Our Dear Governor Warren:*
> *You caused old people to receive $50.00 each month instead of $40.00 as heretofore.*
> *Thank you very much for now I will be able to buy new glasses and have my eyes treated, I am personally very grateful to you, and so I am writing to tell you.*
> *Thanking you again and again.*
> *Respectfully and gratefully yours,*
> *Mrs. Clara May Smith*
> *Los Angeles*
>
> *May 7, 1943*
> *Mr Governor Warren,*
> *Just a few words to tell you you may not notice this letter but it is going to kick back on you some day we all know Governor Olson was a traitor to the aged but we have no record that he was hiding behind a hand-picked committee like you are doing you had no intention of lowering the age. just a game to get in office Some get 40 a month some get 20 and 20 and 25 why dont you treat all alike ailing people at the age of 60 can not get work. they can not do a days work while our boys are away we do without I wonder what my boy would think if he knew I have 5 lbs of winies in 12 month and no other meat*
> *Mrs. S V Dale*
> *(no city)*
>
> *Source:* Earl Warren papers, California State Archives, F3640: 4030 and 4033.

Warren would do well to collect all of the nice things the Ham and Eggers had said about him. Such statements could be useful when they and the other pensionites inevitably turned on Warren later.[52]

Although he had supported the Sixty-Sixty plan and had not signed the majority report, George McLain was anxious to stay on the governor's good side. And because pensioners would get a $10 raise, why not take some of the credit for it? He reported to a Warren aide that he was making "possibly the strongest radio speech given in Mr. Warren's behalf since the election." In the speech, he announced that "Rome wasn't built in a day. . . . The aged people of California can join in the chorus of Thank God for Governor Earl Warren."[53] However, McLain's era of good feeling was not to last.

Six months after the pension committee reported, McLain was already complaining to a Warren aide about county administration of pensions. A year after the report, McLain's attorney griped to Warren that the McLain organization was under investigation. By 1946, McLain's newspaper was trumpeting "Governor Warren's betrayal of the aged" and endorsing his rival in the upcoming Democratic primary.[54]

Although Warren continued to pay lip service to pensions, California was now experiencing an influx of younger job seekers in the wartime state industries. While the new population brought with it its own social problems, Warren regarded the youthful shift in demographics as a blessing (Warren 1977, 225–26). It would eventually kill the pension issue that had roiled state politics for years. Warren was right, of course, but he misjudged the speed with which the political change away from the politics of aging would occur.

By the mid-1940s, Warren's social welfare interests had indeed shifted. He never again supported a specific figure for state pensions, leaving it to the legislature to raise the amount periodically. Essentially, Warren was willing to let state pension payments rise enough to fend off pensionite pressures (Moley 1951, 223). And he was not averse to taking an occasional public position on pensions if it proved popular. In 1945, for example, Warren identified himself with one Elwood Hoffman, a pensioner whose stipend had been cut because he bought War Bonds.[55] Hoffman's War Bond problem was the kind of endearing political anecdote out of which a later California governor—Ronald Reagan—would make a career.

Warren concentrated his social welfare policy—unsuccessfully as it turned out—on creating a statewide health insurance plan for citizens of all ages. Massive opposition by doctors and conservatives defeated Warren's health initiatives, but he remained a popular governor. In 1946, he ran for reelection, again undertaking a "bipartisan" campaign by filing in both the Democratic and Republican primaries. As he had in 1938 in his attorney general race, Warren received both parties' nominations; he won in the general election with little opposition. Warren had thus become the first California governor since Hiram Johnson to win a reelection bid. But despite changing state demographics—and Warren's evident popularity—the pensionites were not about to be forgotten.

Myrtle Williams: Queen for a Year

Although striking a more moderate pose than other pensionites, George McLain followed the Ham and Eggs administrative formula. He employed his own advertising agency to handle his organization's media propaganda, taking a substantial commission in the process. And, of course, there was a radio program (and later a television program). McLain even managed to mirror the Allen brothers' sometime neglect to pay payroll taxes for the staff. He completely dominated his organization, which came to be called the "California Institute for Social Welfare," operating it with a rubber-stamp board. With his appointment to the pension committee in 1943, McLain was able to raise his public profile above those of competing pension groups. He emerged as the major pension player in the state (Pinner, Jacobs, and Selznick 1959, 34–46).

McLain's appeal in organizing went directly to the pocketbook. Potential contributors to his organization were encouraged to view their donations as investments. "Would you spend five dollars to get back $60 to $300 a year increase in your pension checks?" Truly committed contributors could pay extra and take out "life memberships." Apart from lobbying, members also received personal assistance in confronting the welfare bureaucracy (e.g., filing claims and appeals). And publications were offered on legislative developments.

Broadcasts were conducted in a folksy manner with McLain referring to himself as "Uncle George." Like a contemporary radio or TV preacher, there were continued "emergency" fund-raising appeals: "Unless we can raise some money very quickly, our radio programs will cease," he warned. The preacher element was even more present in the closing of each broadcast with a prayer. Although the references were typically Christian, McLain was interdenominational when it came to fund raising. At least one of his Social Welfare clubs had Jewish membership and conducted its business in Yiddish (ibid. 115–18, 146–57). Townsend's prewar link to notorious anti-Semite Gerald L.K. Smith and the Allens' postwar link to Smith were not mirrored in the McLain organization. McLain also cultivated supporters in the black community.

The Allens and others still in the residual Ham and Eggs movement went on proposing ballot propositions that never got off the ground (and involved themselves in a money laundering scandal concerning campaign funding). Meanwhile, McLain continued to build his organization. He focused on pressing the California legislature to raise state pensions incrementally and provided assistance to members having problems with program administrators. A Townsend plan pension proposition was placed on the California ballot in 1944 but lost by a two-to-one margin. Notably, McLain signed the official ballot argument *against* the state-level Townsend plan. He was anxious to eliminate the competition for pensionite support.

McLain's official targets of attack were the "private interests" dominating the legislature and the bureaucrats and social workers administering Old Age Assistance. He accepted Social Security and the accompanying welfare state that had arisen from the New Deal. This was something the Ham and Eggers and the Townsend folks never did. McLain's line was basically that improvements in the existing system were needed. And once the competition of the other pensionite groups was out of the way, it was McLain's turn to put his own proposition on the California state ballot.

Of course, there was certainly opposition to be overcome. In the late 1940s, California still had a generous system of state pensions compared with the national average. There were plenty of complaints about burdens to taxpayers and a foreshadowing of the modern charges that Social Security recipients are "greedy geezers." But such charges simply made the elderly more defensive and desirous of an organization to defend their interests. McLain's organization became an early version of the modern-day AARP, providing benefits, communications, and political advocacy. It put out its own newspaper and possessed "the latest direct mail machinery and gadget" (McWilliams 1951, 297). And it exercised political muscle with precinct captains organized around the state. Some members of the legislature openly admitted to being on McLain's payroll (Cresap 1954, 62).

Three years after World War II ended, McLain was ready to make a major political move.[56] California's state pension premium above the national average had eroded from its 87 percent peak in 1940 to 45 percent by 1948 (Bond et al. 1954, 240). So McLain put on the 1948 California ballot a constitutional amendment raising monthly payments for aged and blind recipients from $60 to $75. The changing power dynamics of pension politics were particularly apparent in that year; competing Townsend and Ham and Eggs propositions failed to obtain places on the ballot (Fitzgerald 1951, 29).

McLain's Proposition 4 moved the authority for administering the program from the counties to the state. The amendment created an elected state Director of the Department of Social Welfare. But for an interim period it effectively named his associate, Myrtle Williams, as state director! Williams and McLain co-owned the Williams Advertising Agency, which like the Allens' earlier Cinema Advertising Agency was able to generate profits from a supposedly nonprofit movement (ibid. 69). (Discreet press accounts of that period do not further explore the McLain–Williams relationship.)

Apart from its administration provisions and monthly stipend increase, Proposition 4 entailed a considerable liberalization of state pension rules. Age limits were lowered from sixty-five to sixty-three. Relatives' responsibility was eliminated. Income and property eligibility rules were substantially relaxed. No charges were allowed for health services provided by public hospitals to pension recipients. Moreover, the costs of these liberalizations were designated by the proposition as liens against all monies in the state treasury. Elderly pensioners would have first call on state funding. And counties would no longer contribute anything to state pension expenses.

Apparently, McLain's proposition had not been expected to win and only a limited campaign was launched against it. Governor Warren at the time was campaigning as the Republican vice presidential candidate with running mate Thomas Dewey. To the extent he was concerned with state ballot measures, it was with Proposition 13, which would have apportioned the state senate by population had it not been defeated by voters. When Proposition 4 passed by a narrow margin (50.9 percent), the governor—who would have been off to Washington and the national stage had the Dewey–Warren ticket won—was now confronted with an immediate state problem.

Myrtle Williams (and through her George McLain) was about to come into possession of all state and county machinery relating to pensions. But Warren and the state legislature would have to pay the bills for the increased pension, lower age limits, and other enhancements. McLain would get the benefit in the eyes of his elderly constituents; Warren and the legislature would get the costs. And the costs appeared to be considerable. Various estimates were flying about, ranging up to $100 million annually.

Actual costs to the state appear in retrospect to be about half that amount. As Table 5.1 shows, monthly pension expenditures during the first (and only) year of the Myrtle Williams administration rose by about $7 million per month (December 1948–December 1949). The federal government picked up roughly 40 percent of overall expenditures, so the annualized cost after a year of operation was about $50 million. These costs included the higher stipend (in a year when consumer prices *dropped* by 2.1 percent), relaxed eligibility rules, and lowered age limits.

Demands were heard almost immediately for Governor Warren to

Table 5.1

Summary of State Old Age Assistance Program, December 1948–December 1949

	December 1948	December 1949	December 1950
Number of recipients	198,301	272,706	268,357
Of which:			
Recipients aged 63–64	0	16,654	0
Average monthly grant	$61.16	$70.74	$67.13
Total monthly expenditure			
($ millions)	$12.1	$19.3	$18.0

Source: California, Department of Social Welfare, *Preliminary Statistical Release,* various issues.

call a special election to repeal Proposition 4. Opponents included the surprised empire of dispossessed counties (although the proposition eliminated their pension expenses) and taxpayer and business groups who were enraged at the costs (Fitzgerald 1951, 78–82). But Warren was reluctant to commit himself to repeal of a pension initiative that had just been passed (Figure 5.4). In his address to the legislature in early January 1949, he said the lawmakers would simply have to come up with the money for the new system. Legislators, apart from dealing with the financial implications, began to question the initiative process itself, introducing various bills to make it more difficult to place propositions on the ballot in the future.

McLain, meanwhile, was clearly at his influential peak. Carey McWilliams, normally an astute observer of California politics of that period, predicted in 1949 that within a decade "McLain may be as familiar a figure in Washington as he is today in Sacramento" (McWilliams 1951, 299). Of course, such a leap to national prominence depended crucially on McLain's maintenance of control of the California pension system. McWilliams thought that McLain would be able to hold on, but others were determined to prevent that outcome.

Opponents of Proposition 4 could also see that McLain's future depended on controlling California's pension system. Thus, after the proposition passed, McLain himself remained a key target of attack. A legislative committee investigated McLain and his organization's finances. Embarrassing disclosures were made—a mini-version of the congressional investigation of Francis Townsend in the 1930s (see chapter 4). McLain's expenses seemed to exceed his income. He lived rent-free

Figure 5.4 **Letter to Earl Warren Asking Him Not to Support Repeal of McLain's Newly Enacted Proposition 4**

Nov 18 1948
Dear Governor Warren -

> *The opposition to Pension Bill No 4 on the ballot are using every means known to knock it out. If you don't hear from the voters direct the opposition may win out. I for one voted for it and will again. The measure was fairly won and we the people as voters for the measure expect you to keep your word and put Old Age Pension Bill #4 into effect. And the statement made by the Tax Payers Assn. To the effect that the voters were confused because there were 18 other issues on the ballot is a weak one. I ask you why the voters were not confused on the other 17 issues? Higher taxes dont frighten me either I am used to them.*

> *The Pension Bill #4 is made a law by the voters and the voters expect you to abide by it and enforce it.*

Yours very respectfully

Roy W. Ward
Los Angeles

Source: Earl Warren papers, California State Archives, F3640: 4010.

in an apartment owned by his organization, which was taking in $500,000 annually. Witnesses also testified that McLain was controlling the State Welfare Department through Myrtle Williams. And there were complaints about some McLain associates that Myrtle Williams appointed to various state positions. Among the appointees was the son of Townsendite California Senator Sheridan Downey (Pinner, Jacobs, and Selznick 1959, 46–48, 243–48).

Although they could not push Warren to call a special election, the opponents of McLain's successful proposition mounted a repeal drive for the November 1949 ballot. They succeeded in putting before the electorate Proposition 2, which would repeal the transfer of pension administration to the state but leave the increased dollar amount intact. Indeed, monthly payments to the blind were raised by another $10 to attract additional votes and support from agencies assisting the sightless.

McLain had his supporters too, chiefly Democrats. These included

Augustus Hawkins (a black assemblyman originally elected on the EPIC ticket in 1934 and who went on to a career in Congress). Sam Yorty, a Democratic assemblyman who was anti-EPIC in 1934, also supported McLain. Yorty later became mayor of Los Angeles. In addition, supporting McLain's cause were U.S. Senator Sheridan Downey and James Roosevelt, son of FDR, who was contemplating running for California governor in 1950 (ibid. 54). Governor Warren remained aloof for a time and McLain threatened him with a recall. At the same time, letters were pouring into the governor's office urging he do something about repealing Proposition 4. Many of these letters were the result of a campaign by the state Chamber of Commerce.[57] (see Figure 5.5)

Eventually, however, Warren came out in favor of repeal (Fitzgerald 1951, 85–87). McLain's political allies—and his loyal pensionite supporters—could not resist the tide. And the repeal proposition passed by 57.5 percent, returning California's old-age assistance administration to the local county authorities. Myrtle Williams was out of her state job. She took it rather well, declaring, "I certainly wish to abide by the expressed will of the people." Her successor later scoffed that "fortunately, she didn't know enough and didn't have enough ability to disrupt too many things" at the Department of Social Welfare (Earl Warren Oral History Project 1977, Schottland, 31).

Some tightening up on pension administration appears to have occurred after Williams left office, however. As shown in Table 5.1, figures for December 1950, a year after repeal became effective, depict a slight decline in the caseload (partly due to the reexclusion of those aged sixty-three and sixty-four). A decline in average payments per recipient (in the face of an increase of consumer prices by 5.9 percent) is also reported.

To the extent that Warren turned his attention to the elderly thereafter, it was through various conferences on the problems of aging. Essentially, he sought to widen the terms of the discussion away from just pensions to areas such as mental and physical health and age discrimination in employment. When the Townsendites invited Warren to speak to their convention, he sent instead his new head of the Department of Social Welfare, Charles Schottland, successor to Myrtle Williams. Schottland spoke to the Townsendites about creating work opportunities for seniors, much to the dismay of Dr. Townsend himself (ibid. 32–33).

Soon Earl Warren no longer had to worry about California's lingering pensionite movement at all. Not long after the Eisenhower adminis-

Figure 5.5 Letter Protesting Warren's Support for Repeal of McLain's Proposition 4

Oct 15 49
Dear Gov Warren

I have felt deeply impressed to write you for I think if you realy knew the condition of the old people and the Blind, you would take action, to prevent these repealers from putting us on the county or poor house or our helpless relatives.

I gave three Sons in the 1ˢᵗ World War and was at that time a widow, and was in poor health but had to make my living, but in later years married again during depression one day we rec a letter from the county to come to L.A. and sign some papers to get yelp, in fact we had very little but had to sign away all we had and become a pauper, but Gov Olson was in office at that time and he ordered all the papers sent back to the people, and my Husband was put to work, he passed away in 1940, in my younger days I was a mission worker, and visited the poor farm, I talk with the people who were there from every walk of life, I have lately visited rest homes, and hospitals, and find many people paying their way with pensions, who have nothing and if they had patients their relatives have to make up the difference to amount of $125.00 a month, now just think what it will mean to them, when so many people are homeless and out of work. I am sure if you could see the conditions, you would take a different attitude toward this Election and help the poor and needy and old people who have helped with their families to make america what it is to day.

A deeply Interested voter
Yours truly

Mrs Christine Watson
Monrovia, California

Source: Earl Warren papers, California State Archives, F3640: 4013.

---

tration took office, Warren was appointed Chief Justice of the U.S. Supreme Court. Schottland also was able to escape California's remaining pensionites through a federal appointment. He became commissioner of Social Security.

Aftermath

George McLain began trying to unseat Earl Warren—who first gave him statewide prominence—for the governor's support of repealing

Proposition 4. Warren was depicted as a traitor to the pensionites, as his predecessor Culbert Olson had once been. In the 1950 gubernatorial election, McLain backed Democrat James Roosevelt against Warren's bid for a third term as governor (after McLain threatened to run himself). Roosevelt's campaign literature on old-age security said he would "fight for an adequate Federal retirement plan, provide pensions sufficient to meet the high cost of living, return pension administration to the State government, [and] remove the so-called relatives' responsibility clause." The McLain influence on these pledges, especially the latter two, is evident. Apart from the pensionites, organized labor also criticized Warren for having supported the repeal of McLain's proposition in 1949 (Earl Warren Oral History Project 1976c, Haggerty, Appendix III, 16).

A campaign aide to James Roosevelt later characterized McLain as "a force to be reckoned with" and indicated that "We were very fortunate to get his [McLain's] support" (Earl Warren Oral History Project 1976a, Post, 25). But McLain's support was not enough to provide a victory for Roosevelt. Among other problems faced by the Democratic candidate was a distinct lack of enthusiastic support by President Truman for Roosevelt's candidacy. Roosevelt, now to his regret, had championed a dump-Truman effort at the 1948 Democratic National Convention. Everyone in the know then was sure that Truman would lose to Dewey in the fall election. And James Roosevelt had hoped to induce Dwight Eisenhower (!) to become the Democrat's nominee. Truman on various occasions had nice things to say about Warren, who had always needed crossover Democrats to win his various elections. In the end, Earl Warren became the only California governor elected to three terms in office.[58]

McLain's 1951 report to his constituents tells of his unsuccessful efforts to push various bills through the legislature. The report names friends and enemies in the legislature and sets the stage for a new McLain ballot initiative in 1952 (McLain 1951). The 1952 proposition would have transferred authority for old age assistance back to the state and added a cost of living adjustment and other benefits. The official argument for that proposal (Proposition 11) read:

> The elderly need relief from their misery and suffering. We need to honor our elderly (as God said to Honor thy Father and Mother).

But by this time the state was losing its elderly tilt. The rapid influx of younger people during World War II and afterwards had irrevocably shifted California's population toward its current youthful position. Moreover, after somewhat uncertain prospects during the 1940s, federal Social Security had been substantially broadened and enhanced in 1950 by Congress. Its role as a public pension program was rapidly growing relative to state-run plans (Berkowitz 1997, 25–28).

Thus, even with God's alleged endorsement, McLain's 1952 proposition failed to pass, along with a related measure.[59] McLain's final proposition to appear on the ballot did so in 1954 and would have raised state pension payments from $80 to $100 a month. It was also defeated, effectively ending the ballot wars in California over pensions for the elderly. Nonetheless, McLain thereafter pushed—unsuccessfully—for legislation to put old age assistance back under state control as it had been under his 1948 proposition (California Institute of Social Welfare 1956? 50–51).

Various other political initiatives followed as well. In 1960, a presidential election year, McLain and his organization attempted to elect a slate of delegates pledged to him at the Democratic National Convention. Apparently, he hoped to defeat a delegation pledged to Governor Edmund "Pat" Brown (who was running as a favorite son) on grounds that Brown had not done enough for old folks. Although McLain did not succeed, his slate did draw 600,000 votes. But there may have been more involved for McLain in 1960 than just political disagreements with Brown about pensions.

McLain was attempting to obtain funding from the Federal Housing Administration (FHA) at the time for a senior citizen housing project in Fresno, California. He apparently was selling subscriptions in the "California League for Senior Citizens," the organization slated to build the project. Subscribers were promised that they would eventually live in the Fresno project or others to be built like it. The FHA was suspicious of McLain's financial ability to manage such a project and even if he really intended to build it. McLain sought assistance of then-Vice President Richard Nixon (a Californian), who was to be the Republican candidate for president in 1960. He apparently hinted at an endorsement of Nixon in exchange for help with his FHA problems and won at least some inquiries and follow-ups from officials on Nixon's staff.

As he had in relationships with other California politicians, McLain could easily move from hot to cold. In 1949, while serving in the U.S. Congress, Nixon had endorsed the *repeal* of McLain's 1948 state takeover of state pensions.[60] He could not have been one of McLain's heroes back then. But in 1960, as noted above, McLain nonetheless turned to Nixon for aid on his housing project. Only two years later, when Nixon ran unsuccessfully for governor of California against incumbent Brown, McLain turned against the former vice president. He denounced Nixon for his stand on welfare, saying Nixon's policies would cause "wholesale suffering and actual starvation" to the aged, blind, and disabled. The intensity of the McLain attacks alarmed officials in the Nixon campaign, who suspected that Brown's organization might be behind the diatribe. In the course of his losing campaign for governor, Nixon was forced to make various statements denying he favored cutting pensions of the elderly.[61]

McLain died in 1965 amid a protest within his League for Senior Citizens. Although the Fresno housing project was completed, another project in the Los Angeles area fell into financial difficulties and remained unfinished and unoccupied. A controversy erupted over alleged financial irregularities. McLain was in the process of suing his opponents for libel when he died.[62] He was the last veteran of the Ham and Eggs movement—the group through which he first became involved in pensions—to maintain even a modicum of visibility in the new youthful California. And with the passing of George McLain, California had finally consumed all of its Ham and Eggs.

Chapter 6

Twenty-First Century Ham and Eggs?

> The elderly are demon voters. The government has created an
> interest group, namely the elderly and it is making political
> activity worthwhile.

Professor Raymond Wolfinger (Tessler and Gottlieb 1999)

History does not repeat itself—not exactly, anyway. But it does leave
behind echoes. In 1999, for example, in an antirecession move, the Japanese government handed out shopping coupons to the elderly and the
young. The coupons could only be used for purchases—not saving—
and had an expiration date to encourage quick spending. One cannot
help but wonder whether some Ham and Eggs acolyte had traveled to
Tokyo during the American occupation and planted a seed that blos-
somed five decades later.[1]

Closer to home, however, the pensionite past is today haunting the
current debate over Social Security and Medicare. The promoters of
Ham and Eggs cut their definition of elderly down to age fifty, thus
incorporating about a third of the California electorate in the late
1930s. But such a low age cutoff will not be needed when the boomer
retirement is at its peak. In 2038, just 100 years after the first Ham and
Eggs proposition appeared on the California ballot, about a third of the
entire U.S. electorate will be aged sixty-five and over (Peterson 1999,
205).

Given these electoral demographics, there is perceived to be a race
to "fix" Social Security and Medicare before the baby boomers retire
and exercise their electoral franchise as frustrated beneficiaries. But it
is naïve to assume that any solution reached well in advance of peak
boomer retirement will be taken as a *fait accompli* by the future boomer-

retiree electorate. Moreover, there is inherent confusion concerning exactly what the problem is with regard to Social Security and Medicare. Today's confusion is likely to frame the retiree political movements of the future.

The Unholy Trinity

A key decision of the Roosevelt administration with regard to the design of Social Security was one to make the government-run pension system resemble a private pension plan. Although private pension plans were comparatively rare at the time, those that did exist often entailed *employee* as well as employer contributions ("contributory plans"). And they generally had a trust fund of some type to finance future benefits. Pension benefits were commonly related by formula to prior wage earnings and work history (i.e., the plans were what are termed today "defined benefit"). The copycat design decision by the New Deal—modeling the government program on private examples—is a critical element for understanding contemporary debate over the financial problems of Social Security and Medicare.

Later in this chapter I will refer to the view of Social Security and Medicare as stand-alone, quasi-autonomous plans as "the Roosevelt model" (although, of course, Medicare came along long after the Roosevelt administration). In contrast, I will use the term "unified budget model" to indicate a view of the two systems as mere components of the federal government's taxing and spending (and transferring). Finally, I will point to a third "demographic" view of the boomer retirement that simply alludes to the coming rise in the number of retirees relative to active workers.

These three alternate perspectives form an unholy trinity in the current debate over the impact of the baby boomer retirement. Which one of these three models is deemed valid very much frames the remedies proposed in anticipation of the baby boom retirement. The model chosen also frames perceptions of equity. Most importantly, the fact that there are three alternative models complicates the public and policy debate. And—as will be seen—the different perspectives make it likely that the controversy will continue well into the twenty-first century, as long as there are significant numbers of boomers collecting benefits.

Put another way, all three views have a degree of validity, although I believe the demographic view best clarifies the dilemma posed by the boomers. But the simultaneous presence of the three perspectives virtually guarantees future acrimony and political turmoil when the boomers retire. And the current debate, which is creating a paper trail of contradictory statements as debaters pick and choose which model to emphasize, is laying the groundwork for that turmoil.

The Politics of Plan Design

As noted, the existing private defined-benefit plans of the 1930s provided a model for the New Deal administration on which a public pension system might be based. A report on private pension plans in the mid-1930s illustrates this point. Of 347 private plans that were adopted or revised in that period, all but 15 had advance funding. Most plans established in the 1930s were also contributory (Latimer and Tufel 1940, 37, 46). So perhaps it was inevitable that the public sector would copy the private domain in these regards. But there was more to it than mere imitation; there was a distinctly political and strategic element.

President Franklin Roosevelt played an important personal role in the overall policy design of Social Security, especially the pension component. In part, his hands-on role may have reflected a void in pre-New Deal American thinking about social insurance. Much of the attention of reformers prior to the New Deal was on mitigating seemingly avoidable risks such as industrial accidents and unemployment. Reformers advocated public policies aimed at pushing employers to reduce these misfortunes. Aging was not a risk that employers could reduce—everyone either aged or died—and so pensions had not been a major thrust of reformist proposals (Moss 1996). In addition, there is the argument—noted in chapter 1—that the experience with federal Civil War veterans' pensions may have discouraged reform interest in more general public pensions.

In any event, the fact that Roosevelt—an individual with great political abilities—took such a direct interest in the Social Security pension suggests a political motivation behind the plan design. The president indicated early on that the basic retirement system should not consist of what executive director of the Committee on Economic Security, Edwin Witte, termed "gratuitous pensions."[2] As governor of New York, Roosevelt had presided over such a gratuitous state scheme for elderly indigents (i.e., one financed from general revenue). He definitely did not want a larger version of that type of program at the federal level.

As noted in chapter 4, Dr. Townsend and his followers were seen by Roosevelt during his first term as potential threats in the upcoming 1936 elections. And unfunded gratuitous pensions seemed to Roosevelt to be akin to what he called "fantastic schemes which have aroused hopes that cannot possibly be fulfilled," code words for the Townsend Plan. Later, when FDR discovered that the plan being proposed by his own administration contained a funding deficit (albeit thirty years in the future), the president insisted on imposing higher payroll tax rates to eliminate it (Witte 1963, 46, 149–51). What is now termed "Social Security" (i.e., a nonmeans-tested pension benefit based on work history), was to be sharply differentiated from means-tested old-age assistance plans in New Deal planning. The latter means-tested state and local programs were to be subsidized by the federal government under the Social Security Act. But they were (and are today) considered "welfare" owing to the means testing.

There were various rationales for creating a general federally run pension system—and later the Medicare system—that would deliberately resemble a private plan. But the key concern was to design a program that could not be readily dismantled by some future Congress. As an observer at the time noted:

> Workers will have made direct contributions for half of their annuities and indirectly they will have paid for most of the employers' contributions as well. When the system is thoroughly established, they will have *earned* their annuities. (Paul Douglas 1936, 172, italics added)

Roosevelt clearly appreciated that point and declared:

> With those taxes in there, no damn politician can ever scrap my social security program (Quoted in I. Bernstein, 1985, 50).

There seemed also to be another motivation in making the Social Security system resemble a private pension plan. As noted, those developing the plan wanted to distinguish between the means-tested old-age assistance program—which they referred to then as a "pension" —and the more general contributory Social Security benefit—which they referred to as an "annuity," an insurance-like term. It was said that the country could not "afford" a general retirement system unless it was set up as a contributory plan. In contrast, the country could afford old-age assistance to indigents because the means-testing element limited its costs.

Executive director Witte testified that "the public cannot afford to pay a pension out of general taxes to everyone that is old regardless of need, whether that amount be $200 a month or $50 a month" (U.S. Congress, Senate 1935, 201). However, from an economic viewpoint, it is not clear why the country could afford a system based on payroll taxes but it could not afford one based on general taxes. A tax is a tax is a tax, after all. It appears that the Townsend proposal may have played a role in what was really a noneconomic rationale on Witte's part. Townsend, it will be recalled, wanted to fund his plan with a transactions tax (a form of general taxation), rather than a payroll tax. And he wanted to give the benefit to everyone over aged sixty, regardless of work history. Whatever Witte and his New Deal planners hoped for in a pension system, they did not want it to look anything like Townsend's proposal.[3]

Witte, it will be recalled, was so upset about the Townsendites that he tried to enlist the FBI in an investigation of Dr. Townsend and his pension organization. While Roosevelt was motivated to discredit Townsend because of the danger he posed in the upcoming 1936 presidential election, Witte appears mainly to have been concerned with the massive income redistribution to the elderly that Townsend was touting.

Possibly there was a sense that without an earmarked payroll tax, Congress would be tempted to make Social Security benefits "too" generous under intense Townsendite pressure. With a fully funded scheme, in contrast, workers and employers would be hit with higher payroll taxes if benefits were raised in the future. Thus, there would be built-in resistance to the upfront costs of excessive benefits. Essentially, workers (or workers and their employers) would finance their own retirements under a fully funded plan.[4] There would be no massive intergenerational transfer. At least, that was the initial thinking.

Private or Public?

Solutions and political calculations of one era, however, create the problems of future generations. The quasi-private Roosevelt design of Social Security has figured prominently in recent debates over "privatization" of Social Security. However, there is historical precedent for that discussion. Attempts back in 1935 to allow a "privatizing" of the system by permitting contracting out of annuities to private insurance companies were only narrowly defeated in Congress (I. Bernstein 1985, 69–70; Jacoby 1997, 212–13). That earlier episode foreshadowed the privatization proposals that came to the fore again in the 1980s and 1990s.

As it turns out, the quasi-private appearance of the plan creates the seeds for its future erosion as a public system; the Roosevelt model does not protect Social Security to the degree the president had supposed. After all, it seems logical to consider substituting a private plan for the public one if the two look much alike. And the notion of having a trust fund similar to that of a private plan immediately raises the question of how such a fund is invested.

Perhaps the best illustration of this point can be found in the means-tested state-administered old-age assistance plan for the indigent elderly contained in the 1935 Social Security Act. That plan had (and has) no specific "contributions"—other than general government revenue. And it had (and has) no trust fund. It does not look like a private plan so no one proposes privatizing it. Without a specific earmarked revenue stream, means-tested old-age assistance would hardly be an attractive takeover target for a private financial services company. It has definite costs but no designated income. And with no identified trust fund for old-age assistance, investment opportunities for Wall Street are absent. There are no funds to invest.

It is ironic, too, that the argument of the 1930s that only a contributory plan with a trust fund can be "afforded" by the nation can be turned on its head. A pension or health plan funded from general revenue can be expensive, but it cannot "run out of funds" or go "bankrupt" (any more than the Pentagon can go bankrupt). Rather, it is up to Congress to allocate resources annually to such programs—or decide not to do so.

A Roosevelt-type plan designed to look like a private system, in contrast, *can* run out of its earmarked funds or go bankrupt, just as any private entity can. Such a private-like system depends on a finite and specific revenue stream of mandatory "contributions" plus "earnings" from its trust fund. It is subject to fiscal "crises," as occurred in the early 1980s, when the trust fund for Social Security almost ran dry (Light 1995). In contrast, its financial health can always be "improved," no matter how expensive the benefits, if the plan's trust fund can be made to earn a higher rate of return through "wise" investments or if additions to its earmarked revenue stream can be developed.

Roosevelt wanted a fully funded pension plan, and the initial plan adopted in 1935 was intended to be just that. There was nothing in the plan, however, that compelled future congresses to keep to that model.

As the president anticipated, the contributory program designed by the New Deal's planners would become an entitlement that Congress would be loath to *abolish*. Conversely, Congress could be moved to make the plan *more generous* than the original Roosevelt program, even in the not-so-distant future. Townsendite pressures would certainly push in that direction. Later congresses could—and did—move the program toward a pay-as-you-go approach and away from Roosevelt's notion of advance full funding.

Indeed, the shift toward pay-as-you-go was made only a few years later in 1939 when the date for initial benefit payouts was advanced from 1942 to 1940. The result of this history of original plan design and later programmatic change has been twofold. *First*, those Americans enrolled in Social Security (the vast majority of the working population and its dependents) feel entitled to whatever promises have been made. After all, they "paid into" the system all their work lives. But *second*, their sense of entitlement is not linked to actuarial balance of the plan or to questions of intergenerational transfers. There is no legal constraint preventing Congress from cutting back on benefits. Nonetheless, there is a strong political constraint arising from that contribution-based sense of entitlement.

Abby's Notch: "Hells Angels of Special-Interest Groups"[5]

> We are notch babies fighting for our rights,
> Here today to bring this cause to right.
> Born 1917 through '21,
> And all we want is true justice done.
> (Notch baby song quoted in Rosenblatt 1987)

The story of the "notch babies" of the 1970s and beyond best illustrates the dynamics of the current plan. Until the late 1960s, U.S. inflation rates had been quite moderate. Social Security was not officially "indexed" to the Consumer Price Index (CPI). However, periodically Congress would raise benefits to offset the erosion by inflation of retiree nominal pensions. Congress made these ad hoc adjustments by raising the level of benefits relative to the individual earnings histories of beneficiaries. Each such adjustment was treated by Social Security actuaries as a one-shot change in the benefit formula rather than as an ongoing process of informal indexation.

But there was a problem with this congressional approach to the inflation adjustment. Individual earnings histories of newly retired individuals *already had* an inflation adjustment for the *starting* benefit. That is, these earnings histories reflected nominal inflation of wages up to retirement along with real wage gains. The difficulty for retirees that Congress was ostensibly trying to solve was that *thereafter* there was no automatic inflation offset.

An overly simple way of thinking about the problem is that the starting pension benefit was "correct" but thereafter its monthly real value was eroded by inflation.[6] By giving all workers under the system an inflation-related benefit boost, Congress was "overcompensating" those persons still working or just retiring in order to offset the impact of inflation on those already retired. Thus, the real value of starting benefits was rising relative to earnings history.

Whether this overcompensation process was a simple error by Congress or part of a general program of raising replacement rates of Social Security pensions is a judgment call. From the shift toward pay-as-you-go in 1939 until the 1972 adjustments (described below), a consensus seemed to develop around implementing general benefit improvements (Achenbaum 1986, 38–60). A long period of prosperity after World War II—combined with a system in which there were many active workers paying in to support a limited number of beneficiaries—made plan improvements politically painless. The system had Roosevelt's appearance of being a stand-alone, private-looking program but without the former president's crucial notion of a full-funding fiscal constraint. Subsequent poor economic performance in the 1970s, however, made further steps toward benefit improvement much more difficult.

In 1972, with the inflation of the 1960s subsiding (and the economy subject to anti-inflation wage–price controls), Congress adopted a procedure that formalized its previous ad hoc practice and made it automatic. The procedure provided explicit indexing of existing benefits *and the starting benefit formula* to the CPI. If inflation had remained modest, and if the economy had continued to perform well (as it had in the past), benefits of the newly retired would have continued to rise relative to those of earlier cohorts. But the process would have remained gradual. Such a creeping increase in starting benefits would have been costly. But payroll tax revenue from a booming economy could have covered at least some of the expense.

Unfortunately, after 1972, a period of "stagflation" set in (i.e., high unemployment and high price inflation). The result was a rapid escalation of benefits of the newly retired due to inflation indexing. At the same time, a "shortfall" of revenue developed that endangered the pension system owing to the impact of a sluggish economy on payroll taxes.[7] Seen as a Roosevelt-type, stand-alone system, the Social Security program moved toward fiscal crisis.

Warned of the shortfall by Social Security actuaries, Congress modified the system of indexation in 1977. In principle, it could have cut back the benefits of those post-1972 retirees who had experienced gains under the 1972 law. But Congress was mindful of the contribution-based sense of entitlement inherent in the Roosevelt design of Social Security. Rather than take away benefits already being received by retirees, or even of those close to retirement age, Congress instead changed the formula prospectively for those born in 1917 or later. Effectively, the new system eliminated the double indexation problem, a process described at the time as "decoupling."

Starting benefits would no longer be subject to indexation (other than though the linkage to the wage history of the beneficiary). But benefits received once a person retired would continue to be tied to the CPI. Rather than create an abrupt shift for those born in 1917, however, Congress provided a transitional formula. The transitional approach pushed those born during 1917 and 1921 *toward* the new formula. Those in that birth-date interval or notch—once they discovered their benefits had been cut relative to pre-1917 cohorts—became known as notch babies.[8] The notch babies were the outcome of the switch in Social Security politics of the 1970s. Sadly for them, the previous ease in raising benefits had come to an end just as the notch babies were nearing retirement.

Many of those in the notch baby cohort discovered their status after a letter complaining of the benefit cut appeared in *Dear Abby*—the widely-read advice to the lovelorn column—on September 5, 1983. As the U.S. General Accounting Office subsequently noted (1988, 57), "'Dear Abby' . . . turned what was a complex technical issue, known to a relatively small number of experts, into an immediate concern of millions of benefit recipients." Abby—a notch baby herself (born 1918)—expressed shock at the inequity Congress had created. She told her readers to write letters of protest to Congress, and a wave of angry missives engulfed the Capitol Building. Two weeks later, after Congress and the Social Security Administration had been besieged with protests, Abby again spoke on the issue. The powers-that-be had hoped for a flat retraction of her earlier column. But the fire had been lit and was not to be so easily extinguished.

Abby's next pronouncement on the notch baby problem came on September 26, 1983. It included mention of the official view that the notch was a generous correction of a previous error. But she did not present this viewpoint as her own; the column was *not* a retraction. Instead, Abby simply quoted various officials. As a counterpoint, she noted that the notch baby interval of 1917 to 1921 "caught most veterans of World War II, a group that had already sacrificed much on behalf of their country." And she concluded, "So, Dear Readers, I leave it to you. Are those born before 1917 being unjustly overcompensated? Or are those born after 1916 being unjustly penalized because of the new computation?"

Abby herself claimed to have received over a million letters on the subject by 1987 (Rosenblatt 1987). As a notch baby, she was not convinced by the official explanations. Her mood may not have been helped by the response she received from officialdom. High-placed individuals apparently told her to stick to advice to the lovelorn and henceforth leave Social Security alone.

Indeed, in 1986, Abby reportedly spoke to a rally of angry notch babies on the steps of the Capitol, one of innumerable such demonstrations.[9] Meanwhile, at a congressional hearing, the House Select Committee on Aging heard from two sisters, Edith and Audrey. Edith, to her later financial distress, was born in 1917, unlike the more prescient Audrey, who was born the year before. As a result, although Edith earned more during her working life, she received less than Audrey from Social Security (U.S. Congress, House of Representatives 1986, vol. VI, 3, 21–22). Said Edith of her position in the notch:

> It is humiliating and a gross discrimination; we have our pride, too. We are not asking for a handout. When we signed up for Social Security I thought everyone would benefit fairly from this program. Seems this is not the case. Why do we have to prove we need it? Those born before 1917 do not have to. (U.S. Congress, House of Representatives 1986, vol. VI, 22)

In the 1930s, state legislatures had found it advantageous and costless (to them) to urge Congress to adopt the Townsend Plan. After all, the Townsend proposal was to be a federal program. That echo of the past was also present in the agitation of the 1980s on behalf of the notch babies. Various state legislatures sent resolutions to Congress urging equity for those born after 1916. Fittingly, given its earlier history of pensionite politics, California was the home of the first legislature to recommend that Congress do something about the notch.

And in keeping with the Townsendite arguments of a revolving (self-funding) system, notch baby proponents argued that giving them a benefit hike would not cost anything. As one said:

> When you give these people more spending power, they create more jobs, and that beefs up the trust fund. So, we don't even think—I don't even think that it will be a loss to the trust fund whatsoever. (U.S. Congress, House of Representatives 1992a, 4)

Congress was able to resist compensating the notch babies despite the considerable agitation. A second fiscal crisis for Social Security had developed in the early 1980s. In 1983, a delicately balanced compromise solution—involving higher taxes and an eventual rise in the normal retirement age—had been developed by a bipartisan commission headed by Alan Greenspan, then a private economic consultant (Light 1995). The Greenspan Commission's compromise was enacted and Congress was in no mood to reopen the painful issue. Moreover, the notch babies—no matter how their cohort was defined—constituted a relatively limited number of people. And organizations such as the AARP opposed their entreaties to Congress on the ground that concessions to the notch babies would undermine the financial condition of Social Security.

Nonetheless, appeals to retirees by other organizations—using the notch baby issue—provided a potential source of revenue for these other groups (U.S. General Accounting Office 1997b). Prominent among the groups testifying at the various congressional hearings in the 1980s and early 1990s on behalf of the notch babies was the National Committee to Preserve Social Security and Medicare. The committee was able to raise over $35 million a year as an advocacy group on various Social Security issues—not just the notch—in the early 1990s. In one embarrassing exchange, the president of this group was forced to admit that she had once opposed adjustments for notch babies in her former career as acting commissioner of the Social Security Administration (U.S. Congress, House of Representatives 1988, 201–3).

Although the National Committee appeared to drop the notch issue by the late 1990s, other groups pressed on, and legislation providing relief for the notch babies continued to drop into the congressional hopper. The Ham and Eggs promoters of the 1930s were able to widen their appeal by lowering the age of beneficiaries to fifty. Notch proponents similarly managed to expand the definition of the notch from the 1917 to 1921 group covered by the transition formula to all those born from 1917 through 1926.[10] This expansion doubled the number of notch babies and ensured that the issue would be both more intense and longer-lived. Even so, the force of mortality steadily eroded the notch constituency (Figure 6.1).

Traditional Values

As noted, Social Security—and later Medicare—were designed to resemble private pension and health insurance plans. This Roosevelt model design, however, tends to obscure the basic issue of the retirement of the baby boomers. The problem is perceived under the Roosevelt model to be one of employer/employee contributions, earnings on trust fund investments, benefit formulas, and actuarial calculations. Those who take the unified budget view—incorporating Social Security into the overall federal budget—tend to focus on government surpluses and deficits and their impact on national saving. But this approach, as does the Roosevelt model, obscures the basic dilemma.

The key issue is simple demographics. At the core of the boomer problem is the political question of how much the active workers of the future will be willing to spend on care of the elderly. Perhaps the best way to see the problem is to consider a hypothetical "traditional" society, one without pensions and social insurance. In such a society—the predominant mode of social organization throughout much of human history—the elderly are supported through extended family networks and by whatever economic assets they themselves have managed to accumulate. Transfers between the generations within the extended families are guided by social norms. No actuaries, government bureaucrats, politicians, academics, or policy wonks at private think-tanks are involved or consulted. There are no trust funds and no unified budgets to consider. What matters is how many mouths there are to feed and how many family members are available to feed them. What matters, in short, is the demographic profile of the extended family.

In such a traditional society, the ratio of supported elderly to active young workers would vary over time within any extended family. Birth rates and death rates would be affected by external forces such as epidemics, famines, warfare, and other natural and manmade disasters. And there would be random internal accidents of births, health status, and mortality. Sometimes there would be good economic times and some-

Figure 6.1 **Letter from Notch Baby to Robert J. Leonard, Chief Counsel and Staff Director, House Committee on Ways and Means**

Mr. Robert Leonard:
> *I see in the paper where you had a meeting on the bill 917, which attempts to erase the S.S. notch inequity. I was to a meeting in Kankakee, Ill for the notch. I'm a notch baby. They say there is a enough money in this S.S. program to correct this thing. We also have 290 Congressmen sponsoring this bill, which is good. I really don't know why some of you people are not doing a thing about this for the help of the Senior Citizens. Us Senior Citizens worked damn hard years ago, so I think it should be corrected <u>now</u>. Otherwise we are <u>voting you out</u> of <u>office</u> in <u>November.</u> Another thing the way the economics is we should have more then a stinky 3.7% raise come January. You sure give the public aid people enough. The public aid people get a <u>check, food stamps, medical care, taxi card</u> and I found out the other day that public aid also pays their $31.90 on their social Security checks. Their probably a quite a few get even that paid. That is not fair to us senior citizens. Sure hope this S.S. notch thing goes through with flying colors. I could use the extra $72.00 a month that I'm be cheated out of.*

Sincerely,
Isabelle Bowers
Kankakee, Illinois

P.S. Another thing the president shouldn't always extend that unemployment every six months. There is work out their If people want to work. But why work if everything is free. My husband is 72 years old and he is still working. They are having a terrible time with the budget too. They shouldn't mix S.S. with that either. The budget & S.S. is too different things.

Source: U.S. Congress, House of Representatives 1992b, 291-93.

---

times bad, depending on such factors as weather and harvests. Norms would vary about how the elderly should be treated and what was their just due.

When times were especially good and the elderly were proportionately few, the then-existing elderly cohort would probably receive more per capita support than their immediate predecessors. Good fortune could be easily shared in such circumstances, perhaps rationalized as appropriate veneration of family elders. Other things being equal, however, a surge in the ratio of elderly to active youths and/or hard times would most likely lead to an adjustment to the norms in the other direction. Under such conditions, per capita family transfers to the elderly would probably be reduced somewhat. And the per capita transfer from the young (to the old) would probably have to rise to meet even these reduced commitments. Both young and old would feel (and share in) the pain of increased dependency and/or difficult times.

Modern society tends to hide such adjustments or at least recasts them in political terms. But ultimately, the income of the elderly—from Social Security or other government transfers, from private pensions, and from past accumulated assets—can be viewed as consumption tickets. With a given collective income, if one group in society acquires and uses more consumption tickets, some other group will have fewer tickets. This logic holds whether the society in question is a primitive tribe of hunter/gatherers or a technologically advanced nation with online financial markets and elaborate social insurance programs. Whether the consumption ticket are labeled private pensions, Social Security benefits, or proceeds from tax-favored 401(k) plans or other assets does not change the basic logic. A surge in the elderly proportion of the population will tend to reduce the consumption tickets available to the young, unless the overall economic pie expands enough to hold everyone harmless.

For contemporary nations, the zero-sum reality of limited consumption tickets can be mitigated for a time at the national level by net borrowing from abroad. As noted in chapter 1, the United States amply demonstrated this point in the 1980s and 1990s by running large foreign trade deficits. But as also noted, at the time the American baby boomers retire similar adverse demographics will also prevail in many other parts of the world. Other societies will be cashing in their foreign assets, including those accumulated in the United States. They are unlikely to be a source of fresh loans. Consumption tickets for elderly American baby boomers will have to be acquired from domestic sources.

Proposed Solutions to Boomer Retirement

Much of the policy discussion surrounding the retirement of the baby boom follows the Roosevelt model, viewing Social Security and Medicare as stand-alone, private-like systems. Serious policy analysts who propose solutions are aware that one could legitimately take a unified budget perspective or the overall demographic perspective. However, they feel constrained to present their pet solutions in Rooseveltian terms, as that is how the issue appears to both politicians and voters. More often than not, the discussion thus ends up focusing on payroll taxes, benefit levels, and the investment portfolio of the trust funds or on various privatization schemes.

Viewed in this Rooseveltian way, the options most often proposed for the pension component of Social Security come down to nine:[11]

- reducing benefits for some or all beneficiaries to cut system costs;
- raising the normal retirement age to cut system costs;
- reducing cost-of-living adjustments and/or modifying the Consumer Price Index to decrease measured inflation, thus cutting system costs;
- means-testing of benefits, reducing the number of beneficiaries and thereby cutting system costs;
- increasing income taxes on benefits, with the tax revenue flowing back into the trust fund, either raising revenue or implicitly cutting benefits—depending on your viewpoint;
- raising Social Security payroll taxes to generate more system revenue;
- investing trust fund money in the stock market with a presumed higher return than on government bonds;
- extending mandatory coverage to uncovered state and local employees, which tends to generate more revenue than expense, at least in the short term;
- using parts of any current or future federal budget surpluses to bolster the trust fund, effectively adding general revenue to other tax revenue.

The more modest proposals—those that seek to preserve the Roosevelt model largely as it has been—focus on a subset of the above options, except for means testing. Means testing is typically frowned on as turning the program into "welfare" (Ball 1998). In addition, some plans call for grafting a mandatory individual savings account onto the existing system (Gramlich 1998). The new account would substitute for lost income and reduced benefits resulting from other modifications to the basic Roosevelt model. These were basically the options that the sharply divided Advisory Council on Social Security reviewed in 1997 (Bureau of National Affairs 1997).

More radical plans completely change Social Security into a minimum income (antipoverty) base, with individual accounts for above-poverty benefits. Or they move toward complete privatization with just individual accounts (Ferrara and Tanner 1998). Proponents of such plans tend to follow the unified budget view and argue that the trust funds are an illusion. Somewhere in the middle are those who believe that the trust funds should be made real through tighter earmarking, even if they are an illusion.

So-called lock box proposals in Congress are designed in theory to ensure that "Social Security is a trust fund for the American people and not a slush fund for big Washington spenders."[12] But legislative earmarking is inherently difficult. As the Congressional Research Service noted: "Simply stated, legislation enacted in the [current] Congress cannot stop some future Congress from passing alternative legislation."[13]

Those who argue for investing the Social Security trust fund in the stock market may also be partly motivated by trying to make the trust fund more "real" (Aaron and Reischauer 1998, 1999). Apart from the higher-return argument, such investment takes the Roosevelt model even closer toward a mimicking of private pension plans than Roosevelt himself had envisioned.

On the other hand, private pension trustees can vote the stock they hold and have discretion over which stock they choose to buy. The prospect of the federal government having such discretion over a large slice of American industry—backdoor socialism—pushes conservatives toward individual accounts—not the trust fund—as the vehicles for stock holding (Feldstein and Feldstein 1999). Indeed, with individual accounts and every worker a mini-capitalist, conservatives see "the division between labor and capital dissolved" with the result being "increase(d) support for free market economic policies" (Ferrara and Tanner 1998, 110).

There tends to be an underestimate, among those proposing more radical reforms, of the political inertia inherent in the American system. Much is made, for example, of Chile's conversion from an underfunded defined-benefit social security system to a program of individual accounts. The fact that this change—whatever its virtues—was accomplished under a military dictatorship is downplayed. Similarly, other radical changes in social insurance in third-world countries were put in force either by autocratic regimes or under the intense pressure of financial crises. Public opinion as a major influence in program design is at best muted under such conditions.

Where democratic governments have put in place significant social insurance reforms, there have also been very different institutions as compared with the United States. For example, in England the Thatcher government developed a plan whereby individuals could opt out of part of the social security program and instead have individual accounts. However, Britain had long had a two-tier social security system in place, with a flat basic pension and an earnings-related tier on top. It had long had an opt-out system from the second tier for employer-run pensions. Thatcher's reform was to add a second opt-out alternative (Mitchell and Rojot 1993, 149–56).

British reforms were thus incremental and enacted under a parliamentary system with a tradition of party discipline. The same system, if proposed for the United States, would not be seen as incremental. And with the lack of political party discipline and divided authority between the president and the Congress in the United States, such a proposal might well run into gridlock.

Because there are different models for looking at Social Security in the United States, rational discussion of the problems posed by the retirement of the baby boom is hindered. Consider the following two statements:

> One of Washington's dirty little secrets is that there really are no trust funds. The government spent that money long ago to finance general government spending, hiding the true size of the federal budget deficit. (Cato Institute researchers Peter J. Ferrara and Michael Tanner 1998, 7)

> Taxes paid by today's workers are used to pay today's retirees. If money is left over, it finances other government spending—though to maintain the insurance fiction, paper entries are created in a "trust fund" that is simultaneously an asset and a liability of the Government. (Nobel laureate economist Milton Friedman 1999)

From a unified budget perspective, the above statements are correct. The federal government has a liability to baby boomers that it matches with Treasury bonds, which are also liabilities. Effectively, "IOU one pension" is "backed" in part by a certificate saying "IOU the money to pay the pension." In that sense, the trust fund is not real and the money seemingly in the fund has already been spent on other government programs.

Note, however, that if a private pension plan held a Treasury security—as many do—we would not assert that the plan did not have a real asset. In fact, such a security is considered to be virtually free of default risk. Yet the proceeds from sale of that asset by the government have been no less spent than those raised by sales to the Social Security trust fund.

It is equally correct to say, from the perspective of the Roosevelt model of Social Security, that:

> The OASDI [Old Age Survivors and Disability Insurance] surplus is invested in government bonds, and the OASDI trust funds are properly credited with all interest on these bonds. This means that this surplus is clearly not stolen from Social Security, as one often hears in political campaigns. (Federal Reserve Board member Edward M. Gramlich 1998, 30)

In fact, it is possible to mix and match between these two perspectives. In an op-ed piece in the *New York Times*, former Nixon administration chief economist Herbert Stein noted that the problem of Social Security could be solved easily. The Treasury should simply create securities to cover its unfunded liability and give them to the trust fund. From a Roosevelt model perspective, the financial problem of the baby boom retirement would be solved. And from a unified budget perspective *on the day of this transaction*, there would be no net impact. The liability created to Social Security would be exactly offset by the asset in the trust fund![14]

Indeed, the proposal by the Clinton administration to save Social Security first by putting the budget surplus into the trust fund is a closely related idea. Effectively, with a surplus, the government would be redeeming outstanding federal debt and giving these claims on the Treasury to the trust fund.[15] The difficulty with such grants to Social Security is that they effectively mix general revenue (or promises of future general revenue) with traditional payroll taxes. In an echo of Roosevelt's bias against "gratuitous" pensions, the comptroller general of the General Accounting Office noted that the proposal "takes us away from an insurance concept and potentially down the road to a welfare concept."[16]

Conspiracy!

The demographic perspective suggests that when the dust eventually settles, baby boomer retirees are going to have lower per capita incomes than they believe is coming to them. Some consumption tickets they hope for will be denied. And younger, active workers may well feel overtaxed. They may resent the fact that one way or another, they have fewer consumption tickets so that their elders can have more.

Of course, if the economic pie were to grow sufficiently, perhaps all generations will feel content. But there are only three ways by which the pie can grow: technological progress, more labor, or more capital. Technology is hard to predict. It would be nice if new technology arrived in sufficient magnitude to provide the boomers with all they might hope for in retirement. However, there is little that public policy—and Social Security reform in particular—can do to assure such a beneficent outcome. But the future labor force and capital stock could be influenced by public policy.

Labor could be expanded by allowing a substantial boost in immigration of young workers, as some have advocated (Kimbell 1997, 21–25). While there may be a deficit in the number of young workers capable of supporting the retired baby boomers in the United States, there is no shortage of such people in the outside world. But national policy, if anything, shifted toward tighter immigration control in the 1980s and 1990s.

Those advocating individual savings accounts as add-ons to Social Security or using federal budget surpluses to enhance the trust fund often portray the virtue of these approaches as an added saving. From added saving comes more investment and a larger capital stock in the future (and a bigger pie to divide). However, time is running out for this solution. Moreover, some added saving—if it occurred—might simply offset a repatriation of foreign capital as other parts of the world deal with their own retiree problems. The likelihood, therefore, is that there will be significant numbers of retired baby boomers who feel dissatisfied with their lot. They will be looking for solutions and someone to blame.

In the late nineteenth century, advocates of coinage of free silver pointed to the "Crime of '73," the date at which the United States returned to the gold standard after the Civil War. This return to the gold standard was seen as a monetary conspiracy directed by bankers and others, sometimes British, sometimes Jewish. The conspiratorial viewpoint went on to play a role in pensionite thinking in the 1930s. It stood in the background of California's Ham and Eggs pension movement with its currency-related component.

Although monetary conspiracy theories are now found mainly on the margins of social thought—in the paranoia of right-wing militias and similar groups—other notions of conspiracy have endured. During the Cold War, the communist conspiracy played a major role in American thinking. The assassinations of John F. Kennedy and Martin Luther King gave rise to considerable conspiratorial theorizing. Popular culture in the 1990s featured conspiracy plots in movies and television (e.g., *The X-Files*).

Conspiracies on virtually any subject can now be easily unearthed on the Internet. And government itself is often the source of conspiracy in popular imagination, thanks to Watergate, Iran-Contra-gate, and other disillusioning episodes. Distrust of government has already led to odd perceptions connected with social insurance. When the Clinton administration proposed its ill-fated health plan, a constituent implored her senator, "Please stop that Clinton plan. . . . I don't want the government to take over my Medicare."[17]

Stolen Nest Eggs

Current debate over Social Security and the retirement of the baby boom generation almost guarantees that future retiree political movements will be built on conspiracy theories of why more is perceived as owed than is being provided. The notion that someone spent the money in the trust fund will be easy to support, based on quotes of the type reproduced above. From the notion that the money was spent when it should have been saved, it is easy to arrive at a darker notion that that money was stolen. A boomer-retiree, cruising some future version of the Internet, could easily find quotes from the past to support such a view:

> To save Social Security, we must first stop *looting* it for spending programs or tax cuts. (Democratic Senator Ernest F. Hollings in 1999; italics added)

"Looting" is a stronger word than "spending." Looting as a concept could be combined with some future retiree's least-favorite recipient of federal spending. The money was looted to pay foreign aid or to pay welfare (i.e., foreigners and welfare recipients did the looting). Growing racial and ethnic diversity in the U.S. population during the twenty-first century could heighten such perceptions. Retirees—reflecting an earlier demographic mix—will be substantially less diverse than the active workers who support them in the future. Just as pensionite politics in the past sometimes took on nasty anti-Semitic overtones, so retiree populism of the future could turn against immigrants and other minorities.

Lost Opportunities

The widespread current assertion that individuals would earn more than the yield on trust-fund Treasury securities by investing on their own will undoubtedly be repeated in the future. Of course, nothing prevents many who save little from voluntarily saving more and investing it as they see fit. Still, there will be an attractiveness to the notion that "they" deprived me of my investment opportunities. One can imagine a political movement of retirees demanding a retroactive reimbursement for the stolen trust funds that were not properly invested—with back credit, of course, for some higher rate of return that should have been earned.

Overcharges

If individual accounts are grafted onto the current system, administration of these accounts could also become an issue in the future. The U.S. General Accounting Office (1999) has noted that the existing collective system of record-keeping for Social Security would require substantial modification to accommodate individual accounts. If account administration is handled by the private sector—through employers or financial institutions—record-keeping costs might be considerable. Depending on how these are handled, the costs might reduce rates of return on the accounts, leading to demands in the future for some sort of retroactive refunds to retirees.

Phony Prices

Changes that were made in the Consumer Price Index (CPI), particularly in the 1990s, could be questioned in the future. Arguments could be made that the changes—which generally reduced the measured rate of inflation and the cost-of-living adjustments under Social Security— produced an *under*statement of inflation. The process by which these changes were developed—which was in fact an interplay of politics and technical economic theorizing—might be seen as conspiratorial in the hindsight of the future. Although the CPI affects only postretirement benefit adjustments, not the starting rate for benefits, such fine distinctions might not be made. Retirees of the future might argue that prices are really much higher than the government is saying and some recompense is due.

Past Assertions

The fact that there was a sequence of reforms of Social Security—each of which was depicted as resolving its financial problems—is itself fodder for conspiracy theorizing. What happened to the money that was "saved" by Jimmy Carter in the 1977 reforms? What happened to the money saved by Ronald Reagan and the Greenspan Commission in the 1983 reforms? Complicated technical explanations in the future about overoptimistic projections may not convince those retirees who are certain that someone took something away from them. In any case, a retiree might ask: "Why is it *my* fault that *they* didn't put enough money away?"

Healthy Skepticism

Curiously, the flurry of proposals for resolving the problems of Social Security pensions—whether seen as a Roosevelt-model, unified budget, or demographic issue—have not been matched with comparable discussion of Medicare options. To the extent there has been debate, it has loosely tracked that surrounding Social Security. Conservatives favor some form of privatization with defined-contribution vouchers to purchase commercial insurance, thus replacing the current defined-benefit program. Liberals, not surprisingly, favor retaining the existing structure. Meanwhile, the public responds favorably to generalized promises to "save" Medicare (Reischauer, Butler, and Lave 1998).

The political debacle faced by the Clinton administration when it proposed a comprehensive national health plan during 1993 and 1994 may have discouraged discussion of Medicare. But viewed through the lens of the Roosevelt model, Medicare is expected to experience financial problems well before the pension element of Social Security. And it is not a small program; annual federal outlays for Medicare are roughly half the size of those for Social Security pension and disability payments.

Although New Deal planners originally considered including health insurance in Social Security, opposition by organized medicine caused the idea to be dropped. Efforts at establishing national health insurance under the Truman administration similarly were killed by strong opposition. State initiatives, such as Governor Earl Warren's attempts to enact a California health insurance plan, also died in the 1940s. However, continued agitation ultimately produced sufficient congressional support for enactment of Medicare (for the elderly) and Medicaid (for welfare recipients) in 1965 (Berkowitz 1997, 32–35).

It is not necessary to peer far ahead to see the issues that will surround health care for the elderly in the future. The pension component of Social Security is determinate, in that each recipient receives a set amount of money based on a defined-benefit formula. Medicare—and for that matter private health insurance—is more ambiguous. Some health expenditures are covered; some are not. Even covered items may not be fully reimbursed. As the federal government and private insurers have sought to reduce health costs, service delivery has been repeatedly altered. Managed care and Health Maintenance Organizations (HMOs) have been promoted as cost-effective substitutes for traditional fee-for-service plans.

The result has been symptoms of public discontent ranging from anti-HMO jokes and cartoons to movies in which HMO and health insurance executives are the villains.[18] In the political realm, legislation providing various patient entitlements has been featured at the federal and state levels—for example, a guaranteed minimum duration hospital stay for maternity. Such enactments represent a reaction to public complaints about health care rationing.

As the baby boomers age into years in which health problems become more and more common—and potentially life-threatening—such complaints will become more and more pointed. The essence of managed care is to put more decision making in the hands of the insurer/provider and to limit free patient choice. Thus, legislation returning decision making to the patient moves the system toward the old fee-for-service approach, with its inherent expense. There is a built-in collision between cost control and patient decision making, which was already becoming politicized in the 1990s.

Indeed, unlike the experience of the 1930s and 1940s, health care could well become a more important political mobilizing issue than pensions when the baby boomers retire. Pensions are clearly an issue for the elderly, but health care quality—although a more significant concern for the old than the young—still affects all age groups, as the issue of minimum hospital stays for childbirth illustrates.

The Best Is Unlikely to Be

Ultimately, however, it is impossible to know what issues and currents of thought will appear most salient in 2020 or 2030. Perhaps the issues then will revolve around something as seemingly far removed from support of the elderly as global warming. Perhaps it will be something more closely connected to the state of the economy or government budget. The point is that political entrepreneurs of that future era will have incentives to tie popular issues to support of the elderly in a saleable package. One lesson from Ham and Eggs and the other pensionite movements of the past is that such movements do not have to "win" to be profitable enterprises for their founders. Another lesson is that even if such movements do not succeed in enacting exactly what they propose, they can nevertheless influence the course of events and policy outcomes.

As the twentieth century closed, the general public was in a "what-me-worry?" frame of mind. It was not ready to focus on the problems posed by an aging society, apart from an amorphous desire that Congress and the president should "save" Social Security. This distancing from the issue left the debate in the hands of policy wonks.

In that limited debating circle, liberals have been prone to view the issue in Roosevelt-model terms. Thus, the coming problem of Social Security is seen as readily resolved through relatively minor changes in payroll taxes, trust fund investments, and benefit formulas. Conservatives have been prone to focus on the "unified budget" approach, viewing the issue as the overall shift in federal budget toward care of the elderly. Their remedies center on shifting such care out of the budget and into the private sector. In both camps, there has been a disproportionate focus on the pension element of Social Security and a relative neglect of Medicare.

But the demographic view makes it clear that it is not the locus or format of the supporting institutions that is critical. And the problem of boomer retirement arises whether support is paid out as pensions or to cover medical services. The shift in income distribution toward the elderly is the key issue for the future, and the potential political organization of the elderly is likely to keep the issue alive for decades.

History teaches that expectations and perceptions of equity go beyond promised incomes in government programs. The pensionite agitation in the 1920s and 1930s did not arise because of a retrenchment on explicit earlier promises of support. In that period, relatively little was promised to the aged, either publicly through social insurance or welfare, or privately through pension plans. Yet California, with its concentration of elderly voters, became a hotbed of demands for government support of the aged. Even without a reneging on formal prior promises by government, the elderly of the past in California and elsewhere thought that more was owed to them than was being delivered.

History also teaches that the issue of elderly support cannot be resolved through a one-time change in policy aimed at addressing such concerns. Pensionite agitation in California continued as long as the state had a disproportionately older population and electorate. Passage of the federal Social Security Act in 1935 did not settle the matter, nor did Governor Earl Warren's promised enactment of a boost in old-age assistance payments when he first took office. There was always someone to say that the reforms were inadequate.

"Grow old along with me," wrote the poet Robert Browning; "the best is yet to be."[19] For the American polity in the coming decades, Browning's outcome seems most unlikely.

Notes

Chapter 1. Will the Boomers Have Their Ham and Eggs?

1. Nonetheless, the projection did have about the correct percentage of the elderly (those sixty-five years and over) as a percent of the total population.

2. There have been calls to take Social Security "off budget" in the future so that it will not "count" in calculating the official federal budget surplus or deficit.

3. Under a ruling of the Financial Accounting Standards Board, as of late 1992 employers must record unfunded liabilities for retiree health insurance on their balance sheets. Some employers were faced with large liabilities not previously recognized. Their choice was to recognize these liabilities and/or establish financial vehicles to fund their retiree health plans. As a result, many decided to cut back or eliminate their programs. For details on these requirements, see Employee Benefit Research Institute 1997, 272–74.

4. The paragraphs that follow draw heavily from Putnam 1970, 15–31.

Chapter 2. Ham and Eggs

1. The most famous result of the taxpayer revolt was Proposition 13 of 1978, drastically reducing property taxes. The Butcher-Forde agency, which managed the campaign for Proposition 13, found the mailing lists it had developed as lucrative sources of contributions. A subsequent exposé revealed that the agency was soliciting contributions by mail and using the revenue to put out yet more mailings, leaving little revenue—after its fees were deducted—for the underlying taxpayer causes and ballot propositions it claimed to represent. See Weber 1996.

2. A chronology of the Ham and Eggs movement and profiles of its various characters can be found in Moore and Moore 1939. The text below relies heavily on this account.

3. A variation on the Price suicide forms the basis of the above-mentioned movie *Meet John Doe*. In the film version, a reporter (Barbara Stanwyck) fakes a letter to the editor in which John Doe says he will commit suicide if the world does not improve. A political movement is inadvertently started, and the newspaper has to come up with a "real" John Doe to take the part of the nonexistent letter writer. A naïve character played by Gary Cooper is persuaded to take the part.

4. Owens was subsequently ousted from the Utopian Society (Fitzgerald 1951, 36).

5. "SEC Gets Ban on Order of Plenocrats, Pledged to Retrieve Depression Losses," *New York Times*, December 9, 1937, 39; "Wins Security Suit: The SEC Reports Chicago Jurist Upholds its Contentions," *New York Times*, April 16, 1939, 22.

6. Aficionados of contemporary militia groups and others on the far right (and—sometimes—far left) will recognize these conspiracy theorics.

7. The Fisher "ideal" index bears his name and is currently in use to measure the quantity and price of the U.S. gross domestic product.

8. As it turned out, the date of initial pension payments was advanced to 1940 when the rise in the Social Security trust fund exceeded expectations. This change of dates is usually considered the point of shift toward "pay as you go" in Social Security.

9. The national income accounts report annual earnings of full-time equivalent employees in 1938 to be $1,247. Average weekly earnings of manufacturing production workers were $22.

10. There are no figures for state gross domestic product at that time. However, in 1940, California had 5.2 percent of the U.S. population (6.9 million people out of 131.7 million). Nominal GDP for the United States in 1940 was about $100 billion, so a rough estimate of California's GDP would be $5.2 billion. There were about 1.7 million people aged fifty and over in California in 1940. If half of them were paid $1,300 annually, the cost would have been $1.1 billion, about 21 percent of the state's estimated gross product. (A subsequent increase in the proposed Ham and Eggs pension to $30 a week would have raised this estimate to 25 percent.)

11. There are no figures for the California money supply. In 1940, a total of $6.76 billion in currency was in circulation in the entire United States, and the narrowly defined money supply was $39.65 billion. Applying the California/U.S. population ratio to these figures produces the estimates in the text.

12. A response to Fisher's letter to FDR disowning Ham and Eggs was sent to Fisher on September 12, 1938. (President's Personal File 3385.)

13. Details of what occurred are unclear. A memo to the files on Ham and Eggs and the Allens in the Franklin D. Roosevelt Library dated September 23, 1938, refers to "'Fog Horn Murphy' Mess, which is now pending in the Federal Courts here in Los Angeles." It goes on to explain that "these cases refer to some Mexican radio station which interfered with stations in this country" (President's Personal File 3385). Moore and Moore (1939, 33-36) provide a discussion of the radio scheme, although with a slightly different spelling of the name of the Mexican partner. The station in question, XERB, did get on the air eventually, but it may have been without the participation of the Allens, given their lack of ready cash. At one point, Lawrence Allen sued the U.S. marshal for releasing the radio equipment to others involved in the Mexican project. *Allen v. Clark, United States Marshal, et al.*, 22 F. Supp. 898 (1938).

14. *Barbachano et al. v. Allen et al.*, 192 F.2d 836 (1951). Willis Allen had hoped that filing for personal bankruptcy would cancel the damages awarded against him. However, he was ordered to pay, nonetheless.

15. Presidential broadcast of August 15, 1938. Transcript in President's Personal File 3385, Franklin D. Roosevelt Library.

16. Transcript of press conference 479, August 26, 1938, and report of the Controller dated August 25, 1938, in President's Personal File 3385, Franklin D. Roosevelt Library.

17. Telegram of August 27, 1938, in President's Personal File 3385, Franklin D. Roosevelt Library.

18. Ham and Eggs pamphlet from President's Personal File 3385, Franklin D. Roosevelt Library.

19. Roosevelt's statement appeared in a public letter dated October 31, 1938, to George Creel, a conservative Democrat who had been defeated in the Democratic gubernatorial primary in 1934 by Upton Sinclair. His statement reads, "As for the '$30 every Thursday' plan I have never concealed the fact that I am against it. I hope it will not be tried—because on the one hand I feel quite sure it will not work and because on the other hand I feel quite sure we can evolve from the present Social Security statute methods of obtaining security for old age which will work better and better each year. But the plan is wholly a State issue . . ." (President's Personal File 3385, Franklin D. Roosevelt Library).

20. Letter to Hoover from Edwin Watson, Secretary to the President, in President's Personal File 3385, Franklin D. Roosevelt Library.

21. "Gerald L.K. Smith Dead: Anti-Communist Crusader," *New York Times*, April 16, 1976, 30.

Chapter 3. The Nonpension Ingredients of Ham and Eggs

1. Pinner, Jacobs, and Selznick (1959, 265) applied the term "political entrepreneur" to George McLain, the Ham and Eggs veteran and founder of his own pensionite movement as described in the previous chapter.

2. Hamilton was born on the Caribbean island of Nevis as the illegitimate son of a woman of Jewish origin.

3. Fisher's use of the term had a different meaning from the barter idea of Tradex. He had in mind a monetary policy aimed at stabilizing an index of commodity prices.

4. Sinclair had dabbled in Hollywood, apart from his above-mentioned film project with Sergei Eisenstein. He wrote a biography of producer William Fox, initially with Fox's active cooperation. Fox did not want the book published in the end, but Sinclair published it anyway, antagonizing Hollywood's top executives. MGM and United Artists spearheaded the Hollywood side of the anti-Sinclair campaign (Starr 1996, 148).

5. The third-party candidate, Raymond Haight, running on the "Commonwealth" ticket, had earlier also run unsuccessfully in the Republican primary against Merriam. He depicted himself as a middle-of-the-road candidate between two extremes. After the primary, Haight was offered the nomination of the EPIC Democrats for attorney general by Sinclair, but he turned it down. It is unclear how the vote for Haight would have gone had he not run. Supporters of Merriam at one point offered Haight various inducements to withdraw, including $100,000. They evidently thought he would pull votes from Merriam (Singer 1974, 384–85, 395). But others believe his ultimate support came at the expense of Sinclair (Gottlieb and Wolt 1977, 212).

6. The lack of a specific dollar amount for pensions is puzzling, given the figures named for other aspects of the Long program. Bennett (1969, 141) reports that no pension amount was specified because any amount other than the $200 per month in the Townsend plan led to protests from the elderly Townsendites. But it is unclear why the $200 figure was not adopted (or exceeded) by Long.

7. Smith's pro-Nazi sentiments entangled him in legal troubles during World War II.

After the war he campaigned against Eisenhower as "Ike the Kike" and called for deportation of blacks and Zionists. See "Gerald K. Smith Dead; Anti-Communist Crusader," *New York Times*, April 16, 1976, 30.

8. The Lundeen bill was pushed by an alliance of communists, social workers, and Farmer-Laborites. (Lundeen was a Farmer-Labor representative from Minnesota.)

9. With his monetarist leanings, Coxey named his son "Legal Tender."

10. C.H. Douglas (1937, 146) wrote that "the authenticity of this document [the 'Protocols'] is of little importance."

11. Pound's grandfather had owned a lumber company that issued a scrip-currency. Pound saw this scrip as real money because it was based on the value of a productive enterprise (Pound 1935, overleaf).

12. Ham and Eggs pamphlet in President's Personal File 3385, Franklin D. Roosevelt Library. Roosevelt press conference 479 transcript, August 26, 1938, from the same library.

13. A Social Credit-type proposal surfaced in Japan in 1998 in the form of a plan to give consumers special time-limited vouchers to raise consumer demand and end that country's recession.

14. The Bradbury Building in downtown Los Angeles, built in 1893, was said to be inspired by Bellamy's futuristic views. Of course, it in fact looks like the latest in modernity at the time it was built and is often used as an exotic movie set, as, for example, in the film *Blade Runner*.

15. Frederick Taylor originated scientific management in the late nineteenth century. He asserted there was one right way to carry out various production tasks. Time and motion studies were to be used to determine this one right way.

16. In the 1950 campaign for one of California's U.S. Senate seats, Boddy ran in the Democratic primary against Helen Gahagan Douglas—and lost. Douglas then ran against Republican Richard Nixon, who characterized her as the "pink lady." Although Nixon is usually seen as the originator of the charge that Douglas was a communist sympathizer, Boddy in fact campaigned against her in the early primary on a similar theme.

17. The National Industrial Recovery Act was later declared unconstitutional.

Chapter 4. Townsend Versus Social Security

1. Letter from Roosevelt to Frank E. Gannett (president of the Gannett newspaper chain) of March 1, 1935. Gannett had defended Roosevelt's gold policy against Hoover's attack in a newspaper column. The Supreme Court decision upholding Roosevelt on gold had been issued in mid-February 1935 (Official file 229 [gold], box 5).

2. Letter from Victor E. Wilson of September 3, 1935, summary of letter from Dan Tobin (Teamsters) of January 17, 1935, letter from Edwin E. Witte of December 11, 1935, Official File 1542 (Townsend), Franklin D. Roosevelt Library.

3. Letter from the Postmaster General of April 16, 1935, in Official File 1542 (Townsend), Franklin D. Roosevelt Library.

4. FBI files on Townsend were made available to the author under a Freedom of Information Act request. The FBI had received complaints from private citizens about the Townsend operation earlier, but had found no cause to become involved. Director J. Edgar Hoover forwarded the files to postal authorities for investigation of mail fraud. Relevant materials concerning the Witte request include Holtzoff to

Hoover, October 4, 1934; Witte to Holtzoff, October 5, 1934; and FBI interview with Witte, November 8, 1934. The last document indicates that the Los Angeles office had been instructed to make a "discreet" investigation of the Townsend organization. A former Townsend organization employee wrote to Witte alleging mail fraud and failure to pay female employees the California minimum wage; this letter was passed on to the FBI (Shuster to Witte, November 19 and 27, 1934). The FBI did not seem especially desirous of pursuing Townsend but did compile information. It closed the Los Angeles investigation at the end of 1935 with a note indicating that the local U.S. attorney did not believe successful prosecution could be made (Hanson report, December 30, 1935).

5. Tamm to Hoover, February 25, 1936 (FBI files).

6. Included was a file on an F.E. Townsend, who may or may not have been Dr. Townsend (Hoover to Bell, February 26, 1936, FBI files). Subsequently, during the hearings, the FBI did turn over a criminal file of one individual to the Bell committee (Tamm to Hoover, June 3, 1936, FBI files).

7. Bell to Jones, March 16, 1936; Jones to Bell, March 21, 1936; Listerman to Hoover, May 1, 1936; Hoover to Listerman, May 13, 1936 (FBI files).

8. The Los Angeles FBI office was asked to file a fugitive complaint against Townsend. On orders from Director J. Edgar Hoover, the FBI remained aloof from the case (Hoover to Keenan, December 18, 1936; Hoover to Los Angeles office, December 18, 1936 [FBI files]).

9. White House press release dated April 18, 1938. President's Personal File 3385, Franklin D. Roosevelt Library.

10. See the previous chapter on the Union Party campaign. Townsend reportedly distanced himself from Smith for the latter's fascistic tendencies during the 1936 campaign (FBI memo on Smith dated May 23, 1942).

11. Townsend's letters to the *Long Beach Press Telegram*, in which the earliest versions of the plan appeared, are reproduced in the appendix to Gaydowski 1970a. See also Townsend, 1943, for these letters.

12. Letter to James Davis from Roosevelt, March 6, 1935, President's Personal File 6678 (Townsend clubs), Franklin D. Roosevelt Library. Young Davis wanted to know the President's views for a speech at school. The letter from FDR cautions him, however, to keep the communication confidential.

13. Letter of April 27, 1948, from Townsend addressed to "Members of Progressive Citizens of America, Friends of the Independent Progressive Party, and the Townsend National Recovery Plan" on file at Southern California Library for Social Science and Research.

14. Papers of Gardner Jackson, container 72 (Townsend), Franklin D. Roosevelt Library.

15. Townsend's FBI files contain various such letters. The FBI apparently took no action other than filing the letters. Townsend apparently spoke at a rally of a pre-World War II communist organization calling for America to stay out of the war. Between the time of the Hitler–Stalin pact and the Nazi invasion of the Soviet Union, the Communist Party espoused an isolationist line.

16. Also included in Downey's 1936 book on the subject is a reprint of a radio address by Downey's brother urging in general terms a fight against unemployment without any specific plan for how this fight might be undertaken.

17. Prof. Hansen did not support the Townsend Plan, but the early American

Keynesians were concerned about a tendency for the economy to stagnate at a low level due to excessive saving.

18. To estimate the non-Depression level of GDP per capita in 1935, a mid-point interpolation of real GDP was taken between 1929 and 1941. The non-Depression nominal GDP in 1935 was then estimated as the ratio of actual nominal GDP to real GDP times the interpolated figure. The resulting estimate is about $100 billion. Current Census estimates suggest an elderly population level in 1935 somewhat higher than the figures used in discussions of the Townsend Plan. It appears that more than 12 million people were aged sixty and over in that year, a little under a tenth of the population.

19. "Baby Doctor for the Millions Dies," *Los Angeles Times*, March 17, 1998, A1, A19–A20 (italics added).

20. In congressional testimony, Townsend said he assumed that 7.5 million people would take the pension out of the 10.4 million which were then assumed to be eligible. (As noted above, current Census estimates suggest a larger fraction of the population fell into the sixty-and-over category than the data used in 1935.) It was unclear exactly how Townsend scaled down from 10.4 million to 7.5 million. He said that a million people would not apply and some elderly would not be citizens. Even with his 7.5 million, however, the non-Depression proportion of GDP in 1935 would be 18 percent and the actual proportion would be 25 percent (U.S. Congress, House of Representatives 1935, 698).

21. See the statement of Robert R. Doane in U.S. Congress, Senate 1935, 1244. Doane assumed the economy was functioning at the 1929 level. His tax collection estimate was $18 billion, an amount consistent with Townsend's estimate of 7.5 million beneficiaries.

22. The bill is reproduced in Neuberger and Loe 1973, 319–29.

23. The material on Margett may well have been that provided by the FBI, although file deletions in the material obtained by the author under the Freedom of Information Act do not make clear whose files were turned over. See the previous citations.

24. Letter from Edwin E. Witte to Merril G. Murray of the Social Security Board, dated December 11, 1935, Official File 1542 (Townsend), Franklin D. Roosevelt Library.

25. Letter from Townsend to Roosevelt dated March 2, 1937, Official File 1542 (Townsend), Franklin D. Roosevelt Library.

26. Nichols to Tolson, May 16, 1939 (FBI files).

27. Letter from Townsend to Roosevelt dated May 26, 1940, Official File 1542 (Townsend), Franklin D. Roosevelt Library.

28. See materials related to Paul McNutt's recommendation in the Townsend folder for years 1941 to 1945, Official File 1542 (Townsend), Franklin D. Roosevelt Library.

29. Folder on "Townsend Plan for National Insurance" in the collection of papers of President Nixon held at the National Archives, Laguna Niguel, California.

Chapter 5. Gerontocracy's Last Stand: Earl Warren and Uncle George

1. Later in his career, some of Earl Warren's opponents would claim that Warren's father was in fact a company spy for the railroads (Cray 1997, 19). There is no support for this allegation.

2. Warren's slate was officially "uncommitted" as Hoover was in eclipse after losing to Roosevelt in 1932. In the course of the 1936 delegate campaign, Warren apparently antagonized Hoover by telling him that the uncommitted slate could win only if Hoover promised he would not be a candidate (Cray 1997, 79–80; Warren 1977, 112).

3. Much of the material in this section is drawn from documents contained in the Earl Warren collection of the California State Archives, particularly folders related to the 1938 attorney general campaign.

4. The "pirate" reference is reported in a letter from Thomas I. Coakley to Warren dated August 2, 1938.

5. The sheet music ("On With Roosevelt"), published in 1938 by E.B. DuBain Publishing Co., Hollywood, is contained in the California State Archives, Earl Warren collection, F3640:279.

6. "Report Warren Would Kill Pension Plan if Elected," *Peoples World*, August 9, 1938, clipping from scrapbook in box containing files F3640, folders 317–39, Warren collection in the California State Archives.

7. Kegley brochure for primary of August 30, 1938, contained in the California State Archives, Earl Warren collection, F3640:257.

8. Roy Owens was a candidate for governor in the Democratic primary.

9. The Progressive Party was a remnant of Theodore Roosevelt's breakaway "Bull Moose" campaign for President in 1912. Progressives controlled the Republican Party in California but thought it advisable to create a separate party for their approach to government. The cross-filing system of which Warren took advantage dates from this period as Republicans wanted to be able to run on both the Republican and Progressive tickets (Cresap 1954, 16; Harris 1961, 4).

10. A letter to Warren from Mrs. J.M. Laughlin of October 29, 1938, references a radio speech previously given by Kegley on behalf of Mayor Shaw.

11. Letter from Warren to Albert Hershman, November 1, 1938.

12. Letter, dated October 14, 1938, from Warren to Bateman, contained in the California State Archives, Earl Warren collection, F3640:223.

13. Letter from Warren to Charles G. Johnson, October 19, 1938.

14. Warren's assistant, Helen MacGregor, received a report from a friend in Santa Monica alleging that Noble's group was receiving instructions from Germany via shortwave radio. She passed this information along to the assistant attorney general, Warren Olney (memo by MacGregor of conversation with Olney dated April 1, 1942). No evidence of such radio instructions was produced at Noble's trials. Noble wrote a letter to the chief of the California Highway Patrol complaining about a police raid on his group, with carbon copies to various officials including Earl Warren (reported in letter from George T. Jeffers to Warren dated April 3, 1942).

15. Noble and his compatriots charged that MacArthur had abandoned his troops in the Philippines. Warren obtained a statement from General Eisenhower indicating the MacArthur had been ordered to leave the Philippines. A folder on the Noble prosecution is contained in the Warren collection at the California State Archives.

16. On appeal, convictions of Noble and the others were reversed on grounds that the Friends of Progress could not be shown to be controlled by the German government and that there had been no calls for the violent overthrow of the American government. Noble's activities are described in the court decision. See *The People, Respondent, v. Robert Noble et al.*, Appellants, 68 Cal. App. 853 (1945). An earlier appeal, on grounds that the defendants were not given a speedy state trial (because they were in the custody

of federal authorities), was dismissed. See 53 Cal *F.K. Ferenz et al., Petitioners, v. the Superior Court of Sacramento County, Respondent.* App. 2d 639 (1942).

17. California Republicans were favored by the disproportionate representation of rural areas, especially at the expense of Los Angeles.

18. Statement of Robert S. Ash of the Alameda County Labor Council. Ash went on to characterize Warren as a good governor. "He was better than anything we had had before, including Olson" (Earl Warren Oral History Project 1976c, Ash, 51).

19. Pollack 1979, 79–80, is an exception. But even he does not develop the political motivation. Severn (1968, 83) finds that "mainly . . . his motives seem to have been those of a public official deeply involved in protective measures and defense planning. . . ." Huston (1966, 59) just says "Distrust of the Japanese was ingrained in Warren, as in thousands of other Californians."

20. At one point, the Wilson administration sent U.S. Secretary of State Williams Jennings Bryan—the former free silver presidential candidate—to California to deal with the Japanese issue in 1913. Bryan's efforts produced no results (Bryan 1971, 366–67).

21. Warren address to Eagles Convention, June 21, 1942, contained in the California State Archives, Earl Warren collection, F3640:4063.

22. Warren campaign press release 120 in Warren California State Archives, folder F3640:541.

23. Special Agent's Report no. 1586 by agent G.W. Griffin dated March 23, 1942.

24. Poll by California Associates contained in loose-leaf binder in folder F3640:544, Warren California State Archives.

25. Townsend to Warren, April 23, 1942; MacGregor to Townsend, April 30, 1942; undated, unsent draft letter of Warren to Townsend; telegram of Warren to Townsend and letter of Warren to Townsend, both of May 19, 1942.

26. Speech of May 30, 1942 contained in Warren California State Archives, file folder F3640:529.

27. Letter of June 12, 1942, from Paul F. Fratessa to Raymond Haight. An undated memo, apparently from Warren aid William T. Sweigert, summarizes the Fratessa letter and adds background information.

28. Memo of June 15, 1942, Chatters to CW and Miss Baxter. (Baxter is apparently Leone Baxter of Campaigns Inc. CW is apparently Clem Whitaker, the other partner in the firm.) Warren later fired Whitaker, making an enemy who was later active in the campaign against Warren's plan for health insurance (Earl Warren Oral History Project 1976b, Draper, 10–11).

29. "State Eagles' Leader Endorses Warren: Praises Work on Pensions, Social Security," *Oakland Tribune*, July 16, 1942. Clipping in Warren California State Archives, folder F3640:507.

30. Undated Ham and Eggs brochure in Warren California State Archives, folder F3640:4063.

31. Radio address of July 9, 1942 (the day after the Eagles press release on pensions) in Warren State Archives collection, folder F3640:4063.

32. Telegram, Warren to Johnson, July 3, 1942.

33. Radio broadcast of September 7, 1942, by Lawrence Allen.

34. "Olson Pension Plan Scored by R.L. Haight," *Contra Costa Gazette*, August 3, 1942, clipping in Warren California State Archives, folder F3640:507.

35. Radio broadcast of October 1, 1942.

36. Radio broadcast of November 1, 1942.

37. Letter of September 11, 1942, from Paul F. Fratesa to Warren.

37. Quoted in Richard Harvey 1959, 254.

39. Clipping from unknown newspaper dated November 1, 1942, in Warren California State Archives.

40. Letter of November 4, 1942, McLain to Warren.

41. Letter of December 11, 1942, McLain to Warren.

42. Letter of December 22, 1942, Haight to Warren.

43. Letter of November 10, 1942, Helen R. MacGregor to George H. McLain.

44. Telegram from Myrtle Williams to Sweigerd (*sic*), February 16, 1943.

45. Address of Lawrence W. Allen to Pension Committee of March 11, 1943, attachment to letter of March 19, 1943, Paul F. Fratessa to W.T. Sweigert contained in Warren California State Archives, folder F3640:4028.

46. Memorandum Re Hearings on Old Age Pensions, Assembly Hall, State Building, Los Angeles, March 11, 1943.

47. Shortly after the enactment of the majority report (see below), Townsend had a change of heart. In August 1943, he announced that he had decided that state initiatives could set examples for the eventual goal of a federal plan. See *Townsend Weekly* of August 7, 1943, in Warren California State Archives, folder F3640:4065.

48. Ibid.

49. Letter to Warren dated March 31, 1943, from John C. Cuneo et al.

50. Letter from Ralph T. Fisher to Warren dated April 7, 1943, in Warren California State Archives, folder F3640:4030.

51. Undated statement of Roy Owens in Warren California State Archives, folder F3640:4029.

52. Letter from Thomas Coakley to W.T. Sweigert, June 3, 1943, in Warren California State Archives, folder F3640:4063.

53. Letter from McLain to W.T. Sweigerd (*sic*) of May 13, 1943, with copy of radio address in Warren California State Archives, folder F3640:4030.

54. Memo of W.T. Sweigert to file of September 17, 1943; letter of March 4, 1944, and telegram of March 17, 1944, William D. Campbell to Warren, in Warren California State Archives, folder F3640:4031 and F3640:4067.

55. Mr. Hoffman's pension was cut because the bonds represented financial assets exceeding the allowable limit. Warren promised that the problem would be fixed, but several months later Mr. Hoffman wrote an angry letter to Warren complaining that the eligibility rules had not been changed. Newspaper clippings on the Hoffman episode can be found in Warren California State Archives, folder F3640:4034. The letter from Hoffman to Warren of February 2, 1946, is in folder F3640:4035.

56. Some of the material below is drawn from the Herbert Phillips collection in the Warren California State Archives. Phillips, a columnist for the *Sacramento Bee,* chronicled state politics.

57. Memo from M.F. Small to Warren of May 20, 1949.

58. Term limits now prevent a recurrence of a three-term governor.

59. McLain's unsuccessful Proposition 10 sought to prevent use of public funds to influence legislation. He apparently thought this ban would nullify the opposition of groups such as the County Supervisors Association to his other proposals.

60. The George McLain file at Nixon Library and Museum, Yorba Linda, California, contains various documents related to the proposition. In a letter to constituent W. F. Cooper dated November 22, 1949, Nixon refers to the 1948 arrangements as "dangerous to our democratic form of government."

61. Documents related to this episode and the 1960 FHA matter appear in the George McLain folder in the President Nixon files held at the National Archives office at Laguna Niguel, California. A letter from Nixon campaign official Lois Gaunt to H.R. Haldeman of October 13, 1962, indicates that the Nixon campaign was getting more mail on the elderly issue as a result of the McLain attack than on any other issue. She suggests researching any links between McLain and "patsy" (presumably Pat Brown) and the sending of a mass mailing to the elderly. Haldeman replied in an undated note to "go ahead—I'll pay for it—do not put thru regular budget."

62. "George H. M'Lain, Pension Worker" (Obituary), *New York Times*, July 13, 1965, 33.

Chapter 6. Twenty-First Century Ham and Eggs?

1. The Japanese plan differed in a fundamental respect from Ham and Eggs. The coupons were redeemable at face value, a value that could be maintained because they were distributed by the central government. And no stamp tax had to be paid to keep the coupons valid.

2. The committee was established by the Roosevelt administration in 1934 to draw up plans for a social insurance program. Its recommendations evolved into the actual Social Security Act of 1935.

3. Witte's reference to $200 a month clearly links his rationale to opposition to Townsend.

4. There are alternative accounting definitions of "full funding." However, whatever definition is used will act as a constraint on raising benefits as long as there is a rule that benefits be completely funded.

5. This phrase appears in Noah 1988.

6. There is, of course, no "correct" benefit. Any formula relating the starting benefit to earnings history is arbitrary and a value judgment of Congress.

7. Taxable wages had risen faster than price inflation in the past. But in the 1970s, price inflation outran wages.

8. Details concerning this episode—including a history of congressional hearings on the notch baby "problem" up through 1994—can be found in U.S. Commission on the Social Security "Notch" Issue.

9. "Dear Abby: Please Come Join Our Protest," *Journal of Commerce*, September 17, 1986, 12A.

10. Nominal wage growth of successive cohorts causes benefits to rise. Thus, if average benefits are diagramed, those born in 1927 (and subject to the new formula) roughly "catch up" with those born in 1916 (who were subject to the old formula).

11. The summary here—except for the last point—is based on U.S. General Accounting Office, 1997a.

12. J. Dennis Hastert, Republican House Majority Leader, quoted in "GOP Leaders Hail Social Security 'Lock Box,' Say Sen. Abraham Will Introduce Legislation," *Daily Labor Report*, March 11, 1999, A12.

13. Quoted in "Clinton Plan Would Set Aside 57 Percent, Not 62 Percent of Surpluses, CRS Study Says," *Daily Labor Report*, March 1, 1999, A13.

14. In the future, from the unified budget perspective, there would remain a deficit when the boomers retired as benefit spending exceeded tax revenues.

15. The 1999 Clinton proposals included both the Social Security and Medicare

trust funds with some revenue invested in the stock market. They also included creation of a new type of individual retirement accounts.

16. Quoted in "General Revenue Transfer Plan Could Undercut System's Structure, Officials Say," *Daily Labor Report*, February 23, 1999, A12–A13.

17. "The Weirdest Year," *Economist*, November 5, 1994, 24.

18. The subplot of *As Good As It Gets*, a 1997 film, involves a boy denied proper treatment by an HMO. That same year, in *The Rainmaker* a young lawyer sues a health insurance company that denied payments for a critical illness for fraud.

19. In the poem "Rabbi Ben Ezra," Stanza I.

References

Aaron, Henry. 1982. *Economic Effects of Social Security.* Washington, DC: Brookings Institution.

———. 1997. "A Bad Idea Whose Time Will Never Come." *Brookings Review* 15 (Summer): 17, 19, 21, 23.

Aaron, Henry J., and Robert D. Reischauer. 1998. *Countdown to Reform: The Great Social Security Debate.* New York: Century Foundation Press.

———. 1999 "Should We Retire Social Security? Grading the Reform Plans." *Brookings Review* 17 (Winter): 6–11.

Achenbaum, Andrew W. 1986. *Social Security: Visions and Revisions.* New York: Cambridge University Press.

Ainsworth, Ed. 1966. *Maverick Mayor: A Biography of Sam Yorty of Los Angeles.* Garden City, NY: Doubleday.

Allswang, John M. 1991. *California Initiatives and Referendums, 1912–1990: A Survey and Guide to Research.* Los Angeles: Edmund G. "Pat" Brown Institute of Public Affairs, California State University, Los Angeles.

American Legion, Americanism Committee. 1942. *"Since Dec. 7": Enemy Propaganda in Southern California.* American Legion, report no. 2.

Ball, Robert M. 1998. *Straight Talk About Social Security: An Analysis of the Issues in the Current Debate.* New York: Century Foundation Press.

Barocas, Victor S. 1997. "The Future of Social Security: An Interview with EBRI President Dallas L. Salisbury." *ACA Journal* 6 (Summer): 24–28.

Bartlett, John Henry. 1937. *The Bonus March and the New Deal.* Chicago: M.A. Donohue.

Barton, Bruce. 1931. "How to Fix Everything." *Vanity Fair* (August), 31, 70.

Beaver, Daniel R. 1957. *A Buckeye Crusader.* Unpublished manuscript available from the University of Cincinnati Library.

Bell, James Robert. 1956. *The Executive Office of the California Governor Under Earl Warren, 1943–1953.* Doctoral dissertation, Department of Political Science, University of California, Berkeley.

Bennett, David H. 1969. *Demagogues in the Depression: American Radicals and the Union Party, 1932–1936.* New Brunswick, NJ: Rutgers University Press.

Berkowitz, Edward D. 1997. "The Historical Development of Social Security in the United States." In *Social Security in the 21st Century,* ed. Eric R. Kingson and James H. Schulz. New York: Oxford University Press, 22–38.

Bernstein, Irving. 1985. *A Caring Society: The New Deal, the Worker, and the Great Depression.* Boston: Houghton Mifflin.

Bernstein, Melvin Harry. 1970. *Political Leadership in California: A Study of Four Governors.* Doctoral dissertation, Department of Political Science, UCLA.

Bollens, John C., and Grant B. Geyer. 1973. *Yorty: Politics of a Constant Candidate.* Pacific Palisades, CA: Palisades.

Bond, Floyd A., et al. 1954. *Our Needy Aged, a California Study of a National Problem.* New York: Henry Holt.

Brinkley, Alan. 1982. *Voices of Protest: Huey Long, Father Coughlin, and the Great Depression.* New York: Knopf.

Brinton, J.W. 1936. *The Townsend National Recovery Plan: The Solution of Your Problem.* 3d ed. rev. Chicago: Townsend National Recovery Plan.

Bryan, William Jennings. 1971 [1925]. *The Memoirs of Williams Jennings Bryan.* New York: Haskell House.

Bureau of National Affairs. 1997. "Excerpts from Volume I of Report of 1994–1996 Advisory Council on Social Security, Issued January 6, 1997." *Daily Labor Report*, Special Supplement, January 7.

Burke, Robert E. 1953. *Olson's New Deal for California.* Berkeley: University of California Press.

California Institute of Social Welfare. n.d. [1956?]. *How the California Legislature Votes on Social Welfare.* Los Angeles: California Institute.

California Pension Plan. 1938. *Ham and Eggs for Californians.* Hollywood: California Pension Plan.

California, Secretary of State. 1938. *Proposed Amendments to Constitution, Propositions and Proposed Laws to Be Submitted to the Electors of the State of California at the General Election to Be Held Tuesday, November 8, 1938, Together With Arguments Respecting the Same.* Sacramento: California State Printer.

———. 1939. *Proposed Amendments to Constitution, Propositions and Proposed Laws to Be Submitted to the Electors of the State of California at the General Election to Be Held Tuesday, November 7, 1939, Together With Arguments Respecting the Same.* Sacramento: California State Printer.

———. 1944. *Proposed Amendments to Constitution, Propositions and Proposed Laws to Be Submitted to the Electors of the State of California at the General Election to Be Held Tuesday, November 7, 1944, Together With Arguments Respecting the Same.* Sacramento: California State Printer.

Cantril, Hadley. 1941. *The Psychology of Social Movements.* New York: Wiley.

Caplan, Jerry Saul. 1947. *The CIVIC Committee in the Recall of Mayor Frank Shaw.* Master's thesis, Department of Political Science, UCLA.

Cleland, Robert Glass. 1947. *California in Our Time: 1910–1940.* New York: Knopf.

Cole, Jeffrey Ian. 1985. *Born to the New Art: CBS Correspondents and the Emergence of Broadcast News, 1930–1941.* Doctoral dissertation, Department of Political Science, UCLA.

Coogan, Gertrude M. 1935. *Money Creators: Who Creates Money? Who Should Create It?* Chicago: Sound Money Press.

Costa, Dora L. 1998. *The Evolution of Retirement: An American Economic History, 1880–1990.* Chicago: University of Chicago Press.

Coughlin, Charles E. 1933. *The New Deal in Money.* Royal Oak, MI: Radio League of the Little Flower.

———. 1936. *Money! Questions and Answers.* Royal Oak, MI: National Union for Social Justice.

Cray, Ed. 1997. *Chief Justice: A Biography of Earl Warren.* New York: Simon and Schuster.

Cresap, Dean R. 1954. *Party Politics in the Golden State.* Los Angeles: Haynes Foundation.

Crouch, Winston W. 1943. *The Initiative and Referendum in California.* Los Angeles: Haynes Foundation.

Davis, Donald G. 1967. "The Ionaco of Gaylord Wilshire." *Southern California Quarterly* 49 (December): 425–53.

Davis, Mike. 1992. *City of Quartz: Excavating the Future in Los Angeles.* New York: Vintage.

Domanick, Joe. 1994. *To Protect and to Serve: The LAPD's Century of War in the City of Dreams.* New York: Pocket Books.

Douglas, C.H. 1937. *Social Credit,* 3d rev. ed. London: Eyre and Spottiswoode.

Douglas, Paul H. 1936. *Social Security in the United States: An Analysis and Appraisal of the Federal Social Security Act.* New York: Whittlesey House.

———. 1968 [1933]. "Foreword to the Agathon Press Edition." In *Insecurity: A Challenge to America,* ed. Abraham Epstein. New York: Agathon Press.

Downey, Sheridan. 1936. *Why I Believe in the Townsend Plan.* Sacramento, CA: Author.

———. 1939. *Pensions or Penury?* New York: Harper and Brothers.

———. 1940. *Highways to Prosperity.* Chicago: Townsend National Weekly.

Earl Warren Oral History Project. 1971. "Earl Warren's Bakersfield." Transcript of interviews, University of California, Berkeley.

———. 1976a. "California Democrats in the Earl Warren Era." Transcript of interviews, University of California, Berkeley.

———. 1976b. "Earl Warren's Campaigns: Vol. I." University of California, Berkeley.

———. 1976c. "Labor Leaders View the Warren Era." University of California, Berkeley.

———. 1977. "Earl Warren as Executive: Social Welfare and State Parks." University of California, Berkeley.

Employee Benefit Research Institute. 1997. *Fundamentals of Employee Benefit Programs,* 5th ed. Washington, DC: EBRI.

Epstein, Abraham. 1928. *The Challenge of the Aged.* New York: Vanguard Press.

———. 1968 [1933]. *Insecurity: A Challenge to America.* New York: Agathon Press.

Farrelly, David, and Ivan Hinderaker, eds. 1951. *The Politics of California: A Book of Readings.* New York: Ronald Press.

Feldstein, Martin, and Kathleen Feldstein. 1999. "Washington Shouldn't Be on Wall Street." *Los Angeles Times,* January 29, B8.

Ferrara, Peter J., and Michael Tanner. 1998. *A New Deal for Social Security.* Washington, DC: Cato Institute.

Finlay, John L. 1972. *Social Credit: The English Origins.* Montreal: McGill-Queens University Press.

Fisher, Irving. 1933. *Stamp Scrip.* New York: Adelphi.

———. 1935. *Stabilised Money: A History of the Movement.* London: George Allen and Unwin.

———. 1936. *100% Money.* New York: Adelphi.

———. 1963 [1922]. *The Purchasing Power of Money,* 2nd rev. ed. New York: Augustus M. Kelley.

Fitzgerald, Bill Edward. 1951. *Pension Politics in California.* Master's thesis, Department of History, University of California, Berkeley.

Ford, John Anson. 1961. *Thirty Explosive Years in Los Angeles County.* San Marino, CA: Huntington Library.

Fowler, Gene, and Bill Crawford. 1987. *Border Radio.* Austin: Texas Monthly Press.

Friedman, Milton. 1999. "Social Security Chimeras." *New York Times,* January 11, A17.

Furst, Thomas Martin, Jr. 1949. *Technicist Empiricism: A Critical Evaluation of the Doctrine of Technocracy, Incorporated.* Master thesis , Department of Political Science, UCLA.

Gale, William G., and John Sabelhaus. 1999. "The Savings Crisis: In the Eye of the Beholder?" *Milken Institute Review* 1(3): 46–56.

Gaydowski, John Duffy. 1970a. "Dr. Townsend and His Plan, 1867–1934." Master of Arts thesis, Department of History, UCLA.

———. 1970b. "Eight Letters to the Editor: Genesis of the Townsend National Recovery Plan, Introduced by J.D. Gaydowski." *Southern California Quarterly* 52 (December): 365–82.

Gottlieb, Robert, and Irene Wolt. 1977. *Thinking Big: The Story of the Los Angeles Times, Its Publishers, and Their Influence on Southern California.* New York: G.P. Putnam's Sons.

Gramlich, Edward M. 1998. *Is It Time to Reform Social Security?* Ann Arbor: University of Michigan Press.

Greenstein, Paul; Nigey Lennon; and Lionel Rolfe. 1992. *Bread and Hyacinths: The Rise and Fall of Utopian Los Angeles.* Los Angeles: California Classics Books.

Grenier, Judson. 1974. "Upton Sinclair: The Road to California." *Southern California Quarterly* 56 (Winter): 325–36.

Hanne, Daniel. 1998. " 'Ham and Eggs' Left and Right: The California Scrip Pension Initiatives of 1938 and 1939." *Southern California Quarterly* 80 (Summer): 183–230.

Harris, Joseph P. 1961. *California Politics,* 3d ed. Stanford, CA: Stanford University Press.

Harvey, Richard Blake. 1959. *The Political Approach of Earl Warren, Governor of California.* Doctoral dissertation, Department of Political Science, UCLA.

Harvey, William H. 1963 [1895]. *Coin's Financial School.* Cambridge, MA: Belknap Press of Harvard University Press.

Henstell, Bruce. 1984. *Sunshine and Wealth: Los Angeles in the Twenties and Thirties.* San Francisco: Chronicle Books.

Hofstadter, Richard. 1955. *The Age of Reform: From Bryan to F.D.R.* New York: Vintage.

Hollings, Ernest F. 1999. "Dipping Into the Social Security Bank." *New York Times,* February 5, A27.

Holtzman, Abraham. 1975. *The Townsend Movement: A Political Study.* New York: Octagon Books.

Huston, Luther A. 1966. *Pathway to Judgment: A Study of Earl Warren.* Philadelphia: Chilton Books.

Irving, John A. 1959. *The Social Credit Movement in Alberta.* Toronto: University of Toronto Press.

Jacoby, Sanford M. 1997. *Modern Manors: Welfare Capitalism Since the New Deal.* Princeton, NJ: Princeton University Press.

Johnson, Frederick L. 1989. "From Leavenworth to Congress: The Improbable Journey of Francis H. Shoemaker." *Minnesota History* 51 (Spring): 166–77.

Katcher, Leo. 1967. *Earl Warren: A Political Biography.* New York: McGraw-Hill.

Kaufman, Bruce E. 1996. "Why the Wagner Act? Reestablishing Contact With Its Original Purpose." *Advances in Industrial and Labor Relations* 7: 15–68.

Kayden, Xandra, ed. 1997. *California Policy Options: 1997.* Los Angeles: UCLA School of Public Policy and Social Research.

Kazin, Michael. 1995. *The Populist Persuasion: An American History.* New York: Basic Books.

Key, V.O., Jr., and Winston W. Crouch. 1938. *The Initiative and Referendum in California.* Berkeley: University of California Press.

Kimbell, Larry J. 1997. "The California Economy: The Long Term Outlook." In Kayden, ed., 1997, 1–29.

King, Peter H. 1997. "Then as Now as Now as Then. . . . " *Los Angeles Times,* December 3, A3.

Kingson, Eric R. and James H. Schulz, eds. 1997. *Social Security in the 21st Century.* New York: Oxford University Press.

Kotlikoff, Laurence J., and Jeffrey Sachs. 1997. "It's High Time to Privatize." *Brookings Review* 15 (Summer): 16, 18, 20, 22.

Latimer, Murray Webb, and Karl Tufel. 1940. *Trends in Industrial Pensions.* New York: Industrial Relations Counselors.

Leader, Leonard. 1972. "Los Angeles and the Great Depression." Doctoral dissertation, Department of History, UCLA.

———. 1980. "Upton Sinclair's EPIC Switch: A Dilemma for American Socialists." *Southern California Quarterly* 62 (Winter): 361–85.

Leonard, Stephen J. 1993. *Trials and Triumphs: A Colorado Portrait of the Great Depression with FSA Photographs.* Niwot: University of Colorado Press.

Lindsay, Cynthia. 1960. *The Natives Are Restless.* Philadelphia: J.B. Lippincott.

Light, Paul. 1995. *Still Artful Work: The Continuing Politics of Social Security Reform,* 2d ed. New York: McGraw-Hill.

Loeb, Harold. 1933. *Life in a Technocracy: What It Might Be Like.* New York: Viking Press.

Mallory, J.R. 1954. *Social Credit and the Federal Power in Canada.* Toronto: University of Toronto Press.

Mann, Robert. 1992. *Legacy to Power: Senator Russell Long of Louisiana.* New York: Paragon House.

McLain, George. 1951. *The Story of the 1951 California Legislature: How the Conspiracy to Wreck the State's Social Welfare Program Was Exposed!* Los Angeles: California Institute of Social Welfare.

McWilliams, Carey. 1951 [1949]. "Pension Politics in California." Reproduced in Farrelly and Hinderaker 1951, 295–99.

———. 1973 [1946]. *Southern California: An Island on the Land.* Santa Barbara, CA: Peregrine Smith.

Merriam, Frank F. 1935. *Old Age Pensions and the Budget.* Address delivered over NBC in a statewide radio program (March 4), pamphlet collection, UCLA.

Mitchell, Greg. 1992. *The Campaign of the Century: Upton Sinclair's Race for Governor of California and the Birth of Media Politics.* New York: Random House.

Mitchell, Daniel J.B. 1986. "Inflation, Unemployment, and the Wagner Act: A Critical Reappraisal." *Stanford Law Review* 38 (April): 1065–95.

Mitchell, Daniel J.B., and Jacques Rojot. 1993. "Employee Benefits in the Single

Market." In *Labor and an Integrated Europe*, ed. Lloyd Ulman, Barry Eichengreen; and William T. Dickens. Washington, DC: Brookings Institution.

Moley, Raymond. 1951. "Knight of Nonpartisanship: Earl Warren." In Farrelly and Hinderaker 1951, 220–28.

Moore, O. Otto. 1947. *Mile High Harbor.* Denver, CO: Associated Publishers.

Moore, Winston, and Marian Moore. 1939. *Out of the Frying Pan.* Los Angeles: DeVorss.

Morris, Charles R. 1996. *The AARP: American's Most Powerful Lobby and the Clash of Generations.* New York: Random House.

Moss, David A. 1996. *Socializing Security: Progressive-Era Economists and the Origins of American Social Policy.* Cambridge, MA: Harvard University Press.

National Industrial Conference Board. 1936. *The Townsend Scheme.* New York: NICB.

Neuberger, Richard L., and Kelley Loe. 1973 [1936]. *An Army of the Aged: A History and Analysis of the Townsend Old Age Pension Plan.* New York: Da Capo Press.

Newton, Jim. 1997. "Hayden: From Radical Youth to Political Maturity, Challenger's Credo Has Been to Make Moral Vision a Reality." *Los Angeles Times*, February 23, A1.

Nixon, Edgar B., ed. 1969. *Franklin D. Roosevelt in Foreign Affairs,* 3 volumes. Cambridge, MA: Harvard University Press.

Noah, Timothy. 1988. "Notch Babies: 'The Issue from Hell.'" *Newsweek*, January 25, 18–19.

Old Age Revolving Pensions, Ltd. 1936. *The Townsend Plan: National Recovery Program*, 2d ed. Chicago: Old Age Revolving Pensions, Ltd.

Organisation for Economic Cooperation and Development (OECD). 1996. *Aging in OECD Countries: A Critical Policy Challenge.* Paris: OECD.

Orloff, Ann Shola. 1993. *The Politics of Pensions: A Comparative Analysis of Britain, Canada, and the United States, 1880–1940.* Madison: University of Wisconsin Press.

Perry, Lewis B., and Richard S. Perry. 1963. *A History of the Los Angeles Labor Movement, 1911–1941.* Berkeley: University of California Press.

Peterson, Peter G. 1996. *Will America Grow Up Before It Grows Old? How the Coming Social Security Crisis Threatens You, Your Family, and Your Country.* New York: Random House.

———. 1999. *Gray Dawn: How the Coming Age Wave Will Transform America—and the World.* New York: Times Books/Random House.

Phillips, Ronnie J. 1995. *The Chicago Plan and New Deal Banking Reform.* Armonk, NY: M.E. Sharpe.

Pinner, Frank A., Paul Jacobs, and Philip Selznick. 1959. *Old Age and Political Behavior: A Case Study.* Berkeley: University of California Press.

Pollack, Jack Harrison. 1979. *Earl Warren: The Judge Who Changed America.* Englewood Cliffs, NJ: Prentice-Hall.

Pound, Ezra. 1935. *Social Credit: An Impact.* London: Stanley Nott.

President's Personal File 3385, Franklin D. Roosevelt Library.

Putnam, Jackson K. 1970. *Old-Age Politics in California from Richardson to Reagan.* Stanford, CA: Stanford University Press.

Quadagno, Jill. 1988. *The Transformation of Old Age Security: Class and Politics in the American Welfare State.* Chicago: University of Chicago Press.

Rasmussen, Cecilia. 1997. "A Mayor Who Stood for Reform." *Los Angeles Times*, November 16, B3.

Reeve, Joseph E. 1943. *Monetary Reform Movements: A Survey of Recent Plans and Panaceas*. Washington, DC: American Council on Public Affairs.

Reischauer, Robert D., Stuart Butler, and Judith R. Lave, eds. 1998. *Medicare: Preparing for the Challenges of the 21st Century*. Washington, DC: National Academy of Social Insurance.

Richardson, James H. 1954. *For the Life of Me: Memoirs of a City Editor*. New York: G.P. Putnam's Sons.

Roosevelt, Nicholas. 1936. *The Townsend Plan: Taxing for Sixty*. Garden City, NY: Doubleday, Doran.

Rosenblatt, Robert A. 1987. "Disparity in Benefits: Retirees Try to Whittle 'The Notch.' " *Los Angeles Times*, March 14, Part 1, 1, 26.

Rosenstone, Robert A. 1970. "Manchester Boddy and the *L.A. Daily News*." *California Historical Society Quarterly* 49 (December): 291–307.

Sass, Steven A. 1997. *The Promise of Private Pensions: The First Hundred Years*. Cambridge, MA: Harvard University Press.

Schlesinger, Arthur M., Jr. 1959. *The Age of Roosevelt: The Coming of the New Deal*. Boston: Houghton Mifflin.

———. 1960. *The Age of Roosevelt: The Politics of Upheaval*. Boston: Houghton Mifflin.

Schwartz, Stephen. 1998. *From West to East: California and the Making of the American Mind*. New York: Free Press.

Severn, Bill. 1968. *Mr. Chief Justice: Earl Warren*. New York: David McKay.

Sinclair, Upton. n.d. *We, the People of America and How We Ended Poverty: A True Story of the Future*. Pasadena, CA: National EPIC League.

Singer, Donald L. 1974. "Upton Sinclair and the California Gubernatorial Campaign of 1934." *Southern California Quarterly* 56 (Winter): 375–406.

Skocpol, Theda. 1992. *Protecting Soldiers and Mothers: The Political Origins of Social Policy and the United States*. Cambridge, CA: Harvard University Press.

Squier, Lee Welling. 1912. *Old Age Dependency in the United States: A Complete Survey of the Pension Movement*. New York: Macmillan.

Starr, Kevin. 1996. *Endangered Dreams: The Great Depression in California*. New York: Oxford University Press.

———. 1997. *The Dream Endures: California Enters the 1940s*. New York: Oxford University Press.

Stein, Herbert. 1999. "How to Solve Almost Everything." *New York Times*, February 3, A19.

Sterling, William, and Stephen Waite. 1998. *Boomernomics: The Future of Your Money in the Upcoming Generational Warfare*. New York: Ballantine.

Stone, Irving. 1948. *Earl Warren: A Great American Story*. New York: Prentice-Hall.

Taft, Philip. 1968. *Labor Politics American Style: The California State Federation of Labor*. Cambridge, MA: Harvard University Press.

Tawa, Renee. 1999. "War Brides: The Last Living Confederate and Union Widows Tell All, From How They Met Their Much-Older Husbands to the Way a Long-Ago Conflict Continues to Dominate Their Lives." *Los Angeles Times*, June 13, E1, E3.

Tessler, Ray, and Jeff Gottlieb. 1999. "Vote for Cityhood Shows Seniors' Political Power." *Los Angeles Times*, March 4, A1, A23.

Townsend, Francis E. 1941. *The Townsend National Recovery Plan: New Reference Book.* Chicago: National Townsend Weekly.

———. 1943. *New Horizons (An Autobiography)*. Chicago: J.L. Stewart.

Ulman, Lloyd, Barry Eichengreen, and William T. Dickens, eds. 1993. *Labor and an Integrated Europe.* Washington, DC: Brookings Institution.

U.S. Bureau of the Census. 1932. *Fifteenth Census of the United States: 1930, Unemployment, Volume II, General Report, Unemployment By Occupation, April, 1930 with Returns from the Special Census of Unemployment, January, 1931.* Washington, DC: GPO.

U.S. Commission on the Social Security, "Notch" Issue. 1994. *Final Report on the Social Security "Notch" Issue.* Washington, DC: GPO.

U.S. Congress, House of Representatives. 1935. *Economic Security Act: Hearings Before the Committee on Ways and Means*, 74th Cong., 1st sess. Washington, DC: GPO.

———. 1936. *Hearings Before the Select Committee Investigating Old-Age Pension Organizations*, 74th Cong., 1st sess. Washington, DC: GPO.

———. 1986. *Reductions in Social Security Benefit Levels: Hearing Before the Select Committee on Aging.* Washington, DC: GPO.

———. 1988. *Report of the General Accounting Office on the Notch Issue: Hearings Before the Subcommittee on Social Security of the Committee on Ways and Means.* Washington, DC: GPO.

———. 1992a. *Social Security and Public Pension Pitfalls: Joint Hearing Before the Subcommittee on Retirement Income and Employment and the Task Force on Social Security and Women of the Select Committee on Aging.* Washington, DC: GPO.

———. 1992b. *Social Security "Notch" Issue: Hearings Before the Subcommittee on Social Security of the Committee on Ways and Means.* Washington, DC: GPO.

U.S. Congress, Senate. 1935. *Economic Security Act: Hearings Before the Committee on Finance*, 74th Cong., 1st sess. Washington, DC: GPO.

U.S. General Accounting Office. 1988. *Social Security: The Notch Issue*, GAO/HRD-88–62. Washington, DC: GAO.

———. 1997a. *Retirement Income: Implications of Demographic Trends for Social Security and Pension Reform*, GAO/HEHS-97–81. Washington, DC: GAO.

———. 1997b. *Social Security Advocacy: Organizations That Mail Fund-Raising Letters*, GAO/HEHS-97–69. Washington, DC: GAO.

———. 1999. *Social Security Reform: Implementation Issues for Individual Accounts*, GAO/HEHS-99–122. Washington, DC: GAO.

Van Dalsem, Newton. 1942. *History of the Utopian Society of America: An Authentic Account of Its Origins and Development Up to 1942.* Los Angeles: Board of Directors of the Utopian Society.

Walker, Mabel L. 1936. *The Townsend Plan Analyzed.* New York: Tax Policy League.

Warren, Earl. 1977. *The Memoirs of Earl Warren.* New York: Doubleday.

Warren, George F., and Frank A. Pearson. 1935. *Gold and Prices.* New York: Wiley.

Watkins, T.H. 1993. *The Great Depression: America in the 1930s.* Boston: Little, Brown.

Weaver, John D. 1967. *Warren: The Man, the Court, the Era.* Boston: Little, Brown.

Weber, Tracy. 1996. "The 'Darth Vaders of Direct Mail.'" *Los Angeles Times*, March 3, A1, A24–A25.

White, G. Edward. 1982. *Earl Warren: A Public Life*. New York: Oxford University Press.

Whiteman, Luther, and Samuel L. Lewis. 1936. *Glory Roads: The Psychological State of California*. New York: Thomas Y. Crowell.

Witte, Edwin E. 1963. *The Development of the Social Security Act*. Madison: University of Wisconsin Press.

Zanger, Martin. 1974. "Upton Sinclair as California's Socialist Candidate for Congress, 1920." *Southern California Quarterly* 56 (Winter): 359–73.

Zimmerman, Tom. 1980. "Ham and Eggs, Everybody!" *Southern California Quarterly* 62 (Spring): 77–96.

Index

About the Author

Daniel J.B. Mitchell is Ho-su Wu professor of Human Resource Management at the Anderson Graduate School of Management and the School of Public Policy and Social Research, U.C.L.A. Professional activities have included memberships on the Executive Boards of the Industrial Relations Research Association (both national and Southern California), the North American Economics and Finance Association, and the Institute of Industrial Relations Association. Professor Mitchell is now president of the North American Economics and Finance Association. He has also served on the nominating committee of the American Economic Association and on the editorial boards of various academic journals. He is editor of the *Issues in Work and Human Resources* series published by M.E. Sharpe, Inc. and began a term as co editor of the journal *Industrial Relations* in 1997.

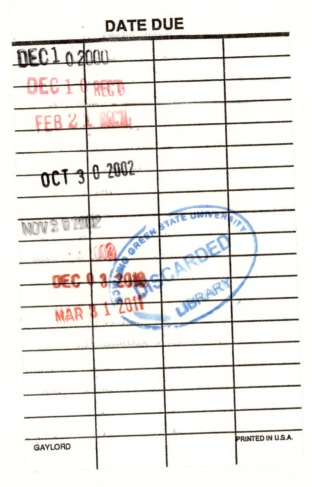